Thomas Alfred Davies

How to make Money, and how to keep it

Thomas Alfred Davies

How to make Money, and how to keep it

ISBN/EAN: 9783743317413

Manufactured in Europe, USA, Canada, Australia, Japa

Cover: Foto ©Lupo / pixelio.de

Manufactured and distributed by brebook publishing software (www.brebook.com)

Thomas Alfred Davies

How to make Money, and how to keep it

HOW TO MAKE MONEY,

AND

HOW TO KEEP IT.

By THOMAS A. DAVIES,

AUTHOR OF COSMOGONY, OR MYSTERIES OF CREATION, AND ANSWER TO HUGH MILLER AND GEOLOGISTS.

NEW YORK:
G. W. *Carleton & Co.*, 499 *Broadway.*
LONDON: S. LOW, SON & CO.
MDCCCLXVIII.

Entered according to Act of Congress, in the year 1867, by
THOMAS A. DAVIES,
in the Clerk's Office of the District Court of the United States, for the Southern District of New York.

THE NEW YORK PRINTING COMPANY,
81, 83, *and* 85 *Centre Street,*
NEW YORK.

CONTENTS.

CHAPTER I.
First Step in Money-making and Saving, . . . 11

CHAPTER II.
What is a Fortune, and what an Independence? . 16

CHAPTER III.
Fountains of Wealth, ... 22

CHAPTER IV.
Labor and its Representative Money, ... 32

CHAPTER V.
The Seeds of Fortunes, ... 58

CHAPTER VI.
How to make Money, ... 81

CHAPTER VII.
Manual Labor, ... 108

CHAPTER VIII.
Apprentices, ... 118

CHAPTER IX.
Clerks, ... 129

CHAPTER X.
Farming and Growing, ... 139

CHAPTER XI.
Mechanical Business, ... 152

CHAPTER XII.
Retail Merchandising, ... 174

CHAPTER XIII.
Manufacturing Business, ... 182

CHAPTER XIV.
Wholesale Merchandising, ... 191

CHAPTER XV.
Brokerage and Commission, ... 201

CHAPTER XVI.
Intellectual Labor.—Lawyers, ... 209

CHAPTER XVII.
Intellectual Labor.—Physicians, ... 219

CHAPTER XVIII.
Intellectual Labor.—Professional Salaried Persons, 225

CHAPTER XIX.
Investments, ... 234

CHAPTER XX.
How Money is Lost, ... 245

CHAPTER XXI.
Earnings and Savings, ... 254

CHAPTER XXII.
Banking and Insurance, ... 273

CHAPTER XXIII.
Life Insurance, ... 288

How to Make Money.

CHAPTER I.

FIRST STEP IN MONEY-MAKING AND SAVING.

Can I make money?—Will I?—Yes, and more.—Tenure of a dollar or of property.—Why is my money mine?—Good government sure tenure by law.—Watch politicians.—Property in danger.—See to your political principles.—Rights of citizens invaded.—Stand from under.—Analogy.—How to secure rights.—Sheriff.—*Posse-Comitatus*.—State troops.—United States troops.—All the States.—Millions of men.—Success or downfall of government.—Read Constitution and laws.—Read on—or stop.

READER, if you have a dollar, or work for one, you are interested in the contents of this book. You have looked at the title, and it excites your cupidity if it does not please your fancy. But you say to yourself—Will it teach me how to make money? If the directions are followed, it will. Will it show me how to keep it? It will. It will do more than that—it will show you how to make money with money. We have much knowledge which we do not use to advantage, and you may not apply the principles here laid down; if so, you will probably be no better off by its reading.

By what tenure do you hold the dollar or property you have, or get that which is your due? Nine-tenths of persons, and possibly a larger proportion, never heard this idea suggested. In other words, why is not your property mine? Simply because we have a government, a social compact; and one of the laws of that government is, that what belongs to you is your own, and not some other person's. This is the fundamental law, the practice and usage of all people. Then comes the direct question to every one—Are you interested in having what is your own? The reply is certain. I am. Then you are directly interested in preserving the government and observing the laws, which alone can secure you in these rights, and also in maintaining the rights of others in like manner. For you cannot expect to be maintained in yours unless you extend to others the same protection.

The moment, then, that one knows that what he has or what he can get depends upon equal laws and equal justice to all, and that the titles of property rest solely upon the law, such person has made one step forward on the long road, in not only making money, but in keeping the title to it when made. You cannot do better, then, than watch your politicians (who generally have no money), and see that they enact such laws as are proper, and that they do not pass your money or hard earnings into their own pockets or those of their friends. It is the opinion of many that there is a little too much of this thing done in the country about these times.

You may always know, then, when the title of your property is in danger, or when your own rights are in danger, from these signs. When you see unequal laws passed, or see one or any number of citizens deprived of legal rights, you may wisely conclude your turn will come next. You may wisely conclude, too, that when one legal right of a citizen of a State is taken from him, the next step may be to deprive you of your right of tenure to property. These are the first evidences of decay in the strength of your government, and probably of its final dissolution and downfall.

As a mere money-making and money-saving means, a steady, just government, with laws well observed by all, even if no higher motive existed, is the first great idea. You may always look for the reverse in the actions of those who have nothing to lose and everything to gain. If, then, you wish to be well grounded in the principles of money-making and money-saving, inform yourself of your political position, and canvass carefully the effect of your political action. Know what *principles* you are advocating by your vote—whether they will tend to disturb or steady the monetary affairs of the State or country, or whether they are for the good of the whole.

One principle is certain in this country—that when sections undertake to manage other sections which have the right to manage themselves and their own affairs, look out and stand from under; trouble is in the wind and future. Look to your dollars, your securities, and to your lives. As much as men can do in bodies-politic is to manage themselves and their own affairs well, and let other people's business alone. No more can one body-politic do this successfully or satisfactorily, than one firm can interfere with and manage the affairs of another, without disturbance, trouble, and disaster.

That every reader may understand how important a government and laws are in making money and keeping it, it will only be necessary to cite the process by which individual property rights are maintained in this country. Suppose a property right is invaded, what is the course

of the party to gain redress? The individual applies to
the legal tribunals to adjudicate the case; and upon a
hearing, it is decided favorably, if you please. The next
step is to place in the hands of the sheriff the order of
the court, and he proceeds to collect the amount, and if
the execution is satisfied, well; but if not, and force is
resorted to, to prevent the execution, and the sheriff alone
is unable to overcome it, he calls out his *posse-comitatus*—
that is, a number of citizens who will aid him in securing
the injured parties' rights. If this should not be sufficient, he calls upon the Governor of the State to turn out
the State troops; and if these are not sufficient still, the
Governor calls upon the President for United States
troops; and if they, too, are not sufficiently powerful,
the President calls upon the Governors of the various
States until force enough is obtained—amounting, it may
be, in this country to many millions of men—to maintain
the rights of this one individual. If the government suc-
ceeds—well, then, the government stands; if it fails, in all
probability another would be established upon its ruins.
But the individual would lose his rights, whatever they
might be.

This shows the magnitude of the individual's right, and
the importance to all concerned that such right should
be respected by legislators and all citizens without such
appeal; and that such appeal may result in the total
destruction of the right and the government also, besides
an untold loss of life and property to a large class not in
any way at fault in the matter.

Every one, then, who wishes to make money and keep
it by a secure tenure, should read the Constitution of the
United States and the laws of his own State, and thereby inform himself of his duty as a citizen, this being the

first principle of self-interest; and then see to it that you do this duty faithfully. If not, the reader had better stop where he is, and save himself the trouble of making money to be lost by his own neglect. If otherwise, read on, and act accordingly.

CHAPTER II.

WHAT IS A FORTUNE, AND WHAT AN INDEPENDENCE?

Unanswerable question.—Halo.—Increases as we approach.—Pleasures of a fortune.—Hope.—Anticipations.—Hoarding stigmatized.—Make a show.—No money.—Obscurity.—Poverty—Question which.—Spend or make.—Fear to fall.—False position.—Lavish expenditures.—Approved.—Moral and political duty.—Independence.—What.—Live without labor.—Fixed amount.—All can gain independence.—Labor respectable.—All labor.—No meanness or penuriousness.—Proper economy.—Trouble.—Debt.—Not happy.—Money at interest.—Respectable.—Contentment.—You your owner.—Not mortgaged.—No slave.—Not ashamed to spend, not ashamed to make.

THE answer to the question, What is a fortune? never has been, and probably never will be answered. For what may be a fortune for one is of little account in the millions of another. The nearest definition that can be given to this undefinable amount is, that it is a halo of a mysterious sum of money which recedes, increasing as we approach. It is almost, if not altogether, a universal ambition to acquire a fortune by those who have intelligence enough to understand, or experience enough to know, the pleasures which are supposed to surround its possession. There are peculiar qualities of the human mind brought into action in the pursuit and possession of wealth. The simple acquisition of money to some is a substantial, realized pleasure; while with others the simple possession gives in like manner a heartfelt satisfaction. Then there are those who take no special pleasure in the acquisition, but theirs consists in hope and anticipation of what they will derive in its possession or in the spending of it; while there are still others who make to enjoy the fruits, and do enjoy them by a liberal expenditure in the higher and nobler deeds of the liberal man of fortune and luxurious ease.

Nor can there be found among men a nobler sentiment than stimulates him who labors to acquire means to spend in contributing comfort to those whose misjudgment or misfortunes have placed them in the background of poverty and want. Let such noble men live and enjoy while they dispense; the people should be proud of such examples, and their own consciences will be their own reward. But what more despicable or degraded than the condition of those who have a fortune, and are shrivelled up in penuriousness, meanness, and simple money-hoarding! Such simply hold the means of contributing pleasure and comfort to the deserving, without either enjoying what they possess themselves or deriving any benefit from the various ways of munificence.

The largest class of those who make, or desire to make a fortune, have but one idea—and that is, to be able to make all the external appearance and show of a man of fortune. Display is the great object, and hence many endeavor to put on the exuviæ of a fortune, and expend while they do not possess the means. This is too lamentably the case nowadays; and the result is, that all the substance that would, if saved, in time make a fortune, is squandered in the gratification of a pride only due to him who has accomplished the object. Nor do such individuals gain more than the merited contempt of creditors and sensible people; they generally fail in the end, and sink in after life into obscurity and poverty.

It then becomes a solid question for individuals to

maturely consider, while on the road to fortune, whether they will spend their own or the substance of others—whether they will live as their means warrant, or assume what they really are not? The world generally is not deceived by such appearances, though it may be in some peculiar instances. What real pleasure can there be to live at an altitude in life where there is no foundation to support, and fear of a downfall is for ever haunting the imagination? Such people vainly imagine that they are like the ostrich, who hides his head and conceives his huge, ugly body is in like manner obscured. Respectability does not depend upon false tokens; still, many are satisfied with such a style of life, as the counterfeiter is with his occupation so long as he is not detected in his false position.

Those who possess fortunes in reality are frequently blamed for lavish expenditure, and what is called a waste of money. The more spent of individual fortune, the better for the community at large—for the trades, and for the laboring classes. Nothing is more commendable than judicious expenditure by those who have the fortunes producing incomes. There is a large class, however, who wish to spend as fast as they acquire money. To those, the only object will be to find out how to make it the fastest, that they may have the larger ability to gratify their fancies.' There is a plausibility of argument which may satisfy this class of individuals, found in the fact that they get the gratification by an immediate enjoyment, which delay might cut short in death; or the loss of money after the trouble of accumulating it.

But these are short-sighted views; for all persons owe it to themselves and those dependent upon them to save of their means for accident or misfortune. *It is a moral* and political duty to make themselves and their dependants independent of public or private charity; for if they do not, they spend that which does not actually belong to them. To make oneself independent should be the first great aim of life. Then what is an INDEPENDENCE? The answer to this question is plain; being such an amount of money, safely invested, as will produce an income equal to the necessaries of life. In other words, to be able to live without labor. If one could always be sure to be able to save even something, or enough to keep him from falling a charge either upon public or private charity, there would be no need of an independence. But, as all know, such cannot be guaranteed to any one.

While the fortune, then, is an indefinable amount, the independence is a fixed sum dependent upon the price of necessaries, and the country in which it is required. In some latitudes this amount is very small, while in others it is no immaterial sum. It may be assumed that the interest of five thousand dollars invested at six per cent. would accomplish this object. If, then, the desires and wants are no more, then the individual has an independence, and a fortune too. But the ever-living desire of gain, even when this sum is obtained, will spur on its possessor to further accumulation as a general rule. If, however, he has others dependent upon him for support who cannot earn themselves, he must have as many independencies as there are individuals to support.

There is no able-bodied person, of sound mind, who cannot in this country gain an independence from labor. For all he has to do is to lay aside of what he receives, all that is not required for the necessaries of life; and by looking at the tables at the back of this book he will find that small earnings per day will soon mount up to this standard, and even more. Penuriousness or meanness is not recommended; but on the contrary, will prevent one making the most money with his opportunities. A just and proper economy is the true line, and any one can determine this for himself. No one feels so happy as when he is pursuing a legitimate business, is out of debt, and has some money at interest. From that moment he lives in a new world, is more respected, has more substantial friends, and wields a greater influence among his peers. Not only that, but his very independence of circumstances makes his services in any department of life more valuable, and he can command more money for them, and can hence accumulate faster.

But let one be behindhand, or in debt, or in trouble, or on the anxious seat as to how he will make ends meet to support himself and his family—he is in the power of any one who has any transactions with him. He becomes the suppliant for everything; and cannot, from the nature of things, get as much for what he gives as though the reverse were the case. An independence, then, should be the first thing aimed at, either by male or female; and every nerve and sinew should be strained, and every expenditure scrutinized, till this end shall have been attained. Self-denial should be exercised in everything, remembering always that such a course is not only respectable, but in the end will make you more friends, and more happiness from the beginning to the end of life. You are, then, your own always, and never mortgaged to others, which is a mild term for being the slave of another. The object being here to explain simply what a fortune and an independence are, the manner in which they can be acquired will be explained hereafter.

The independence, although it may free you from further labor to make money by it, does not free you of labor altogether. The little mercantile business required to be carried on to purchase your supplies and attend to the home comforts, is still to be done. If that be to spend three hundred dollars per annum, this is, then, the amount of your mercantile business. Every dollar you spend requires two to make the expenditure—the seller and the purchaser. The man of fortune, who spends his three thousand dollars, has in this way ten times as much labor to perform as he who spends his three hundred dollars; and the man who spends his thirty thousand dollars, does one hundred times as much as the one who spends three hundred dollars.

From this it will be seen that every calling in life has its labor; and even the man of fortune is not free from it; for in addition to that of the expenditure, he has also to see to his investments, to the collection of his income, and such-like; so that all have labor of some kind or another to perform, and hence we conclude that labor is respectable, and none need be ashamed to labor who would not be ashamed to be seen spending a dollar. Only those who have no money, and do not know the process by which it is attained, look down upon honest labor. The laborer stands higher in the scale of usefulness than they, if they have no accumulated labor (money) to compare with him.

So that none need hesitate, who want money, to work wherever they can gain employment; and if they can carry with them knowledge and superior acquirements, their services will be more valuable, but not a whit more respectable, on the great scale of political economy. Bearing this steadily in mind, and profiting by it, you have laid a good foundation for success in acquiring an independence or a fortune.

CHAPTER III.

FOUNTAINS OF WEALTH.

Fountains of wealth open to all.—Beacon-lights—Wealth the great struggle.—The ups and downs.—Not explainable.—Foundations of value.—Machinery of life.—Questions.—How to make services valuable.—Example.—Result.—Same wages most valuable.—Most money.—Best labor cheapest.—Mechanical labor compared.—Best makes most money.—Promotion by care.—Servant girls.—Best make most.—Small fortunes.—Salesmen compared.—Interest.—Pleasant manners.—Attention to business.—Advancement.—Best makes $131,950.—Poorest makes nothing.—Springs that feed the fountain.—Great secret.—Wealth in value of services.

IN this country, the fountains of wealth are open to all. Few avail themselves of the opportunity presented to accumulate a fortune, while every one of able body and sound mind can make himself independent of labor, if not achieve a fortune in time. As far as history, either sacred or profane, leads us back over the toiling masses of mankind, the struggles for wealth stand as beacon-lights above their efforts of every other kind. Within these labyrinths, and at every stand-point of the historian, the eternal desire for gain shows itself in almost every motive, and has nerved to action almost every toiling hand. These struggles spring from necessities implanted in man's very existence; and however high-born or depressed in the scale of life an individual may be, his nature demands sustenance, and whether he labors for it himself or not, some one must fulfil the necessity and till the ground for his sake.

Labor, then, is the living fountain of wealth, from out of whose depths flow the alimental and luxurious streams of life. As the Maker of all things has moulded one particle of water like another, so too, by nature, is one laborer like another. Each may take different positions in life, first up, then below, changing positions at every moment of time, fulfilling laws which are inexplicable by the deepest philosophy. To-day may see one basking in the upper-jeweldom of sunshine ; to-morrow, sunk in deep-down recesses where the smiles of plenty, or the cheering rays of luxury never reach. To-day may see the bubble of circumstance quickly convey one from beneath, and bear him above for a time upon its sparkling glitter ; to-morrow, memory serves to tell his history—in poverty or distress.

Why one particular globule of water is upon the surface, and another just like it, is at the bottom of the ocean, bearing its proportion of the superincumbent weight of others above—or why one individual glides serenely on in the pleasures of life with every want supplied, and another toils in the scorching sun, overtasked with labor, bearing the burdens of others, is beyond the ability of the naturalist or the logic of the political economist to explain. No other solution can be given for the cause of such relations than can be found in what would seem to be a natural axiom—that because an ocean must be made up of globules of water, hence some must be below and perform a heavier duty than those which of necessity must be above ; or that because a community must be made up of individuals, hence some must occupy superior, and others inferior positions. Nor does this necessity grow out of the normal condition of man ; for that is agriculture limited, too, to the supply of the bare necessaries of life, and that agriculture performed with the rudest implements fashioned by the laborers themselves.

Such labor, it will be seen, is the foundation of all values. Its institution caused the necessity for tools to carry it on to advantage; and for these, materials in wood and metals were required, which opened new avenues of wants, till the great machinery of human labor in all its varieties has been set in motion. It will be unnecessary to follow up the dependence of one branch of industry upon another, or their relative importance to the whole; sufficient for the purposes in hand is a glance at the whole, to show that from any or from all, money can be made by individuals by labor in or around this multiplicity of elementary occupations.

But, says the reader, we knew all this before; and what insight does this give towards making money? In order to make money, one has first to be told where it can be had, and by what means; and after that, the best mode of getting the most of it by individual exertion. And now it may be asked—If you want a lawyer to manage an important case, do you employ a poor one? If you are dangerously sick, do you employ a poor physician? If you want a good servant, do you take a greenhorn? If you want a good, capable, and trustworthy clerk, do you hire one having none of these qualities? If you want a good thing of any kind, is it of no consequence whether you employ an honest or dishonest man to get it for you? If you want a good job of carpentry done, do you employ a botch? If you want good masonry put up, do you get a hod-carrier to do it? No matter what may be the experience of the reader in such matters, he will answer all these questions in the negative, and sum up the whole matter by saying—If I want a thing done, I get the best man I can, who will do it cheapest; and at the same time such individual knows that the cheapest is sometimes, and is most generally, the dearest.

But little reflection is required to see that the most valuable services will always bring the most money; and in this principle lies the hidden recess from which flows the stream of independence or a fortune. It must not be forgotten, or passed by, or neglected by any one who wishes to make the *most money* out of his labor or services, no matter what they may be. We give an example. Two mechanics worked upon the same piece of machinery; both from circumstances received the same pay. One was faithful, pleasant in his manners, obliging, polite, agreeable, worked for the interest of his boss, and was careful of material and saving of his time in doing his work to advantage; and did his work well. The other did his work equally well when it was done; but he was snappish, was an eye-servant, was disobliging, uncivil, cut and slashed material to loss; took his ease about everything, and was only careful about one object, and that was to put in his time. Both received the same amount of money each pay-day. The general impression was, that they both were earning money equally fast, and so they would have been as long as they both continued to receive the same amount of money. The truth turned out in the end that the first one had been accumulating standing friends, influence, character, and personal interest; while the other had stood still, if he had not lost what the other had gained. The first probably never cast a thought of a result further than to do his duty as a matter of common honesty, while the other only had the simple thought of getting his wages for his time put in. These men, then, worked upon no idea of making the most money that could be made by their services; for if they had, probably both would have worked better, and had they been informed of the means, both would have been in the way of receiving extra compensation by advancement.

The result was, however, that the boss was applied to to recommend a foreman for some important job at the South; and the *personal interest* he felt in the first young mechanic, coupled with the consideration that he had been faithful and honest, trustworthy and capable, led him to forego his own interest in him as a workman, and recommend him for the promotion which he got.

Let us analyze the two cases, and see whether these two mechanics did absolutely receive the same amount of money for their services. They both received two dollars a day, for this was some time ago. The foreman, however, was to get five dollars a day for five years, and all expenses paid. So that, considering he had to pay his board at home, he got three dollars and a half more a day than he was getting. By looking at the tables at the end of the book, you will find that this amount daily for five years, of three hundred and thirteen days, amounts to $6,425.87, interest added each six months at seven per cent. The other mechanic in the meantime was getting the same as he had. Now the two had worked for the same boss, and in the same shop, two years before the first was made a foreman. It will be seen then by calculation that although both were working for the same pay, one actually received $6,425.87 more than the other. Or for the two years, while they both received the same money apparently, one received in fact $11.51 more than the other per day.

The young man, when he received this sum of $6,425.87,

was just twenty-five years of age, which if improved at compound interest at seven per cent. till he was fifty years of age, would amount to $34,875.98; a snug little fortune, and a certain independence for the remainder of his life, if he had done no more than just support himself in the meantime. This simple case illustrates a very important principle in money-making; any one who works for another, and who cannot or will not apply the lesson to his own condition, will fail to do that which would make his services worth the most money to himself.

Let us examine the principles of action which, whether intentional or not, directly brought about this result, and they will be found as follows :

First.—General deportment, consisting of pleasant, agreeable, and attractive manners.

Second.—Displaying an interest in the interests of his employer, by which an interest was created in the mind of the employer for him.

Third.—Economy in time and material used, by which the employer made money over the ordinary workman, and which all men will remember and reciprocate at the first opportunity.

There is, however, another advantage from such a course of conduct, even though it does not lead to such a large result as the one cited. It is always sure to gain for the individual the highest rate of wages under any circumstances, and we will illustrate it on a very limited scale. Two female servants were engaged in the same house, at the same wages, seven dollars per month. One was careful, attentive, kind, obliging, pleasant, and did all and everything to please, save, and take care of the interests of the household; in other words, made herself an agreeable and useful servant; while the other did what she was told, and took about as much interest in matters as servants generally do who think their whole duty is to do just so much, and get their money for doing as little as possible. It so happened that the family determined to discharge one of the two servants, not wishing to keep both. Reader, can you divine which of the two was discharged? The one was discharged who was the least useful; and now we will just look at the accounts of these two servants for one year only, and see how they stood at the end of it. The one that remained did the work of both, and had her wages raised to ten dollars; the one that left was out of employment three months, and finally was compelled to take a place at six dollars per month.

The first received for her year's work $120. The second received $54. The necessary expenses of the first for dress, etc., was $40, leaving $80 clear gain. The second paid three months' board at $9 per month, and the balance of all she received for clothing and other necessaries. So that while they were working together they received the same money; but from the way in which each was valuable or agreeable to the employers—during the time of the next year one received $80 more than the other in cash profit, and got $13 more in clothing and necessaries.

Each of the girls was twenty years old at the end of the year when they worked separately. Let us look what this $80 will accumulate to, if put in a savings institution and improved at compound interest at six per cent. when she arrives at fifty years of age. By consulting tables it will be found that it will amount to $469.40, as being the difference of action of two servant girls in the same house receiving only $7 per month. If she had accumulated the same amount of $80 each year till she was fifty years old, the tables on thirty years, page —, shows that it would amount to $6,329.47, the earnings being 25 cents per day for 313 working days.

The two cases cited are among the lowest classes of labor; and now, for the purpose of a higher illustration, let us take the instance of two clerks in a wholesale drygoods establishment. Both were salesmen, and receiving $1,500 per annum. The one did all that was generally required of salesmen, was regular, registered and made his sales as he should do; and no objection could be found in the way of doing his business, and his employers were satisfied with him, and he was worth to them the amount of his salary. But he was not interested, nor did he look to anything further than his own particular department, nor did he make any special effort to gain custom for the house, or keep an eye out to the general run of the business. The other, on the contrary, was always busy late and early, had something more to do when all had left, and was always found in the store among the first in the morning; was constantly reaching out to get trade and new customers, and keeping an eye on everything that transpired; was never prying, but always aiding any one when he could, and keeping everything in order as far as possible without interference with the affairs of others; made himself, by his agreeable and pleasant manners, popular with customers, and with all those engaged in the house, and by such a course was felt from cellar to garret. Which of these two young men—for they were both twenty-three years of age— earned during the year the most money? We will see. A neighboring house having lost their principal salesman by death, and having heard of, and knowing by sad experience the loss of valuable customers enticed away by this active, winning salesman, they at once applied to him and offered him $2500 a year if he wished to leave his present house. Of course so good an offer was not to be passed unnoticed, and he broached the subject to the members of the house in which he was employed, and asked if they had any objection to his accepting the offer. To which they replied, "We will consider the matter, and let you know in a day or so."

This fact drew the attention of the firm to investigate the sales made by this young man, and it was found that he had brought a large amount of custom to the house, and of all he had sold, no bad debts had resulted. They came to the conclusion that he was more valuable to them than the salary of $1500; and said at once, "We will make your salary hereafter $2500;" and so he remained, and continued to exert himself still more.

Now let us inquire into the financial condition of these two salesmen. The one spent all his salary, for he had more time on his hands about town, and less to interest him than the other; while the other took lodgings near his store, seldom went anywhere, and read most of his time while he was not calculating and figuring about his business. The result was that he spent $500, and saved $1000 of his salary. The next year, when he received $2500, he spent the same, while the other salesman spent all he received as before.

It becomes interesting here to make a calculation on even these low figures. We will make it for two years. The one had nothing to lay to the good—the other had $3000 at the end of two years, or when he was twenty-five years old. This, put at compound interest at seven per cent. for twenty-five years, or until he was fifty, would amount, as shown by tables, to $16,290, or, if he had continued to do the same thing yearly—namely, gain $2000 until he was fifty years of age—it would amount to $131,952; a snug little fortune on comparatively very small earnings.

From these few examples, which can be adapted to any conceivable case, after an examination and study of the tables it will be seen where the fountains of wealth lie. By reflection, the necessary qualifications are made apparent how the most money can be made by increasing the value of the labor. The general principles which result can be stated to be—

First.—Be polite, civil, agreeable, and never fail to make every one you come in contact with interested in yourself and what you are doing.

Second.—Do what you have to do for another so that he may feel that you are working for his interest.

Third.—Do what you have to do in the best way possible, and endeavor to improve on every repetition.

Fourth.—Be honest, candid, dignified, and social. This inspires confidence and increases character, reputation, and influence.

These are a few of the items necessary to reach the fountains of wealth, and to observe them is a sure means of making money; to neglect them is a sure way of losing your opportunity to do so, and will inevitably result in loss.

CHAPTER IV.

LABOR AND ITS REPRESENTATIVE MONEY.

Wade through definitions.—Labor, money.—Most valuable, most money.—Skill controls.—Great lesson of life.—Skill and natural tact.—Neutral minds.—Skill acquired.—Make labor valuable.—Male and female.—Employment only necessary.—Labor represented by money.—Machinery of life.—Unit of action.—Agricultural labor. — Allegory. — Illustration of values. — Natural products and implements.—Exchanges.—Barter.—Labor divided. — Results beneficial. — Commerce established. — Labor compared.—Most skill most value.—Working of commerce.—Profits resulted.—Credit wanted.—Trade from necessity.—Worked well.—New avenues.—People pleased.— Representation of value wanted.—Lucky digging for silver.—Fits the case. Trouble worked out.—Ships built.—Rowing and paddling.—Ingenuity sails.—Against mind. — Delighted.—More ships.—Allegory ends.—Varieties of labor.—Dollar made, dollar saved. Intellectual and manual labor.—Confines of barbarism and civilization. — Combination. — Capital.—First lesson.—Money values.—Aim of life.—Little attention.—Carping.—No extreme. —Light.—Say it.—Better people.—Narrow-minded philosophy. —Choose for yourself.—Hoarding condemned.

IT is unfortunate for a reader who takes up a book with the idea of finding interesting matter within its pages, to be compelled to wade through two or three chapters of definitions. But the one who expects to gain information must at least expect to be taught the meaning of the terms in which the information is to be conveyed. The meaning of the term labor, is no doubt well understood by many; and that money is its representative, is equally well known. But to the money-maker who expects to use labor as the means of procuring it, he must be made aware that there are various kinds of labor, and the same kind varies greatly in quality, and that some kind of labor commands more money for the same time than other kinds, and that the better the quality of labor the higher price it will secure.

A hod-carrier cannot obtain the wages of a mason, although they work at the same general business; nor can an apprentice, or a poor mason, command the pay of a skilful one, although they are each masons. It is apparent, without a lengthy argument or illustration, that labor is valuable just in proportion to its *quality*, and in this respect does not vary from any article of merchandise, or of purchase and sale. As labor, too, is the only means by which value can be created, the rule of its quality extends from the simplest form of labor to the most intricate. The man who handles the shovel can display skill over another who may have equal strength and as good a tool. One banker may in like manner use more skill than another banker having like opportunities and equal capital. One merchant, with small means and poor opportunity, may far outstrip another in making money who may have larger means and a far superior chance.

This difference in the quality of the same kind of labor is called *skill*, and is a controlling feature in fixing the value of labor. It is a general guarantee of success in life, or in the business in which it is displayed. It elevates its possessor above his tradesmen or peers, and makes his labor always in demand. It is an advertisement in his business and an endorsement of ability before the public. It applies equally to *all* descriptions of labor without an exception, and is a controlling quality in the choice of a purchaser when known.

If you wish a mechanical job done, you will employ the

best man you know, by which is meant tne most skilful, and the one who will take the least time in which to do it, and hence will cost the least money. If you wish a physician, or a lawyer, if the case be worth it, and you are able to pay the amount charged, you will procure the best one that you know. If you wish to have a lot of goods purchased by a broker, a commission merchant, or any other expert, you will employ the one who is the most skilful in the market. If you wish a draft collected in foreign parts, you will employ the best banker. If you want your property insured, you will employ the best broker, for he is supposed to know the best companies.

There is no exception to the rule that he who is most skilful commands the readiest employment, and hence it is that every one desirous of making money should fully understand what this skill is. When they shall apprehend what it is, they should then be informed how to obtain it. This is the great lesson of life, and upon its being well or imperfectly learned depends the probable success or failure of the individual. It applies with equal force to the female as it does to the male. The female has within her reach in like manner the power to make herself independent, and still preserve the delicacy of her sex. Let no female, then, shrink from the task of making herself skilful in her avocation, whether it be in the gilded halls of fashion, the more modest one—the recipient of admiration, or the humbler one of the operative, or the climax of female hopes—the matron or mother. Skill will tell in each and every department of female life, and the success of such will measurably depend upon this cardinal of advancement.

Natural *skill* is the adaptation of *natural tact* to acquired knowledge. Natural tact is the natural bent of the mind. Some minds are mechanical, some calculative, some imaginative, some ingenious, some shrewd, some apparently neutral, displaying all qualities alike; some evincing a predominance fitting them for one department of life, and some for another. In the choice of employment it is useless to say that each individual would do well to follow the natural bent of his mind, which would give him tact in his business, and that would tend to give him skill. Skill may be obtained in any department of life by *perseverance* and *industry*, without the presence of natural tact. It is hence so much easier to accomplish, and the labor generally performed so much more agreeably and pleasantly that every person should, as far as practicable, follow the natural bent of his mind in the selection of business. This is well to know when the individual is free to choose; but many persons are thrown into employments accidentally, and in such cases their success may be aided by natural tact and may not.

Skill, whether natural or acquired, is the great guarantee of success in business of any kind. There may be partial or limited success, or through circumstances, a splendid success by the greatest blunderer; but the exception does not detract from the value of the rule. Those who look to these exceptions for a road to lead them to the temple of fortune will wear away their lives in poverty and disappointment.

SKILL is to be acquired by *knowledge* and *experience*. A chapter could be written on the qualities of mind of persons desirous of obtaining a fortune, in order to give a full explanation of the knowledge and experience required for that end, and what *skill* does in various occupations. It is only necessary to speak generally of it here, in order to explain the meaning of *skill*, to show the value of different qualities of the same kind of labor. The more knowledge a person possesses respecting his occupation, the more modes he understands of doing the same thing, and he is enabled to choose the best. If, however, he has never tried either mode, and does not know that it has been tried by others, he is wanting in experience as well as in knowledge, and he is as likely to do it to a disadvantage as he is to do it in the best and most skilful way. Knowledge may be obtained by reading, or orally, or by personal experience, and the greater such may be, the more skilful, as a general rule, is the laborer, it matters not what kind of labor he is performing.

The money-seeker must then understand that to be the *most skilful in his kind of occupation*, it matters not what it may be, is the *first* and *greatest* step towards making money. To be simply satisfied with knowing *how* to perform his vocation, may give him the means of a comfortable living; but if he wants more, he must increase by skill and knowledge the *value* of his labor, and he will have no difficulty in finding a ready market for it; or, as will be seen in a future chapter, must economize his earnings and deny himself everything except the bare necessaries of life until he shall have saved by this means what he fails to make by skill in his business. For let it be remembered that there is no male or female, with able body and sound mind, who can gain employment, that cannot in time make himself independent of manual labor, or independent of the labor of his vocation.

Employment is all that is required, and that is to be obtained by having a knowledge of what you undertake. Skill will prove the way in which the labor will be accomplished for a profitable end, as a general thing. Misfortune may overtake the most skilful. This should not prevent the effort to obtain skill and superiority, but should act as an incentive to prepare beforehand for such contingencies. This must show any one in search of money that labor is the only sure mode of obtaining it. Now it must be shown how labor can be represented by money. The representation of labor by money depends upon the relative value of the different kinds of labor; that is, the relative exchange of one labor for another of a different kind. And in order that the money-maker may understand the principles upon which his labor is valuable in money, and why money will release him from labor, it is necessary to show him how his labor can be represented by money in the first place, and then show him how he can command the labor in like manner of others, or how he can supply his wants with money without labor.

The machinery of life, to the casual observer, seems confused and uncertain. He looks around him and sees such a variety of trades and occupations—such a swarming of people in cities—such worlds of nations all moving together in harmony of life—that it amazes and surprises him. But let him once get the unit of this combined action, and it all reveals itself as simply as the confused crowd of figures in the multiplication table was revealed to his youthful wondering eyes when he became aware of the use of the unit in figures.

Agriculture was the primeval representation of labor, whether that labor was performed by gathering the natural fruits of the earth or by a successful endeavor to reproduce them in kind. The effort to reproduce them required, as we well know, the turning up and the smoothing down, and the general working of the ground.

It matters little whether this labor was performed by one, by two, or by a nation in this manner; there was a time when some rude instrument was used by the agriculturist to supply the place of hands to upturn the earth and work it. We will pass by all anterior modes of interchanges between these primeval agriculturists, and assume the point when they found it convenient or necessary to use implements in tilling the ground; and here the allegory explaining the machinery of society as it now exists begins.

There was in the far recesses of the past a community of agriculturists, and they occupied quite a territory of land productive and beautiful to behold. They gathered the fruits which overhung the land, and lived and increased in numbers. The natural products being insufficient to supply such numbers, and seeing that seeds grew and produced, they turned their attention to planting the seeds in the ground, and they were rewarded with a harvest. They found that digging in the ground with their hands and with sticks was a slow and tedious process; and an ingenious man conceived the idea of making a *hoe*, a rude construction to be sure, made of stone, and a hole in it for a handle. He was enabled to do as much with his hoe as four or five would do with their hands and sticks, and this his neighbors saw, and endeavored to follow his example and make a hoe for themselves. So the inhabitants all set to work to make hoes; but when they went to get the stone out of which to make them, some had, and some had not, the right kind of material; and the result was, some succeeded and some did not succeed in accomplishing their object.

Here was a spur to those who could not make hoes to get them in some shape; and the idea occurred to them to get the man who made the first hoe, and who had plenty of material, to make for them also. So application was made by a near friend to the hoe-man to make a hoe; and being a good-natured and obliging fellow, he consented, and made his friend a hoe. Another and another did the same, till the man found he had no time for anything else, and finally had nothing to eat. "This will not do," said he; "I must have something to live on, even if I disoblige my friends;" and revolving the thing over in his mind, an idea occurred to him. Said he to himself: "If I spend my time in making hoes for my neighbors, why should they not spend their time in raising grain for me?" After reflecting on the thing for a few days, he determined to make a stand, and not make any more hoes; and assigned as a reason that he had nothing to eat, and must go to work and raise something.

The man's neighbors, for whom he had made hoes, saw at once the injustice of taking his time and leaving him to starve. So each one made up in products just what they thought he might have earned at agriculture, and a little more on account of his having the material out of which he constructed them, and sent the amounts respectively to him. Of course the man was pleased, and at the same time amazed at the accuracy with which each one had judged with the other the amount to be given for each hoe. The man reflected upon it for some time, and said to himself: "I have more products given me for my hoes than I could have raised out of the earth in the meantime in making them; and instead of being just as well off as my neighbors, behold I am better off, and have a surplus." The man determined at once to make more hoes, and give notice to those whom he had refused that he would make for them, and take grain in payment therefor. The man was driven very hard to supply all with hoes who wanted them, and the grain poured in so fast upon him that he could not consume it.

About this time it was rumored, that a man living at a distance had made some cloth out of bark in a very peculiar way; and the people in that vicinity found in like manner as with the hoe, that they could get this cloth for grain; and although the cloth they made themselves answered their purposes very well, still this other cloth was handsomer and suited their tastes and fancies better than their own. The result was, that the cloth-man had very soon more to do than he could well attend to himself, and was overstocked with grain. A man who was an agriculturist, and also an ingenious man, knowing this state of things, went and proposed to the cloth-man to leave his agriculture and join him in making cloth. The cloth-man was pleased to have some one to help him, as he had more to do than was agreeable, and at once consented to let the agriculturist join him.

And they commenced working together. But they had not worked but a day or so on the cloth, when it became apparent that the one did twice as much as the other, and twice as well. This did not at first seem to make much difference, as the one was delighted to have some one to help him, while the other was equally delighted, and expected to get as much grain as the one who had worked at the cloth so long. They both worked on very well satisfied with each other, the neighbors bringing in products every day or so, and taking away some of the cloth. It soon became apparent that they all preferred the cloth of the Original Jacobs, and the agriculturist's cloth was left on hand. This did not seem to make any difference, till one day they had none of

Jacob's cloth, and they wished a customer to take some cloth made by the agriculturist. "Well," said the customer, "if you have none of the other I do not care for this, for we can make as good as that ourselves." And so the man went away and would not leave his grain. Then they tried with others to exchange the agriculturist's cloth for grain, but with no better success; and they were both exceedingly unhappy, and did not know what to do.

As the hoe-man had heard of the cloth made at a distance, and had seen some worn by a traveller who had passed his way, and also heard that the man would take grain for his cloth as he had done for his hoes, after thinking the matter over for some days, he determined to have some of the cloth. The next thing occurred to his mind was to know how he was to get it, and how he was to get the grain so far. He mused upon it for some time. Said he: "If I go myself and carry my grain, it will take me certainly six days. In that time I can make ten hoes that will bring me ten measures of grain, and they say I shall be obliged to give the cloth-man ten measures more for what I want. So when I get back, my cloth will cost me twenty measures of grain. Let me see; I know a friend going that way, and possibly he would take my grain and get my cloth. I will see him about it." He had scarce ended the sentence when his friend came in and began to speak of this same cloth, and told the hoe-man that he was going to make a journey there to get some of the cloth. "And," said he, "a traveller who has passed this way told me that he heard a man say, who was an agriculturist near by the cloth-man, that they had heard of your hoes over there and wanted some; but it was too far to carry the grain, and they had not come for them. Now an idea has occurred to me to carry some of these hoes over there and see if I can get grain for them, and then the grain being on the spot, I can easily get the cloth—what do you think of it?"

"Well," said the hoe-man, "I see no objection to it whatever. And another thing, Mr. Commerce (for that was his name), I want some of that cloth myself, and as you are going there, could you get some for me also?"

"Certainly," replied Mr. Commerce, "I would willingly oblige you; but I cannot carry either grain or hoes enough to get there and back in a week's time, but will do it as quickly as I can."

Now the hoe-man was a good, honest, and clever soul; and although Mr. Commerce was ready and willing to oblige him, and get his cloth and carry his hoes without compensation, he would not make ten measures of grain or ten hoes out of his, Mr. C.'s, labor without compensation, for he had had a taste of that himself. So he told Mr. Commerce what it would cost him to go, and frankly offered him the ten hoes or ten measures of wheat if he would bring back the cloth with him. Although Mr. Commerce had the reputation of being very shrewd and cunning, yet he had wisdom enough, and principle enough, too, not to extort from the hoe-man more than was fair, and he said he would take the matter into consideration. In a day or so he called again on the hoe-man, and in the meantime he had seen one of his neighbors who had heard of this same cloth, and who also wanted just as much as the hoe-man wanted. Mr. Commerce, being a calculating and really a shrewd man, said to himself: "If I can make something from the hoe-man, and something from my neighbor, who knows but what I may make enough to get my cloth for nothing?" The idea stimulated him greatly, and he went about to see if some one else did not want this cloth also, for they had all by this time heard of it. He was well rewarded, for very many who had raised more grain than they could use, because their new hoes had helped them so much, were anxious to get this cloth, and more particularly since they had heard the hoe-man was going to get some.

The result was, that Mr. Commerce began to count up, and found that if all were supplied it would take all the hoes the man had, and it would be utterly impossible for him to carry so many. So he set his wits to work to see how he could carry them, and finally hit upon an expedient. He conceived the idea of tying the hoes together, and balancing them across the back of an ox, and driving the ox before him to the distant land. The plan was divulged to the neighborhood, and all seemed much pleased, because it amounted to a contraband for each one to go separately.

An unexpected trouble occurred at this juncture, not thought of before by Mr. Commerce, and entirely new to the hoe-man. It now occurred to Mr. C. that he had not grain enough to give for the hoes, and how to arrange that matter he did not plainly see. So he went to the hoe-man, told the whole story to him, and, being a sensible man, he said: "As you will return in a week, and as I have these hoes on hand, and have grain enough to last me some time, and, to tell you the truth, I cannot just now take in so much, but will be able to do so by the time you return, you can take the hoes, and when you do return with the cloth our neighbors can bring in the grain. If this is satisfactory to you, it is so to me."

It is needless to say the parties perfectly agreed with each other, and the entire arrangement was carried out, and all arrived safely at their destination. Mr. Dimity and Mr. Headlong, for these were the cloth-makers, had in the meantime been thinking over the quandary in which they had placed themselves. Mr. Dimity had none of his own cloth, and none on hand except that made by Mr. Headlong. They were talking this matter over when Mr. Commerce arrived in the country. He left his ox some way back upon the road in a little grove, and, tying him to a tree, placed some food before him, and started for the abode of Mr. Dimity with one of his hoes. After a few passing remarks, Mr. C. inquired of Mr. Headlong, for he happened to speak to him first, "if he was the maker of certain cloth, which was considered very good?" To which Mr. Headlong replied in the affirmative, and showed him such as he had made.

"The cloth suits me," replied Mr. C.; "what do you ask for it?" and the price named was just what Mr. C. had supposed it would be. "Whether I take any or not will depend upon whether you can take what I can give you in return for it," said Mr. C. "I have here a hoe, an agricultural instrument, by which much more grain can be raised by one person than with the bare hands and sticks," said Mr. C.

"I have heard of that instrument," said Mr. Headlong, "and some one of my neighbors was saying that he wanted one, as he had heard them spoken of very highly."

"You can try it, and see how you like it; and if you do, then I will make you a proposition," said Mr. C. The result was that Mr. Headlong was pleased with the hoe, and regretted much that this was the only one Mr. C. had brought, as he had seen several who were anxious to procure one. The price was asked, and Mr. C. stated, "that they sold where they were made for ten measures of grain, and it could not be expected to bring them so far and sell them at the same here."

"No," replied Mr. Headlong, "I will willingly give you equal to fifteen measures of grain, payable in cloth, for this one, and if you had more I would take them on the same terms."

"Your offer is very liberal, Mr. H. How many would you take on those terms?"

"All you have," quickly replied Mr. H.

"Then I will let you have thirty," replied Mr. C.

"I do not know that I have cloth enough made to give you all of it now, but I will see," said Mr. H.

The result of the barter was that Mr. C. took back of Mr. Headlong's cloth sufficient to pay for the thirty hoes, and had made the value of fifteen more, and had it in cloth.

Dimity and Headlong sold their thirty hoes to the surrounding neighbors, and received more grain for them than they could have sold their cloth for. In fact, the people were all so well pleased, and so entirely satisfied, that Mr. Commerce became very popular. So much so, that he finally determined to establish himself midway between the countries, so that he might extend his operations to all sorts of things which were just being introduced by ingenuity and labor.

As the people increased in numbers, and the articles of use became more abundant, Mr. Commerce found it next to impossible to exchange one thing for another, and the people who had been so well satisfied with his management heretofore, were becoming clamorous and uneasy. He found that persons came from a great distance, and instead of bringing their goods along, they were compelled to leave them behind; for although they were valuable, and would command other things in exchange at that place, their bulk prevented their profitable removal. Finally he hit upon a plan by which one could remove, leaving his property behind, and take with him the representative in some small article which could be easily transported.

Then the question and main difficulty arose, how this representative should be made. It became evident from experience, as in the case of the thirty hoes which were sold for cloth, that what would represent the hoes where they were made, would not represent them where they were sold. So that Mr. Commerce and all the people whom he consulted saw at once that a hoe could not be represented everywhere by anything but itself, and they were still in trouble. As wants began to multiply, suggested by the great variety of little things made, and people increased also, every one found it very inconvenient to barter for these small things, and in many cases the people had to part with more, and buy more, than they wished to do.

Finally Mr. Commerce, who was an ingenious and very useful man to the people, hit upon a plan which all thought would work well, and be a great benefit to every one. He proposed, that when a person sold anything he should have something to represent the value of the price at which the thing was sold, and the seller should have the right to choose whether he would take other things in exchange, or whether he would take the agreed value, as arranged between the buyer and seller. This seemed to please every one ; but still there was a trouble, and that was, to find something compact which could be used as this representative. Some proposed pebbles, some wood, some bits of leather, and some one thing, and some another. But all such things they found would not do, because dishonest people could make any quantity of them without ever having had in their possession anything which they represented in value.

About this time a lucky circumstance for the people occurred. Some men were digging in the rocks in a neighboring mountain, and discovered a metal called silver; and as they had never seen such a thing before, they labored away some time, only procuring as much as they could hold in their hands. They at once conveyed it to Mr. Commerce to know what it was, and what it was worth, and supposed as a matter of course that he would know all about it.

"This is a strange thing to me," said Mr. C.; "where did you get it?"

"In a neighboring mountain," replied the men.

"Is it abundant?" inquired Mr. C.

"By no means," said the men; "we three have labored hard six days each to get what you have in your hand."

Now Mr. Commerce was a quick-minded man, and his experience had taught him much wisdom. A thought occurred to him, but he did not communicate it to the men, but said to them: "Go back to the mountain and work again for six days, and bring me as much silver as you will all three get, and I will pay you for your labor the same price as though you worked in the field at agriculture." The men were well satisfied and departed, and returned at the end of the six days, bringing just about as much as they had brought at first. Mr. Commerce paid them for their labor, and seeing that they could get as much for this kind of work as they could for any other, with the chance of finding much silver, they returned to the mountain, and worked on steadily. Other men hearing of this silver, started into other mountains, and some did, and some did not, obtain any.

Mr. Commerce, who was constantly making calculations, kept an account of every day's work that was done, either in exploring for, or working at, successfully or otherwise, this silver-getting, till he was satisfied that no great quantity of it could be obtained without a corresponding amount of labor. It had occurred to him before that this silver might be used as the representative of labor; but the exact way in which it could be used had not yet occurred to him. So, after a considerable time, he added up all the days' work which had been done at this silver-getting, and set a man to work dividing up the silver that had been obtained into just as many pieces as there had been days' work done; and he was astonished to find how small the pieces were. He then reasoned with himself in this wise: "If these men have worked faithfully, and I think they have, the result of one day's labor is one of these pieces of silver. Now these pieces of silver are small, and easily conveyed; can we not all agree to make these pieces of silver the standard of labor? Let me see how that will work. Suppose one man cannot do as much as another, how then? As for example, suppose one man should do twice as much as another?" And his own proposition seemed to bother him. But he quickly recovered, and said to himself: "No; this fixing the value of a day's work by a given piece of silver won't do; because the day's works will not all be alike, nor if alike, will they always produce the same value. My experience teaches me that VALUE is a relative term, and that there is *no value* to anything without exchange, or that will produce something to exchange. And, too, I find that the same thing will not always bring the same number of days' work, nor is it of the same value. It seems to me, then, that the *price* agreed upon between buyer and seller, or the *result*, should in some way be represented, and certainly this is the *value* of the thing or things at the time and place as agreed upon by the parties. Now if one thing is five times as valuable as another, if we can represent the value of one thing, we can easily represent the value of another. Just as I have learned in figures where one is the unit, and any number of results can be represented by repeating the unit or dividing it. Now if I can only get the people to agree, why not use one piece of silver to be the unit to represent *values*, or *agreed upon results*, between buyer and seller, as well as use the unit one a figure to represent the unit of results in figures?"

Mr. Commerce was so much elated with the idea that he at once called all the people together, told them the whole story, and asked them what they thought of it. Some thought well of it at once; others did not understand it; and others had so much confidence in Mr. Commerce, since they had always found him useful and honest, that all agreed to it in a body. Since then the results of labor and bargains for labor itself have been represented without difficulty. Everybody took their things to Mr. C.; and having provided himself with sufficient silver for the purpose, was prepared, after they had mutually agreed upon the value of what was sold or purchased, to represent the result in silver, and paid over the balance which was found in favor of the seller or buyer. Soon the people had silver themselves, and they would frequently go to their neighbors and get things for the silver, just as they had formerly exchanged with each other. The plan worked so well that the people flocked to Mr. Commerce for almost everything, and took almost everything to him, and his business increased so that he was compelled to build ships to carry things from one place to another, and have them rowed and paddled by men. This took away so many men from other pursuits that it became a serious matter, and the people were dissatisfied because that raised the price of labor. An ingenious man, seeing what was wanted, set to work and made a ship with sails to it, that would go when the wind blew without either being rowed or paddled. After he had it all completed he told Mr. Commerce about it, and asked him to look at it, and go with him in it sailing. They went, and it happened to be a fine day and a pleasant wind, and the ship went right past the other boats filled with men rowing, paddling, and tugging away, much to their amazement, because they saw no oars or paddles, and saw a few people standing upon the ship doing nothing. When the ship turned about to return, and the ingenious man had set his sails so as to go against the wind, Mr. Commerce was amazed, for he had not till then seen the utility of the thing. He thought that it was quite easy to go with the wind, but he had not seen how it would go against the wind alone.

Mr. Commerce at once made an agreement for the ship, and purchased it, paying a large pile of silver pieces for it; more than the man could carry. The ingenious man had more silver than he knew what to do with; but he went immediately about making others, and the result was the people were delighted, for they saw at once by the explanation of Mr. C. that this invention of sails to the ship gave them just so many more able-bodied men, and increased their total wealth just the value of so many more days' work in the year.

The entire success of this invention to save labor, or rather increase it, induced the people to hold out great encouragement, and offer large rewards to any ingenious person who would in like manner make any article by which more could be accomplished with less labor. For the people saw plainly that every day's labor saved was a day's labor made. The result was, that every species of contrivance to save labor was resorted to. A man made a mill to turn by water, which would require an immense number of men to accomplish the same thing; another made an engine to run by steam, which accomplished wonders.

The people, although much pleased with the first labor-saving machines, and aware that they saved the labor of men, soon found that the labor at first saved had a value nearly, if not quite, equal to manual labor; but as the supply of that kind of labor increased, it diminished in value. The same with the water power and the steam power; although each was the representative of labor, each had its value according to the demand and supply, just like manual labor.

The allegory must end here. Enough has been said to show the rise and progress of commerce from barter to the more easy exchange of the wants of high civilization; from the first form of manual labor in agriculture to higher labor of motive powers. It has been shown, too, from the allegory, how labor can be compared with labor, and that labor, or its equivalent, gives value to all things, and how the things themselves are compared with each other in value, and a difference obtained as the result, and how that result is represented by money.

To the money-maker the lesson is not only necessary, but is valuable, in order to show him what money is, and where to look to obtain it. Nor need he be ashamed to labor, for whoever has money that he has made himself, has labored to obtain it. There can be no escape from the disgrace, if disgrace it be, to labor—and the result of that labor should, perchance, be riches. More and closer than that, even, does the disgrace cling; the man who has a dollar in his pocket, if not given to him, or not dishonestly obtained, has labored for it, and the dollar, before he came in possession of it, was the representative of some one's labor. If labor is a disgrace, then to have money is likewise a disgrace.

Nor can all labor at the same thing. Honest labor makes honest money, and when it finally falls into the coffers of the wealthy, there is no distinction between one dollar and another; and so there should not be, in any rightly balanced mind, any invidious distinction between one kind of labor and another. All honest employments are commendable; nor should any one who is willing to be seen spending a dollar, be ashamed to be seen earning one. Education and refinement are what elevate, and make wide distinctions between individuals; and, generally speaking, the employment is indicative of these possessions. On this account it is that one employment is regarded less or more reputable and more respectable than another. This should be so; for he who arms himself with knowledge, and polishes himself of the asperities of his nature, and is refined and elegant in his manners, commands a higher price for his labor than he who is ignorant and takes no pains to accumulate those qualities. The former has fitted himself for higher duties in life than the latter, and his value as a member of society is greater to the community, and hence more highly esteemed. In the selection of employments choose those, if you can fit yourself for them, in which the compensation is greatest, and be assured they will require the exercise of the greatest amount of skill, and the possession of the greatest amount of knowledge.

The two great natural branches of LABOR, the INTELLECTUAL and the MANUAL, are never entirely separated. There is no such thing, possibly, as purely manual labor without some intellect, nor is there purely intellectual labor without something of the manual. There is nevertheless that which is denominated manual labor, and that which is called intellectual labor, and the two may be said to bound the kingdom of labor on each confine. Between these two extremes all possible combinations of the manual and the intellectual take place. Upon the one confine it is the lingering rays of barbarism, and upon the other the full, sure light of civilization. Those two hands of labor work in unison to produce the great intermediate circulation of the middling classes, and all chime together to make the harmony of society.

As intellectual and manual labor combined, as is seen, produce such admirable results, there is still another combination of each of them, separately or together, with concentrated labor, that produces still higher and more brilliant results. Concentrated labor is money, or what is usually termed CAPITAL. When one man furnishes the capital, and another man does the manual and intellectual labor necessary to manage it, they both really work together, the one with money, the other with labor not yet turned to money.

CAPITAL is the representative of labor, and is obtained as the profits of labor, or is the surplus of the proceeds of labor over expenditure. The one who expects to make money will soon find himself in the possession of capi tal if he is successful. It is regarded by most people as essential to a full and fair start in the world. Be sure, however, that the one who does not know how to make capital will not understand how to handle it safely and successfully if entrusted to him. To know how to make a dollar and save it, is the first lesson of the money-maker, and is generally the key that will lock up safely the fortune. This, if it be no more than a dollar, is capital; small to be sure, but yet it is capital.

When Mr. Commerce wanted to take the hoes of the manufacturer if the latter had refused him the credit, then would have been the time to use capital. For Mr. C. saw that he could make by the operation; and if he had paid down for them, there would have been no need of asking a favor of the manufacturer. But Mr. Commerce got on just as well without as he would have done with the money. Simply because the manufacturer had confidence in him and that his property was safe in his hands.

This allowing persons to take property for a time without paying for it, is called credit, and, as has been seen, is sometimes just as good as ready capital in order to accomplish the objects of trade. If one carpenter borrows the tools of another and uses them, he has borrowed and used capital, and in just as complete a manner as though he had borrowed their market value in money and used it for the same time. Capital may be in money, or it may be in money values; in either case it is the representative of labor, and its name is generally taken to signify money or money values, owned by the possessor.

These definitions and explanations are all deemed necessary, in order to expose the foundations of wealth and show what it is, and on what its getting and possession depend. If money is of no value to supply wants, then it is of no value as a source of comfort and pleasure, and can offer no inducement to the seeker after fortune.

To explain to him how money comes, what it is, and what it will do, is quite as essential as to point out the mode of procuring and the mode of keeping it.

To procure money is the object of the entire toiling world. It has been a source of amusement at times to hear persons condemn the individual who was striving to make an early independence—even go further, and say money was not worth the having. Such people are not honest with themselves, for if they had either the chance or the ability to make money, they would be the first to embrace it. Money-making is a duty—a political duty. How are our institutions of learning to be kept up, our government supported, our churches filled, our school-houses built, our children brought up, clothed, and fed, the aged supported, the cripple aided, the helpless widows and orphans cared for, without money is made by some one? And if the money-maker has the disgrace of doing all this, then such disgrace be our lot, and the lot of those whom we wish to instruct in money-getting and money-saving, for these purposes, and thousands of others equally worthy.

There is no subject in the whole range of life that has received so little attention from the pens of writers as this. Piles on piles, nay thousands on thousands, of books have been written to display profligacy, vice, and ruin, while scarce any have been put forth to urge men to save instead of spending their substance. Education of every sort and kind, from science to spiritualism, is rampant in the land through tall edifices, dotting every acre in our cities, and every town in our country; yet not comparatively a word is breathed to the youth or to the middle-aged to educate them how to get and how to save, or how to use labor and knowledge to the best advantage. The teacher will toil with his pupil for days and weeks to show him the intricate points of a mathematical problem which shall calculate wealth when made, and show him by great labor where he will make his own error when he attempts it unaided ; but not one lisp will he utter to tell him where the leak will probably be in his finances, which, if not guarded, will consign him early to poverty, and later to the poor-house.

This book will probably be met by the press and some carping individuals, as most books of this nature are, by the accusation that it tends to degrade the human heart to money-making—to make the young mean and the old miserly. To all this there is but one answer. You must not educate physicians, because they may give too much poison ; you must not educate in oratory, for fear of the bronchitis or overstrain of the lungs ; you must not educate in religion, for fear of making bigots ; in truth, you must not educate at all, for fear the pupil will run to extremes. Mean and miserly people are uniformly those who have not been educated or brought up in the light of knowledge, but who know just enough of money not to know its real use.

Let the complaining individual choose between two estates—the fear that his son or daughter *might be mean with money*, or poverty and dependence on the charity, and live on the earnings of some other individual. This will test the reason and the soundness of murmurings against a work on educating either the young or the old in the art of making or saving money. Let it go to the extreme even on both sides, that they absolutely are mean and miserly, and in possession of a competency, or are in poverty, subject to the cold charities of the public authorities. Which do you choose? If you are truly honest it is not difficult to make an answer for any parent or friend.

If there can be one ray of light shed by any one upon this subject to make the young or the old economical, saving, and prudent of money, let it shine! If one incentive can be urged by eloquent language, or attractive and bewitching pictures of the future, to nail the well-earned dollar in safety for the hour of need, let the words be spoken, and the pictures be stereotyped. If anything can be done for the young to arrest profligacy, and thence choke out vice, let no man complain even at the risk of not fully educating here and there one who may become mean or even miserly. If any book can be written which will show to any class of people how to be more prosperous, how to increase in means, how to avoid losses, how to avoid reverses of fortune, how to live better and happier, how to be free from charities, and finally how to become better citizens, and better members of society, let the book be printed and spread broadcast over the land.

Let no narrow-minded philosophy meet it in the way, and say "hold!" Let no carping lips say, "You will make misers of our children;" but let them read—not one thing only—the way to save—but let them read the way to make money also—the very lesson which every parent wants early put in practice upon his striving child. It is a false philosophy which pretends to despise money-making, but a true philosophy which condemns in unmeasured terms the hoarding of riches.

CHAPTER V.

THE SEEDS OF FORTUNES.

Parental cares.—Obligations.—Affections.—Visions of the future.—Ambitions.—Education.—Most important neglected.—Married life.—Ignorance.—Company.—Like stripe.—Break up.—Yardstick.—Bare subsistence.—New start.—Ship.—Not a mariner.—Storm.—Shipwreck.—Questions.—Inexperience does all.—Testators.—Lifetime.—Parental anxiety.—Cause of early failure.—No business education.—Embryo merchant.—Suddenly gifted —Swim, my child.—Must learn first.—Unnatural mothers.—Purchasing without knowledge.—At twenty-one, eleven years a merchant.—Calculations.—Astonishing result.—Free from charity.—Seeds of fortune.—Early sown.—Children's business.—Learns how.—Great epoch.—Starts to trade.—First bargain.—Success.—Rules of action.—Time consumed.—First dollar nailed.—Spur to action.—School and collegiate education.—How managed.—Figures.—All can.—Settlement on children.—Easy.—Useless expenses.—Large amounts.—Table.—How to get increase.—Conversation.—Rubbing out values.—Bank bills on your back.—Big loss.—Take care.—Worldly goods.—Independence.—Future.—No poverty.

"Just as the twig is bent the tree inclines." Parents seldom reflect how much responsibility is thrown upon them in the rearing of a child. First, they are bound by affection and by the law, to provide food and clothing for them, and are responsible for all their depredatory acts. Night and morning, day in and day out, they watch over and provide for their wants. The midnight hour surprises the mother in some pleasant task for her young, some little thing which the business of the day crowded out of its legitimate place. And thus the days, and even the years roll away, and as the youth grows the cares continue, and never cease.

Late and early the child is watched to keep it out of harm's way, and then its education begins. The usual religious devotions are lisped over night and morning, and in more mature speech scraps of the Catechism are repeated orally, and at last the herculean task of learning the alphabet is crowded upon the child's memory. The task is accomplished; the child is promising, is smart, and is rather uncommon. Bright visions of the future light up in the affection of the parents as they follow in their mind's eye the gallant young man of twenty-one, captivating crowds of admiring young ladies, or taking the first honors in some high institution of learning, and just about entering upon the path of life which will lead him to honor, wealth, and possibly glory; or a daughter, whose fair form they see gracing the halls of the princely mansion, or drawing around her dazzling beauty the fashion of the land.

These visions are varied at any new feature displayed by the beloved offspring. Ambition seizes possession of the hearts of the parents, and they determine at once to crowd the mind of the child with every sort of knowledge. Teachers are procured accordingly. Music, dancing, French, Italian, Latin, Greek, with reading history, geography, arithmetic, and belles-lettres for the daughter, and a like array for the son. The education becomes complete; the daughter soon enters the round of society; is admired, is courted, is won, and is married. The son graduates respectably; either enters a profession, or goes into commercial life. And now begins the effect of an education which is entirely on a wrong basis, or, rather, the most important thing has been neglected.

The young lady has married either a man who has just been left a fortune, or is out of his time as a clerk, and is ready to go into business on his own account, or some other similar connection; either of which, under the present system of education, will in a very few years lead to the same result in nine cases out of ten. The young woman being suddenly placed in charge of a house, at once finds that she knows nothing of housekeeping, of the value of a single article of household goods, or what the realities of the world are made of. The young man of fortune, her husband, is worse still, if possible; he never was inside of a market, don't know the value of a single article of food, and scarcely of clothing, or how to purchase one article for his table. Ignorance reigns supreme over the household about all matters except what is denominated a good education. There is money enough, to be sure; and as for the price of vegetables and meats, that can be learned very soon—so say they.

The servants are procured, the house is furnished by some one who happens to get the order, and the horses and carriage are at the door. The house is open to company, and the new-married couple are in society. Friends of a like stripe flock around, things run smoothly for a time, the red flag finally hangs out of the window, and the next you hear, the lovely couple have gone to Europe, and in four or five years you may see the rich young man measuring off tape by the yard in some shop that sold him his dry-goods. This is not an overdrawn picture, for the experience of almost every one can recall to mind similar, if not exact, fac-similes of results. If the thing be varied in any way, it may be by the curtailment of the basis of the first start in life, the means spent having reduced the fortune to a respectable living, if not to a meagre support or a bare subsistence.

Whatever may be the circumstances of any who are left with money, not one in a hundred retains the original amount. Depletion is sure to follow, as a rule, even though the desire, the intention, and the effort be to increase instead of diminishing it. The individual who suddenly becomes possessed of wealth by inheritance or chance luck, is in the position of a landsman who suddenly finds himself alone on shipboard out at sea. To be sure the ship is there, the rudder is in place, the sails are all bent, and under a fair and moderate breeze he may have skill enough to hold the helm aright, and if he paid but little attention to it, if the ship was in trim, all would go well. Some skilful and experienced hand had accomplished all this, and a moment's reflection will inform the most superficial mind that such skill and experience were not the work of a day or of a year.

The inexperienced mariner has his inexperienced family on board. From want of attention and care the sails soon become mildewed, and split with the first gust of wind that strikes them; the yards are out of place; one gives way after another, till weakness prevails in every part of former strength and symmetry. The first storm finishes the rigging, and now comes the danger of total shipwreck. If the helpless and ignorant seamen can reach the land in safety with their lives, they little care what becomes of the floating hull. Nor is the management of a fortune less difficult to perform in its way than the management of a ship at sea. Ask the captain of such a vessel whether he would place a son of his in charge of such a ship without his having been well grounded in the theoretical as well as the practical knowledge of seamanship? Ask him whether any degree of affection would induce him to thus expose both the safety of the ship, and the life of his son? Ask him, too, what were the probable chances under such circumstances that the ship, cargo, and souls on board would reach a haven in safety over an ordinary sea-voyage? His answer would undoubtedly be about the same as it would be, if you asked the head of a banking-house what would be the result of his business if entrusted to the management of the youngest and most inexperienced clerk in his establishment.

Though the case is a clear one, that inexperience in any department of life is conclusive evidence of inability, no thought is bestowed, apparently, by testators as to the ability of the heir to take care of what they are conferring. Some there are who do measure all these things accurately in a well-balanced mind; but the cases are as scarce as the skilful management of money by the inexperienced. Nor is it always within the ability of the man of wealth to bestow his own money, for disease or death may overtake him, and leave it for the law of the land to distribute. If he has no interest in the persons who are to be his heirs, then he need take no thought to surround them with defences against sharpers, or give them knowledge of the way to manage what has required every moment of his thoughts, and a lifetime of experience to do well.

Affection prompts the parent to do everything for the child, for his education, as a means of advancement in life. No wish is left ungratified, no money denied for pleasure, no stone left unturned for his gratification. Every want is supplied, even without the asking; every look penetrated to discern the bent of the unfolding mind; every action balanced to note progress in knowledge, and every grace scanned to mark the advance in refinement. The argus eye of the parent is ever watchful, the heart ever anxious. Time rolls on, and the young girl passes away from under this supervision to the cares of her own, and the boy to seek what the parent has heretofore given him. Even in these new conditions everything that devoting parents can confer is still extended to the striving children. They commence to act for themselves, they must purchase for themselves, they must make for themselves, they must find means for themselves, and they must finally manage for themselves.

Now let us examine for a moment what education they have received, either at the school or under the parental roof, to enable them to enter on these duties. Has the parent or the teacher ever taught them the value of a single article which has supplied their wants, as a part of their education? True, the child may have heard the cost or price of this or that; but has the child ever been systematically taught the business of life while under the care of the parent? Has the child been placed in the independent condition with respect to supplying its own wants, and carrying on its own business, as it has been compelled to read and learn, for the purpose of using that learning independent of the parent? Has the child's attention ever been called to the manipulations of life, by the A B C manipulations, in supplying its own wants while under the parental roof? If not, how can you reasonably expect or ask anything but ignorance, and consequent failure for a time, when they are called upon by the parent to act for themselves? Would you expect the child shall be suddenly gifted with that which all experience tells is the result of great experience? Would you expect that child to read before it had learned the letters, speak the language before it had uttered a sound, or in like manner use, handle, protect, invest, and keep money before it had learned the value of a dollar? Would you, if you wished to teach him to swim, take him to a precipice and dash him into the water, and carelessly say to him: "Swim, my child!"

No; such infanticide would send a thrill of horror through your entire being; but you do little less when you allow the child of your affection to be launched untutored into the turbulent sea of life, where failure, want, poverty, and misery, are less welcome than death itself. Your kindness, your affection, your pride, ruin your child before he leaves the parental home. You first unfit him by his antecedents for business and for the affairs of life, and then wonder why he does not thrive; and finally, if so lucky he or you may be, after failure overtakes him, you gather him again to yourself, and renurse and redestroy the little advance he has made. But if circumstances do not thus favor him, he sinks down in despair, and the winds of fortune drift him to and fro like the withered leaves of the forest.

This, all this, is generally the fault of the parent. The early days of the child are spent with an uneducated, selfish nurse, and from her its first impressions of character are received. Among the higher walks of life, and to those especially, these remarks more particularly apply. The mother often cannot afford even to feed the child from her own flesh, but borrows an unnatural substitute. The moment the little creature can talk it is taught to despise everything common, that is, everything that appertains to the realities of life except a love for dress, show, and company. It is unnecessary to repeat the course of education in the nurseries of many of the present day. The absence of all attempts to teach children what will be insisted on in this book shall be taught them, to fit them to become successful men and women, is not now undertaken, even though it be known.

The following remarks respecting the partial preparation of children while under the parental care or while young, in the knowledge of the affairs of life, apply equally to all, the rich and the poor, the high and the low. The main difficulty which all young persons experience when they come to act for themselves is, that they do not know what to do. If a merchant wished to buy a stock of goods to advantage, how do you think he would succeed if he had never bought an article in his life, nor even been present at the purchase of one? No trouble at all about purchasing the stock; that would be simple and easy. He would only have to inquire out who kept this and that thing, and the purchasing would be readily accomplished. He would be just as likely to buy his articles third or fourth-handed, as to buy them of first hands; and if he was so fortunate as to buy them of first hands, he would be as likely to pay one price as another. His first step in merchandizing would probably be his ruin; and when once his capital is gone, and his credit too, he is worse off than a young man without friends or money.

The young beginner, without experience in the manner of purchasing, the value of the articles which he is compelled to purchase, and the little business which he is forced to carry on to supply his own personal wants, may fail as utterly in his first attempt, and probably would, as the man who undertakes merchandizing without knowledge. And if such a beginner had no parent or friend to fall back upon and supply the loss or deficiency, the embarrassment would be about equal in both instances. But if the child had been taught at twelve years of age that he was a consumer, and hence might at that early age become an embryo merchant, and had been furnished with the capital used by the parent to begin to purchase what he himself consumed, an education in value and in the actual business of life would have been begun. When that child had arrived at the age of twenty-one he would have been nine years a practical merchant, and would ordinarily have touched the value of every article of consumption sold in the land. And if such business had been conducted with skill and economy, the profits of it over and above what the parent would have expended in the same thing would be a handsome capital for the young man to commence merchandizing upon, or give him a good start in some other business.

The figures resulting from such a course would astonish the most calculating. The benefits to the child would be enduring; and at every step in his career, from the day he was twelve years old till he was twenty-one, some practical and useful knowledge would be acquired. Nor would this at all interfere with his general education, except to materially aid him in procuring knowledge. It would make him self-confident, improve his reasoning powers, and increase his thought and calculation. He would from necessity be made to know the value of a dollar, which is the first step towards certainly being independent of charity. This word charity sounds harsh upon the ear, though many who are dependent upon it are not ready to admit the fact.

The child is supported by the charity, in one sense, of the parent, till he supports himself. The friend who eats your bread and can get bread in no other way, lives on charity. The old who cannot work, and have no means, in like manner are the subjects of charity. The position of being the recipient of charity is an unenviable one, and it is more honorable to work at any honest employment than accept this boon. If, then, the young can place themselves beyond the charity of the parent even, they will accomplish a great and good work. But this is scarce expected, except when the parent has not the means to support and educate the child.

The seeds of a fortune, if sown to grow, must be sown early. There may be those who will find out later the means of managing for themselves so as to accomplish the object. But the earlier the lesson of economy, self-denial, prudence and skill in handling capital, is learned, the earlier it can be put in practice. The earlier the lesson is taught to the child, of the handling and the having of money for the purpose of being out of the humiliating position of dependence, the less fear there is that it will be sought for with an appetite for hoarding. The child must be taught rightly, or the instruction may act like medicine given in over or under-doses.

There may be objections in the mode laid down here; but if any should suggest themselves to parents they can vary them at their pleasure. What will be done here must be regarded as simply suggestions, not rules of action. It is then suggested that, if the child is hale and hearty, the age of twelve years seems to be early enough to commence the training in miniature or ABC business. They, both male and female, should then be informed by the parent, that after that day they would be required by their aid, or by the aid of some proper person, to purchase every article of clothing which they were to wear, attend to its making, and perform generally the business of their own. That they were to pay for their subsistence to the parent about its cost. That to do this a certain stipend per annum was to be allowed, and a systematic account kept to show the expenditure of every cent and the corresponding amounts received.

In this way the child will early be taught to figure, calculate, and trade. He will also see the value of the boon of parental care, and be made to appreciate it. Let the amount for his expenditure be ample, and at the same time imperative, and one or two domestic failures will give him a foretaste of heavier ones in after years. Let him understand, too, the disgrace of failure—put him in coventry and curtail his privileges, and make him feel early that to go beyond his depth and exceed his right, is morally wrong, as well as personally disgraceful. Make him understand the moral and legal obligation of his contract, for he will readily accept the offer to have the stipend and make his own expenditures. Such is human nature, even in its earliest stages, that responsibility creates self-respect; and such an offer to a boy or girl will be as great an epoch in their history as the day when they legally are beyond the control of the parent.

The difficulty in such an arrangement is that the parents will be the first to give out. At first the idea may strike them favorably; but the trouble will be too great, and they cannot *see the effects of a different course.* Though if one parent will take the trouble, and will persevere to the end, and the result shall be one child educated rightly in his business habits, the book will do good, and the instruction is not in vain.

"And now, my young man, I am going to take you to purchase the first pair of shoes you ever bought; and as we go along we will have a talk together. You know you have got your father's money, which he has labored hard to procure, and every shilling counts one with him. He has also entrusted you with it to expend for necessaries, and as a trustee of that money you must spend it only for such things as are purely necessary, and with his permission only. You may say that you have to-day entered, by your father's consent, upon your A B C manhood. He has done this to educate you in the way of the world. If you use the knowledge you will gain by his kindness in this respect, you will thank the day when you commenced this system of education, and all I can say to you is, persevere in it till your father ceases to give you the means of support."

"We are now at the shoe-shop. What number do you wear?"

"I don't know," replied the boy.

"Certainly I did not suppose you did; but find out, so that when you come again you need not spend a quarter of an hour trying on shoes till you find a pair to fit; for by your ignorance of that fact now, three of us, the shoemaker, yourself, and myself, lose collectively about half an hour of valuable time—yours for play and study, mine for writing, and the shoemaker, who, because everybody is equally ignorant, has to charge more for his shoes. What kind of shoes do you want?"

"I do not know; such as mother gets me, I suppose," replied the boy. "Yes, calf-skin, thick soled."

Now I must give you a few rules about purchasing, which you should remember.

Find out before you start just what you want. This will save time, and keep you from buying what you do not want, or cheap bargains, which are always the dearest in the end.

Ask for the varieties of the kind of goods you want, if you desire to select. Ask for nothing else.

To ask to see that which you do not want, out of curiosity, is taking the time of the tradesman by false pretences. It is taking from him by false representations that which is money to him. If he voluntarily offers to show you, look if you please.

Ask the price simply.

If the price and article suit you, take it; and if it does not suit you, leave it, and ask no abatement.

If the tradesman can abate, and wishes to sell at a lower rate, he may himself make the proposition. But if you do it, you imply that he charges more than he can afford to take, and is making an exorbitant profit. It is jockeying on the part of the purchaser, which is both undignified and unmanly.

Be prompt in your decisions.

This is practicable if you know what you want, and it saves much time all around.

Never ask the wholesale dealer to sell you a retail quantity at wholesale price.

For then you both do injustice to the retailer, and you ask the wholesaler to give you the amount of money which is the proper addition to the wholesale price, whether the business be done by one man or by another.

If a tradesman deceives you, go to him no more.

There are more places than one where you can get the same article; and if he deceives you once, he will in all probability deceive you again.

If he sell you a poor article for good, inform him of it.

The chances are, he is as much deceived as you, as false representations make him criminally liable. He will readily correct the error if he is an honest man; if not, you cannot make him honest by complaint at law, though that might be your duty.

If you find you have deceived yourself in a purchase, keep the goods.

The seller cannot find eyes and judgment on both sides of a bargain; do not then blame him, but blame yourself.

Treat tradesmen with respect and politeness.

The buyer and the seller, in all honest and necessary dealings, stand on an equal platform. They are each necessary to the other, and are, for the time, equal to each other—the one holding the goods, the other the money. Be polite and civil to them, and you will generally provoke the same civility in return.

Be discriminating in values.

There may be a hundred articles of the same kind and same price, but one may be of much better quality and more valuable than another; and in order that you shall get the most for your money, you must select the best out of the lot.

With these very general, but by no means all the suggestions which might be made to you, we will now enter the shoe-store, and you may make your first purchase.

The young beginner completed his purchase, his shoes were good, the amount of money paid a little less than the parent usually gave; for, somehow, the merchant thought he would not put on the extreme price to such a novice, and the whole transaction was eminently satisfactory to all parties. It is not difficult to see what qualities of the mind were called into exercise by this simple practical lesson. The boy would at once begin to examine such articles, inquire what they were made of, and of their various qualities, the kinds of leather used—

how it was made, and where; till following up these suggestions, his mind would ramify into every avenue of knowledge of such practical nature and utility. Such information would store his mind with facts highly essential to the vigorous attainment of other learning, as the mind would have external exercise highly beneficial to its energetic action.

It is but too apparent that all this will consume much time of some one. But a common education in letters cannot be obtained without a long series of care on the part of the teacher, and the expenditure of time on the part of the pupil. At the present time this business education is commenced when all other education is finished, and the pupil begins to use it before he has learned the lesson. The result is, that the education is too expensive in most cases, involving the inexperienced in debt and trouble which it takes half a lifetime to wipe away. Human action must be excited by an object in order to prove effective; and hence, if you wish the child to aid in this sort of education, you must not only extend to him a motive, but you must show him some advantage which he is to reap from all this labor on his part. If you can accomplish that, you will even find him foremost in his desire to accomplish something.

You need not teach children that it is pleasant to have money, for as soon as they find out that money will buy a whistle, a top, or a rocking-horse, that lesson is learned. Nor will they be slow in discovering every attribute of a fortune. But should they be so obtuse, the parent or guardian should instil into their minds the cardinal *virtue* and *duty*, that is, to *labor for and have money*, in order that they may neither be a charge upon the public nor upon their friends. With this *moral and political duty* constantly held up before their minds, they will see that the object for which they are striving is not mercenary and mean, but that it is the highest and first duty of man, and is in every way commendable and praiseworthy.

The independence should be sought for with care and with thought, as being next best to knowledge. Nor is knowledge necessarily superior to one's duties to his neighbor, himself, and to the public at large. Then, in order that the youth may be excited to acquire a business knowledge and plant his first dollar in security as the seed of an independence or of a fortune, he must be told what that dollar will accomplish towards this desirable end. He must be taught how a dollar can be *lost* as well as *earned*, and that it, like the seed placed in the ground, requires fencing in, to protect it from being destroyed.

The incentive to make money should be explained; and the same care and attention which will make the little business of the child profitable will make the larger business of the man profitable also. The business of the man is prosecuted for profit and a living; the business of the child can be made the same by proper arrangement. The parent can either allow a commission to the child on the amount of his expenditure, *if the business be well done*, or allow him to make his profit out of the difference between his income and expenditure. The child must feel, as the merchant feels, that he has the *chance* of making something, or he will be discouraged and take no interest in his little business.

The parent will have accomplished all his duty in one direction if he gives his child a business education as well as an ordinary school or collegiate one, and fits him to avail himself certainly of what the parent can do still further for him. The moment one becomes a parent they have a money obligation thrown upon them to make a certain kind of independence for another. How, asks the reader, can this be done? The answer is simple, and the course is equally so. What is the parent's wish? Does he wish to give the child a collegiate education?

We will suppose this first, and suppose, too, that the means are limited, and the prospect, under ordinary circumstances, is, that they will not be *able* to do so. Let us see. You will be able to give him the ordinary education, probably, to fit him for college; if not, we will show how that can be done. We will suppose that this will cost two hundred dollars, and his collegiate education will cost one thousand dollars. Now suppose you commence his primary education at thirteen years old, and his collegiate education at fifteen. Now let us see what is to be done to get the money. You have twelve years to make the two hundred dollars in, and fifteen years to make the one thousand dollars in. How much have you got to save daily (three hundred and eighteen working days), improved every six months, to have the amount? You commence the first year the child is born, and continue the same each day of the twelve years. Look at the tables of earnings for *ten* years; 5 cents per day gives $199.89 at 5 per cent., $210.26 at 6 per cent., and $222.29 at 7 per cent. By the *one year* table you find that 5 cents per day gives for two years (one double) $15.85 at 5 per cent., $15.88 at 6 per cent., and $15.92 at 7 per cent. So that if the parent put aside every day 5 cents, when the child was 13 years old, there would result $215.74 if improved at 5 per cent., $226.14 if improved at 6 per cent., and $238.21 if improved at 7 per cent. We ask, is there any one who could not lay aside $15.90 per year, or 5 cents per day, to educate a child?

Let us now examine as to the $1,000 necessary for the collegiate education. The parent has from the time the child is born till he is say 16 years old to lay aside this amount, that is, 15 years. Look at the 15 years' accumulation table, and you find that 15 cents a day, improved at 5 per cent., gives $1,030.62; improved at 6 per cent. gives $1,116.83; improved at 7 per cent. gives $1,211.84. Is there any one scarcely in this country who cannot lay aside 20 cents a day, or $63.60 per year, besides supporting himself?

Assume, if you please, that the parent is well off, and wishes to make a settlement of a stated sum upon the child when twenty-five years of age, for the purpose of going into business, or settling himself comfortably, or as a marriage gift, possibly, to a young lady. Suppose it to be $10,000. How much would the parent be obliged to lay aside, improved at seven per cent., to accomplish that object? Look at the *twenty-five year* table of improved earnings, run down the column under seven per cent. till you find the nearest sum to it. You find $10,251, and find that fifty cents per day, accumulated at seven per cent., has done the business. There is scarcely a family where this amount is not frittered away daily, and even more.

But suppose there were five children, each requiring this sum, the whole amount would be but $2.50 per day, for 313 working days, for 25 years, or a gross sum of $51,255. There are very few families who could not save this sum from their expenditures without feeling or missing it. It amounts to but $15 per week, or $910 per annum; or $3 per week per child, or $182 per year per child. There would, however, be but little use in putting this sum in the hands of a child not educated as before spoken of, in the ways of business, as in all probability it would be lost in a short time, and the reasons will be apparent if the reader reads this book through. If, however, any doubt would exist in the mind of the parent, the sum could be placed at interest, and the interest only given; or, still better, purchase an annuity, which would place the child beyond want during life.

How much money is uselessly spent on children—uselessly because it neither educates, nourishes, feeds, clothes, nor is advantageous to them; but is generally a great disadvantage to them, by teaching them that every whim or want can be supplied, and thereby giving them a taste and an education to spend rather than earn.

It is within bounds to say that every child of fair, well-to-do parents has one hundred dollars a year spent upon him, by parents, which could be dispensed with; that is, in extra cost of clothing, toys, and a thousand and one things. That is 31 cents per day on an average, say till he is 11 years old, and at least 50 cents from then till he is 21 years old, an average say of 41 cents for twenty years. Now it will probably astonish any one to find what sum this will be, supposing that it is spent only 313 working days of each year. By turning to the twenty-year table of earnings we find that this sum, improved at 5 per cent., gives $4,324; improved at 6 per cent. gives $4,838; improved at 7 per cent. gives $5,424; improved at 8 per cent. gives $6,096.

The amount of 41 cents is far inside the real useless expenditure in nine cases out of every ten. Let any one but calculate the amount spent by any one of his children during this period, and he will find that it approaches near a dollar, and often more. But suppose it to be a dollar, we find the amount at 21 years to be, improved at

7 per cent. $13,232, a snug little capital to commence life with, or purchase an annuity to make him independent of want.

Over is a table which shows what an expenditure of $10 made from the age of one year to 25 years will cost, or will produce if compounded at 7 per cent. at 30, 40, 50, 60, and 70 years. That is, if the same amount in money had been put at interest, how much it would amount to at those periods.

This table explains itself. It will be seen by that, that an expenditure of $10 at 1 year of age if invested at 7 per cent., would be $76.12 at 30 years of age, $149.74 at 40, $294.57 at 50, $579.46 at 60, $1,139.89 at 70, $2,242.24 at 80 years of age, and so on. And if repeated every year to the end of twenty-five years, the result would be the gross sums of each line added up for the various ages, 30, 40, 50, 60, 70, and 80. Thus it will be seen what ample provision can be made for a child by a little self-denial and a judicious investment of a very trifling sum each year—a sum that would never be missed from the household expenditures.

In like manner, by reference to the tables of earnings in the back part of the book, say for twenty-five years, either the child or the parent can see that the saving of a cent daily will amount, at 7 per cent., to $205 when he is twenty-five years old; of 5 cents per day, to $1,025; of 10 cents a day, to $2,050; of 25 cents a day, to $5,125; of 50 cents, to $10,250, and so on. Is it saying too much to assert that an independence for a child is within the reach and power of almost any one? But, says the reader, "I may be able to get the money, but how can I get the increase?" We say read on; you will find out that in time as you progress.

TABLE

Showing an expenditure of $10 at any age from 1 to 25 years, and the amount such would be if improved at compound interest at 7 per cent. at 30, 40, 50, 60, 70, and 80 years of such person's age.

YEARS OLD WHEN SPENT.	At 30 years.	At 40 years.	At 50 years.	At 60 years.	At 70 years.	At 80 years.
1	$76 12	$149 74	$294 57	$579 46	$1,139 89	$2,242 24
2	71 14	139 95	275 30	541 56	1,065 32	2,095 65
3	66 49	130 79	257 29	506 13	995 63	1,958 55
4	62 14	122 24	240 45	473 02	930 49	1,830 32
5	58 07	114 24	224 73	442 07	869 62	1,710 67
6	54 27	106 77	210 02	413 15	812 72	1,598 76
7	50 72	99 78	196 28	386 12	759 56	1,494 17
8	47 41	93 25	183 44	360 86	709 87	1,396 42
9	44 30	87 15	171 44	337 25	663 43	1,305 06
10	41 41	81 45	160 23	315 19	620 03	1,219 69
11	38 70	76 12	149 74	294 59	579 46	1,139 89
12	36 17	71 14	139 95	275 30	541 56	1,065 32
13	33 80	66 49	130 79	257 28	506 13	995 63
14	31 59	62 14	122 24	240 45	473 02	930 49
15	29 52	58 07	114 24	224 73	442 07	869 62
16	27 59	54 27	106 77	210 02	413 15	812 73
17	25 79	50 72	99 78	196 28	386 21	759 56
18	24 10	47 40	93 25	183 44	360 86	709 87
19	22 52	44 30	87 15	171 44	337 25	663 43
20	21 05	41 40	81 45	160 22	315 19	620 03
21	19 67	38 70	76 12	149 74	294 57	579 46
22	18 38	36 17	71 14	139 95	275 30	541 56
23	17 18	33 80	66 49	130 79	257 29	566 13
24	16 05	31 59	62 14	122 24	240 46	473 02
25	15 00	29 52	58 07	114 24	224 73	442 07

Now, young boy or girl, there is a word to be said to you. Clothing first costs money, and it costs money also to replace it. If you had a $10 bill would you sit down and rub it out on the pavement till you had nothing of it left? Would you consider any one sane whom you would see doing such a thing? What would you think, then, of one who would thus use a $100 or $200 bill? It is easy to tell what you would say if you saw any one doing such a thing, that they were out of their mind or were wanting in intellect. If they had a fortune and could not find objects of charity to bestow it upon, such rubbing out of value may be a justifiable amusement. But if they had not, it is a moral and political wrong; and probably the public charity or that of friends would have to replace the loss or pay the bill. They might do the same, in result, with dress, and your foolish notions might regard them as stylish. The reader is left to finish up the balance of the argument.

The child, however, should regard his apparel as so many bank bills, and use it accordingly. If the child rips, tears, uselessly wears out, or destroys his clothing, he does no better or worse than he who sits upon the sidewalk and rubs out a bank bill, and has nothing to show for it but his folly. Then, to make money, be careful of what you have—use good clothing for the best purposes, and old for uses where the new would be destroyed or uselessly defaced. *Think* of the bank bills on your back, and think how long you can make them last and look fresh and appropriately neat. It is but a common event to damage your dress ten dollars in a day; this, in fifty years, would produce about two hundred dollars—quite a heavy loss; and, if saved, an equally large gain.

The same care and thought should be had about all things which are useful and cost money; and he will probably have more of this world's goods and be quickest independent of labor who attends most closely to such suggestions.

No expenditure should be made by parent or child, if they have not yet attained an independence, without first considering the cost, as referred to in that scale. Not what it costs to-day, but what it costs on the day fixed for the independence. If the same amount of thought, energy, time, toil, and sacrifice, be made in properly spending, investing, and generally caring for money after it is got, as there is in getting it, there would be no danger as to the result. None would be without an independence, few without a fortune, and none in distress, poverty, or want, who could gain employment.

CHAPTER VI.

HOW TO MAKE MONEY.

Means of money-making. — Diversity.—Selection.—Stand by.—
Chance and choice.—Different aims.—Relative wants.—Mark
and abide.—Most accomplished.—Commerce a failure.—Not so
always.—Chances in Boston.—Fail as a class.—A strong bank.
—One per cent. in Philadelphia.—Two per cent. in New York.
—Bankrupt act.—Chances in Cincinnati.—Chances in New
York, Boston, and Philadelphia.—Nearly all fail.—Shrink with
terror.—Mercantile business same as banking well done.—
Causes of failure not explained.—Will be.—Would pay best.—
Business example.—Kid-glove merchant.—Failure.—Ignorance
alike.—Course.—End.—It must make.—Merchants and banks.
—Fault somewhere.—Success and failure hand in hand.—Employer and employed.—When most valuable.—Manners make
money.—How.—Losses by same.—Example.—Others.—Little
element.— Great results. — Bad manners expensive.— Metal
merchant.—Incivility and ignorance.—Loss $196,401.—Expensive amusement.—Great principle.—Lose or gain.—Fire.—Loss
$30,000.—General principles.—All make money.—Danger just
here.—" Every one to his trade."—Beware.—Look out.—The
made dollar.—Stop and read.—Where the trouble lies.

THE means of making money are as various as the employments into which individuals enter. There is no occupation which yields more than the sum required for support, that does not afford an opportunity for gain. There is a choice of such employments; some producing more money than others for the same time and the same labor. It is well to look to that difference in the selection to be made. But when the occupation *is* once entered upon *never leave it while there is a reasonable demand for either the articles dealt in or the kind of labor bestowed.* This cardinal in money-making of course only applies to those who are thus engaged, and not to the one who has made an independence, and can *afford to make the sacrifice* of a change; for a change from one business to another is expensive, involving generally a loss of the capital, of skill and knowledge acquired, and time both in making the change and in acquiring skill in the new business.

The diversity of business makes diversity of employments; and as a general thing, those who engage in them have no intelligent choice in the matter. They are either selected by the parent, or by the youth who has not the remotest idea of the detail or of the profitableness of what he is about to engage in. What usually attracts both, however, is the fact of some one having *done well* or *made a fortune in that kind of business.* Some are driven from necessity to take whatever offers in the way of employment, relying upon chance for something better or for advancement. Whatever may be the kind of employment which fate or choice has given one, there is about as much chance to make an independence by one as in the other. That is, taking into account the gains and necessary expenditures attached to each, the result relatively is about the same, as will be seen hereafter.

What is a fortune for a laboring man, accustomed to the society of his peers, and only spending what that grade of life requires, does not compel as much money to fill his necessities, or even his desires, as the merchant of liberal education, of extended acquaintance among the refined and educated, demanding expenditures commensurate with such a walk in life. The two individuals are on entirely distinct bases of necessary wants, live in two distinct worlds, and are laboring in different extended spheres. The same is true of every grade or walk in life; nor is there an exception from the scullion to the king. This is the machinery of society; and, right or wrong, so we find it, and so we treat it.

The fortune is only to be measured by that condition where the possessor is satisfied with the supply of a given number and description of wants. Should the individual be content with what the interest of five thousand dollars would command, then this sum *is* his independence and his fortune also. But if his independence from charity was just this sum, and he was unhappy because he had not the means of gratifying other and more expensive desires, he might keep out of the poorhouse, or swing clear of the charity of friends, but he would not possess a fortune. The independence may be measurably fixed in amount, but the fortune is the child of the rich man's imagination. It may be rated much, or comparatively small, just in proportion to his satisfaction.

Each grade of business has generally its relative portion of income and relative proportion of expenditures; not altogether from the necessities attaching to the business itself, but from the general supposed necessities attaching to the position and wants of the persons conducting it. Generally, then, what is a fortune in one business, is a small fraction of one in another. The question, then, is with every individual to decide what rank in life he will aim at, in order to settle the amount of the fortune to be obtained in business. Few will be able to make a mark, and abide by it; but individual imperfections do not affect a sound principle.

Some businesses are incapable, from the very nature of them, of great extension. They are limited, and the money to be made from them is likewise limited. The first guarantee of success is to be *satisfied with the business you are engaged in*. For it can be conclusively shown that one business is just about as good as another in its results in the long run. The next qualification for money making in such business is *knowledge respecting it in every possible relation, and skill and tact in its application to accomplish most with the least expenditure of time and capital.*

All works published upon business and money-making seem to hold up to the applicants for fortunes the inducements of commerce as the great field for wealth. But, if the statistics furnished are to be relied upon, merchandizing is the last occupation in which to look for a fortune, provided merchandizing is carried on in the usual way. But a failure of ten thousand locomotives to perform well, or their giving out from a defect in some of their parts, would not condemn the present beautiful specimens of such work. The failure of one man in merchandizing should not necessarily indicate the failure of another. We take the liberty of making an extract of some statistics found in that very excellent work, " Freedley's Practical Treatise on Business," respecting mercantile success, headed :

"CHANCES OF SUCCESS IN MERCANTILE LIFE IN BOSTON.

" On the evening of the 28th of February, 1840, GENERAL HENRY A. S. DEARBORN delivered an address at an agricultural meeting of the members of the Legislature, which embraced a statement that startled many, and attracted the attention of business men in all parts of the country. Freeman Hunt, Esq., of the *Merchants' Maga-*

zine, wrote to General Dearborn for a copy of his remarks, made in connection with that statement, which he placed at his disposal. General Dearborn was Collector of the Port of Boston for nearly twenty years, and was therefore enabled to notice the vicissitudes in trade, and his statements are confirmed by the remarks of a Boston merchant, which are here appended. He is speaking of the superior advantages of a residence in the country, and observes:—

"'In England, the pleasures, and privileges, and blessings of the *country* seem properly understood and valued. No man there considers himself a freeman unless he has a right in the soil. Merchants, bankers, citizens, men of every description, whose condition of life allows them to aspire after anything better, are looking forward always to retirement in the country—to the possession of a garden or a farm, and to the full enjoyment of rural pleasures. The taste of the nobility of England is eminently in that direction. There are none of them who, with all the means which the most enormous wealth can afford, even think of spending the year in London, or of remaining in the confinement, noise, and confusion of the city, a day longer than they are compelled to do by their parliamentary or other public duties.

"'There is, in this respect, a marked difference between England and France. Formerly, the nobility of France were scattered broadcast over the territory, and had their villas, their castles, and chateaux, in all the provinces of the kingdom. But the monarchs, anxious to increase the splendor of their courts, and to concentrate around them all that was imposing and beautiful in fashion, luxury, and wealth, collected the aristocracy in the capital. The natural consequence was that the country was badly tilled, and agriculture made no advancement, while England was making rapid and extraordinary progress in the useful and beautiful arts of agriculture and horticulture, and now, in her cultivation, presents an example of all that is interesting in embellishment and important in production. We are the descendants of England; yet on these subjects we have reversed the order of taste and sentiment which there prevails.

"'Happy would it be for us if our gentlemen of wealth and intelligence would copy the bright example of the affluent and exalted men of England. If, after having accumulated immense fortunes in cities, they would carry their riches and science into the country, and seek to reclaim, to improve, and render it more productive and beautiful. * * * *

"'It is an inexplicable fact that even men who have grown rich in any manner in the country should rush into cities to spend their wealth; and it is equally as remarkable, that those who have accumulated fortunes in the city shudder at the idea of going into the country, where wealth might be safely appropriated to purposes of the highest utility, pleasure, and refinement.

"'There prevails, in this, rather too much ignorance, false sentiment, and unworthy prejudice. The city must, of course, be regarded as the proper seat of active business in all the branches of commerce and navigation. But when a large portion of life has been spent in these harassing pursuits, and men have acquired the means of competence and independence in the country, why they should not seek to enjoy the refreshing exercise, the delightful recreations, and the privileged hours of retirement and reflection which a rural residence affords, was a mystery which it was impossible to solve.

"'It was not merely the ungovernable influence of a city life upon health that was most deeply to be regretted. Many an uncorrupted young man from the country, impelled by a reckless passion for gain, has there early found the grave of his virtues. But too many instances might be pointed out, in which the acquisition of property has proved as great a curse as could have befallen them. The chances of success in trade are likewise much less numerous, and are more uncertain than men generally believe, or are willing to allow. *After an extensive acquaintance with business men, and having long been an attentive observer of the course of events in the mercantile community, I am satisfied that,* AMONG ONE HUNDRED MERCHANTS AND TRADERS, NOT MORE THAN THREE, IN THIS CITY, EVER ACQUIRE INDEPENDENCE. *It was with great distrust that I came to this conclusion; but, after consulting with an experienced merchant, he fully admitted its truth.* Infinitely better, therefore, would it be for a vast portion of the young men who leave the country for the city, if they could be satisfied with a farmer's life. How preferable would it have been for those who have sought wealth and distinction in cities, if they had been satisfied with the comforts, innocent amusements, and soothing quietude of the country; and, instead of the sad tale of their disasters, which must go back to the parental fireside, the future traveller, as he passed the humble churchyard in which they had been laid at rest with their laborious ancestors, might truthfully repeat these emphatic words of England's gifted bard :—

"Some village Hampden that, with dauntless breast,
The little tyrant of his fields withstood;
Some mute, inglorious Milton here may rest;
Some Cromwell, guiltless of his country's blood."'

"The following confirmatory remarks of an intelligent gentleman from Boston appeared in the *Farmers' Library* :—

"'The statement made by General Dearborn appeared to me so startling, so appalling, that I was induced to examine it with much care, and, I regret to say, I found it true. I then called upon a friend, a great antiquarian, a gentleman always referred to in all matters relating to the city of Boston, and he told me that, in the year 1800, he took a memorandum of every person on Long Wharf, and that, in 1840—which is as long as a merchant continues in business—only *five* in *one hundred* remained. They had all, in that time, FAILED, OR DIED DESTITUTE OF PROPERTY. I then went to a very intelligent director of the Union Bank—a very strong bank. He told me that the bank commenced business in 1798; that there was then but one other bank in Boston, the Massachusetts Bank, and that the bank was so overrun with business that the clerks and officers were obliged to work until twelve o'clock at night, and all Sundays; that they had occasion to look back, a year or two ago, and they found that, of the *one thousand accounts* which were opened with them in starting, only *six* remained; they had, in the forty years, either *failed or died destitute of property*. Houses, whose paper had passed without a question, *had all gone down in that time*. Bankruptcy, said he, is like death, and almost as certain; they fall singly and alone.

and are thus forgotten; but there is no escape from it, and he is a fortunate man who *fails young*.

"'Another friend told me that he had occasion to look through the probate office a few years since, and he was surprised to find that over 90 per cent. of all the estates settled there *were insolvent*. And, within a few days, I have gone back to the incorporation of our banks in Boston. I have a list of the directors, since they started. This is, however, a very unfair way of testing the rule, for bank directors are the most substantial men in the community. In the old bank over *one-third* had failed in forty years, and in the new bank a much larger proportion.

"'I am sorry to present to you so gloomy a picture, and I trust you will instil into your sons, as General Dearborn recommends, a love of agriculture; for, in mercantile pursuits, they will fail to a dead certainty.'

"CHANCES OF SUCCESS IN BOSTON, PHILADELPHIA, AND NEW YORK.

"Nahum Capen, Esq., Editor of the *Massachusetts State Record*, makes some interesting statements on the subject in the following letter which he wrote to the Hon. Truman Clark, to be presented at one of the legislative agricultural meetings held weekly during the session of the Legislature at the Senate Chamber.

"'BOSTON, *March* 2, 1847.

"'HON. TRUMAN CLARK :

"'MY DEAR SIR—In accordance with your wishes, I send herewith such statistics in regard to failures in

Massachusetts, as I received last year, in reply to a circular I sent to every town in the commonwealth, for the purpose of colleƈting information for the *Massachusetts State Record.* As these returns were imperfeƈt, I deferred any publication of them till another year, when probably I should have the means of doing the subjeƈt ample justice.

"'Number of towns represented, 144; estimated population of ditto, 242,186; number of farming towns, 79; manufaƈturing and farming, 56; number engaged mostly in navigation, 9; number of failures reported, 357.

"'*Business of Bankrupts.*—Farmers, 59; manufaƈturers and mechanics, 182, including 70 boot and shoe manufacturers; laborers, 9; innholders, 1; speculators (farmers), 4; ministers, 1; traders, 63; business not stated, 48. * *

"'It does not appear, from my returns, how many farmers failed in consequence of becoming speculators, intemperate, or indolent men. It seems to me that an industrious, temperate, and frugal farmer can hardly do otherwise than succeed. Small gains, gradually accumulated, are safer and surer than large profits and sudden fortunes. Their influence is favorable to the growth of good morals, and they do not endanger the habits of prudence.

"'If Governor Carver had invested £70 on his arrival in the country at compound interest, the accumulated sum at this time would be sufficient to buy the whole State of Massachusetts, and it would exceed the banking capital of the United States.

"'If a young man at twenty-one were to lease a farm and make an annual profit of one hundred dollars, and invest both principal and interest from year to year, for twenty-five years, his fund would amount to $5,000. If he were to own the farm, he might have a fund at interest of $10,000 in twenty-five years.

"'A trader, however, may begin with a capital of $10,000 on the credit system, as now managed, and in twenty-five years there are ninety-seven chances to every one hundred, that he will be $10,000 in debt beyond his means to pay.

"'This percentage of success and failure has been alluded to, at your discussions, as being true of Boston. I believe it to be nearly correct. I have been advised by very intelligent gentlemen, who have the means of knowing, *that not more than* ONE *per cent. of the best class of merchants succeed without failing in* PHILADELPHIA, *and that not more than* TWO *per cent. of the merchants of* NEW YORK ULTIMATELY *retire on an independence, after having submitted to the usual ordeal of failure.* These calculations are based, it must be observed, upon periods of twenty-five and thirty years.

"'The lot of the merchant is one of great labor and anxiety, compared to that of the farmer. He labors harder, his life is shorter, and he is less sure of a competency in old age.'

"A contributor to the *Merchants' Magazine* states that it is said 'that but *one* eminent merchant, and his death is still recent, has ever continued in active business *in the city of New York*, to the close of a long life, without undergoing bankruptcy or a suspension of payments in some of the various crises of the country.' It is also asserted by *reliable authority*, from records kept during periods of twenty to forty years, that, of every hundred persons who commence business in Boston, ninety-five at least die poor; that of the same number in New York not two ultimately acquire wealth, after passing through the intermediate process of bankruptcy; while in Philadelphia the proportion is still smaller.

"By the statistics of bankruptcy under the uniform bankrupt law in 1841,

"The number of applicants for relief under that law were 33,739
"The number of creditors returned . 1,049,603
"The amount of debts stated . 440,934,615
"The valuation of property surrendered 43,697,307

"If this valuation were correct, nearly ten cents would have been paid on every dollar due; but what was the fact?

"In the Southern district of New York, one cent was paid, on an average, for each dollar due; in the Northern district, thirteen and two-thirds, being by far the largest dividend. In Connecticut, the average dividend was somewhat over half a cent on each dollar.

"'In Mississippi, it was . . 6 cents to $1,000
" 'Maine . . . . ½ cent " 100
" ' Michigan and Iowa . . ¼ " " 100
" ' New Jersey . . . 4 cents to 100
" ' Tennessee . . . 4½ " " 100
" ' Maryland . . . . 1 dollar to 100
" ' Kentucky . . . 8 dollars to 1,000
" ' Illinois . . . . 1 dollar to 1,500
" ' Pennsylvania, East Virginia, South Alabama, Washington, nothing.

"*Palmer's Almanac*, 1849.'

"'After making every possible allowance for the enhancement of this enormous amount of debt by inflation of values, speculative prices, etc., the proportion of $400,000,000, lost by those of the 1,049,603 creditors who were engaged in proper and legitimate business, must still have been immense, and may justly be charged against the profits of our regular commerce. These things being so, our system of trade should be characterized, not as a system of exchange, but as a system of bankruptcy, tending to the ruin of all who engage in it; the exceptions being only numerous enough to prove the rule.

"CHANCES IN CINCINNATI.

"C. Cist, of *Cist's Cincinnati Advertiser*, the statist of that city, published, some two or three years ago, the following result of his investigations :—

"'The avidity with which young men crowd those avenues in life in which there is a chance of making money with rapidity, or of acquiring political or social distinction and eminence, is the more remarkable, when it is apparent, on the surface of the subject, that they are venturing in a lottery in which there are many blanks to one prize. A few acquire the object of their pursuit; the mass sink into obscurity and insignificance.

"'Take, for example, mercantile pursuits. It is the experience and observation of intelligent persons in the East, that there is hardly a firm in existence now which did business twenty years ago; and that nine out of ten in mercantile life, in the long run, amidst the fluctuations of trade, are broken.

"'Let me, however, bring the subject nearer home. I had prepared a list of the principal active business men who were in trade twenty years ago, in Cincinnati, of which a brief extract is all that I have space for in these columns. In place of giving names, I shall distinguish them by numbers.

"'No. 1. Broke; resumed business; has since left Cincinnati.
" 2. Broke; resides in Indiana.
" 3. Broke; and now engaged in collecting accounts.
" 4. Died.
" 5. Now captain of a steamboat.
" 6. Left merchandizing to put up pork, which business he also quit in time to save his *bacon*; independent in circumstances.
" 7. Dead.
" 8. Broke; resides at St. Louis.
" 9. A firm; one of the partners dead; the other out of business; both insolvent.
" 10. Partners; both dead.
" 11. Partners; broke; one now a book-keeper, the other dead.
" 12. Became embarrassed, and swallowed poison.
" 13. A firm; broke.
" 14. A firm; broke; one of the partners died a common sot; the others left the city.
" 15. Broke, and left the city.
" 16. A firm; all its members out of business.
" 17. A firm; senior partner dead.
" 18. A firm; senior partner dead, junior resides at Toledo.
" 19. Is now a clerk, and left Cincinnati, after becoming intemperate.
" 20, 21, 22, 23. Died intemperate.
" 26. A firm; one of the partners in another business; one removed to New York, and one a clerk.
" 27. Broke; and drowned himself in the Ohio.

"'No. 28. Broke ; died of delirium tremens.
"   29, 35, 36, 37, 38. Broke, and removed to other cities.
"   32. Out of business, having broke three times.
"   33. Broke ; now dealing in flour.

"'My list comprehends some 400 business men, of which the above is a sample. I know of but *five now in business who were so twenty years since.* Such is mercantile success.'

"From 'Report of his Majesty's Commissioners for inquiring into the Administration and Practical Operation of the Poor Laws, 1834,' one of the officers gave the subjoined return :—

"'As far as I can recollect, from the books and documents furnished by the bankrupts, it seems to me that fourteen have been ruined by speculations in things with which they were unacquainted ; three by neglected book-keeping ; ten by trading beyond their capital and facile means, and the consequent loss and expense of accommodation bills ; forty-nine by expending more than they could reasonably hope their profits would be, though their business yielded a fair return ; none by any general distress, or the falling off of any particular branch of trade.'

"Another officer states :—

"'The new court has been open upwards of eighteen months, during which period fifty-two cases of bankruptcy have come under my care. To the best of my judgment, not one of them can be attributed to any general distress. It is my opinion that thirty-two of them have arisen from an imprudent expenditure, and five partly from that cause, and partly from a pressure on the business in which the bankrupt was employed—fifteen I attribute to imprudent speculations, combined, in many instances, with an extravagant mode of life. Among these fifteen I find a tailor, in a very small way of business, borrowing money to become the owner of a West India ship trading to Jamaica, a concern with which he was wholly unacquainted; consequently, he was cheated in every way and speedily ruined. A London publican, having a slight knowledge of science, neglects his business here and goes over to France, for the purpose of entering into a contract with the French authorities for the supply of Paris with water. A working goldsmith, never having had £10, takes Saville House, Leicester Square, and engages singers and musicians for the purpose of establishing concerts. The thirty-two classed as failing through imprudences in their mode of, living, include many whose necessities, leading them to resort to accommodation-bill transactions, have become the prey of money-lenders and their attendant harpies, the inferior class of solicitors.'"

From these statistics the money-maker might shrink with terror and internal apprehension of almost certain poverty. But in this list are found some who have succeeded well; hence, if one has done it, another by following the same general course has the same chance. Mercantile business *can* be conducted so as to be profitable, and as *certainly so as banking business.* We hazard nothing in making this assertion; and if authors had not failed to prove the postulate by showing the defects of mismanaged mercantile business, no new works on the subject of money-making would be required. Freedley remarks : " As to the *causes of failures*, we are sorry to say, that we have not been able to find any satisfactory certificate."

We assert that the causes of failure in mercantile or every other business are as apparent as the causes of failure in banking. *There can be no question on this subject.* All banking is not successful ; but if the officers are honest and capable, hopeless failure seldom, if ever, occurs. To make merchandizing as safe as banking is all that the most conservative could desire. Banking, generally speaking, is conducted by individuals who have had large experience in other business, and have been measurably successful. The securities, and, in truth, all the business transactions, are the result of *conference, deliberation*, and *argument*, between several persons *well trained* in business. By this means all *doubtful* operations and securities are excluded, and only those entered into in which all agree.

Mercantile business, on the other hand, is seldom conducted in this way, and hence seldom is successful. Let any man or firm commence dealing in the articles themselves instead of in the paper which represents them, such as the bankers do, and use the same discrimination in judging of credits, have the same amount of capital in proportion to the amount done, and the *mercantile business would pay the best*. The losses would be no more, and the profits greater. Who are these who go into business of this nature? A, has a son who has agonized in kid gloves a term of three or four years as clerk in some well regulated establishment, or perhaps who has never seen the inside of any business ; A, is anxious to see him do something for himself, and has money. He inquires about, and the son looks around also, to see if there is not some chance of business. Some house already established hears of this amount of money with a nobody attached to it, and being in want, as most houses are who will consent to take a stranger into their business, agree to the terms, and the young man in kids becomes the tail-end of a sign in gilt, or & Co., patched on by the skill of the sign-painter.

The man in kids has been informed how much his capital will yield him of profits, and hence, as profits are made to live on, he arranges, by means of boarding-house, livery-stable, and the like, a basis of expenditure corresponding with the golden bait held out by the former firm. The capital put in is speedily dispersed to pay borrowed money and such-like little arrearages of the firm, and the balance runs smoothly into paying the first notes which become due for merchandize already sold and lost. The new firm obtains new credit, more goods are purchased than ever, more business is done, and the books show heavy gains. The young man in kids reports the result to his delighted father, and the swollen income of the young man makes him at once a prodigy in the family, and a speculation among the dowagers who are looking out a suitable match for their daughters. His society becomes sought after, he is invited to dinners, balls, parties, and evening sociables ; and finally finds himself engaged, then married. All are delighted ; money flies right and left ; for, from appearances and from what the book-keeper reports, after all such abatements of income there is a large balance left. No one need be told that the affairs of the firm soon become involved ; a general smash-up takes place; and the members, after a year or two spent on what little money each could gather from the crumbling ruins for immediate want, then either take up some new business, or, profiting by sad experience, begin anew.

This is but one phase of embryo mercantile life, and may be regarded as an extreme one; but the formula will answer for almost any unsuccessful case by making substitution of other states of life and circumstances. If ignorance be substituted for the kid-gloves in this formula, a still larger class of failures will be portrayed, and so on with the entire catalogue of qualities which insure the same result. There are, however, cases of failure having few of these elements in them. Firms may be prudent, careful, and successful for a series of years, and then be borne down by misfortunes *apparently* beyond their control. As a means, however, of money-making, *certainly* no surer business can be found if properly conducted. It is based in the necessities of life, and money and profit *must* flow out of it. The manner of conducting it rightly is alone necessary to be known, and when known, followed, and success will attend in almost every instance; the exceptions will be so few that they may be set down to incompetency.

The direct cause of mercantile failure can in most cases be traced to the banks with which they do their business. This is a serious evil; but there is no remedy for it except in the individuals engaged taking proper views of the initiatory steps. The firm opens an account with a bank or banks, and deposits all its spare funds. As long as the surplus funds last the bank will lend on good paper presented, and sometimes longer. The merchant, manufacturer, or mechanic, soon bases his course of business upon the implied and possibly agreed upon amount or line of discount. New enterprises are gone into, legitimate in their nature, but requiring a little more money than anticipated, and the balance in the bank account is reduced. The argus eye of the president or cashier lights upon the figures, and the application for a new loan is refused. As helpless in the hands of the banks as poverty, he is bound to seek money from other sources; he applies to an outside money-lender, and is met with the singular question: Why will not your bank do your paper? Distrust seizes upon him, and now the man must submit to a deep shave, and the piling on of securities till he cramps himself, or else he must stop.

The bank, on the other hand, notwithstanding the implied bargain, and the fact that he has paid all as yet, finding that he is compelled to resort to shaves, concludes that his paper is not safe, and finally runs out his discount line. If he survives, and has been able to maintain himself, they grant him a new favor, and squeeze him anew when the time comes. These repeated a few times ruin the borrower, when he cannot succeed in getting money outside or in the bank, and failure is the consequence. The bank, however, cannot be said to be in fault, for they are bound to be secure, though there may be fault bound up in the transaction between the parties which it is difficult to determine how far of right it belongs to the one, or how far to the other.

These difficulties and dangers can all be avoided, and the manner will be explained hereafter; the point now in hand being to show *how* the *most* money can be made in every department of life—the handling it after it is made being quite a different trade. The one may be well understood by a person, and he be successful, and the other not understood in the first element, and hence success, failure, and poverty, go hand in hand through life with the same individual.

How to make the most money out of every occupation in life is a study. There are two great classes to be considered with this view, the employer and the employed. The employers make money by the services of the employed, while the employed receive money for their services to the employers. So far as making money, both are governed by the same general principles. To make the services of the employed valuable is the object of the employers, and they make money just in proportion as they are valuable for the money paid. While the employed should see to it that their services are as valuable as the money paid, and if they are more so, they are certain to be rewarded dollar for dollar. Hence it is the object, or should be the object, of the employed to be as valuable as possible to the employer.

How is this to be accomplished? A merchant who trades with you is in reality employed by you, and you pay for his services by the profit you pay him on his goods. Is it his interest to serve you well? If he does not, he loses your trade, and you go elsewhere. If he deals dishonestly with you, it is not probable that you will return to him to have it repeated. If he is uncivil or impolite, disobliging or uncourteous, you feel piqued, and lose your interest in him and in his establishment, and you naturally look elsewhere to supply your wants. If you find goods equally cheap, and sold by a nice, civil, and attractive man, you will buy of him and leave the other. If you find the first one's goods cheaper, and enough so to pay you for dealing with an unpleasant man, you may buy of him.

Now let us see what it costs the first man to be "uncivil, impolite, disobliging, or uncourteous." This customer may purchase, if at retail, $1,000 in a year, on which the profit would be say $200. If he fails to sell him by reason of a slight feeling in his breast, the merchant would lose $200 at once. This, improved at compound interest at seven per cent. for the ordinary term of twenty-five years of business, would be the neat little sum of $1,084. If he lost one customer of this kind each year from the same cause, he would lose sixty-three cents a day, which, by looking at the tables, if improved at seven per cent. for the twenty-five years, would amount to the splendid sum of $12,915—rather an expensive amusement; while the pleasant merchant would in like manner gain these sums respectively.

Then suppose we take the case of the wholesale merchant dealing in correspondingly large sums. If he lost the custom of a firm, amounting in a year to $15,000, on which there was a profit of $1,500, he would lose, if that sum be improved at seven per cent., in his term of twenty-five years in business, $8,145; or if he did the same every year for the twenty-five years in business, he would lose the sum of $98,199. The reader probably thinks by this time that this little element in business is worth looking at rather carefully.

These calculations are based upon the supposition that the uncivil and civil merchants sell at the same profit. But every one knows that the latter can get more for his goods than the former. The gain, therefore, of the latter will be greater than the loss of the former. But suppose we look at the case where one is compelled to get the same amount of custom by taking off five per cent. more than the other can sell for by reason of his attractive manners. They both sell $100,000 per annum, one making $15,000 and the other making $20,000. The first wins in a 25 year business, by the tables, $47.92 per day, making, improved at 7 per cent., $982,416 at the end of 25 years, while the other makes $63.90 per day, which, improved in like manner, gives $1,310,025, making a difference of $327,609, rather a large sum to lose by mere mannerism, but by no means as large a sum as the civil merchant would make in proportion.

No merchant can afford to be uncivil; and from a knowledge of how many are so in the transaction of their business, can any one wonder why they fail when they add this expense to the other expenses of life? By the term uncivil, as used here, is meant that mannerism in all business intercourse which repels rather than attracts—that which leaves a barb rather than a pleasant and interested remembrance. The more nearly the term, however, takes its full force and meaning, or goes beyond that, the more it becomes as an expensive amusement, and the nearer it brings the employed, no matter who he may be, to failure or greater loss of money.

The more you can, then, by pleasant and kind treatment interest the employer in your business, the more naturally he will be interested in the employed, and *vice versa;* and mutual benefit *in money* will result to both. Let us name a case which actually occurred in New York about thirty years ago.

A country manufacturer came to the city to purchase metal to be used in his business, and, being dressed in rather a rough garb, was not in his personal appearance very prepossessing. But as he always paid cash for what he purchased, and being rather abrupt and eccentric in his way, he did not pay much attention to style. He went to one of the largest metal houses in the city and inquired the price of the material he wanted; the seller, supposing that he was some retail customer wanting to know the wholesale price in order to govern a small purchase, asked the retail price. The manufacturer said he wanted to know the price of a quantity. The merchant asked him how much he wanted. Becoming a little piqued, the manufacturer said, "That is my business." The merchant, still feeling that the countryman was only asking out of curiosity, set his price, and the manufacturer departed, never to enter that store again. Both houses are still in existence, the older members having died, and other partners and younger men carrying on the business.

Now let us examine this case, for it is a large one. For the whole time since, the country manufacturer has purchased on an average $40,000 worth of materials yearly, every dollar of which this New York house could have sold him if they had done so at a right price; and as he was a close buyer, could probably have made 5 per cent. and got the cash. By this little trifling affair that house lost $2,000 a year for 30 years; and if that sum had been saved and improved at 7 per cent. during that time, it would now amount to $196,401; rather an expensive three minutes' talk, springing from ignorance and incivility.

No man in business or money-making can tell what word or action may make him or lose him money. No one will make, in all probability, by chafing those who come in contact with him, while he may lose largely by it. The *most important principle in money-making* is to deal with every one in such a manner that he is *satisfied* and *pleased.* If you have done this to one, you have laid a train of influence, advertisement, and interest, wherever he goes; for it is as natural for persons to speak well of any one, or of any establishment, that has served them well, and in which they are interested, as it is for water to run down hill. To advertise to accomplish the same end would cost much money, so that your mannerism or action may not cost you anything to satisfy and please; while you make dollars by securing an influence that will bring you money from every quarter of the compass. If you want to make money, don't read this and forget it. When one has made a fortune he may do such things, but even then he may lose in like manner. An instance as an illustration, occurred in the lower part of the city about 1839. A fire occurred, and extended to a large warehouse owned by a close-fisted, grinding rich man, about as crabbed and ugly as he well could be. The fire was just taking in an upper story by heated iron window-shutters, and, it was believed, could have been easily extinguished by the firemen. Calls were made for an engine-pipe, when one of the firemen cried out: "This is old S.'s store; let her burn." Whether this was the cause or not, no one could tell; but the warehouse was consumed without insurance, at a loss to the crusty old gentleman's estate of $30,000.

We could go on and give you instances without number where heavy losses, and even fortunes, have been lost or not made by some apparent immaterial act or word which at the moment would pass unnoticed. These, however, are the straws of the money-making life; and, important as they are in themselves, there are a thousand and one other items which conduce more or less to the same end. As general rules, the following may be laid down as the more important:

First.—A settled character for sobriety, honesty, industry, veracity, and trustworthiness.

Second.—Pleasant, agreeable, and attractive manners ; never repulsive, civil without fawning ; dignified, without reserve ; and an even temper, never allowing it to be ruffled in a business transaction.

Third.—Study the interests of those you deal with as well as your own, and let them see and feel it, as that will secure a repetition of transactions, or bring business through those with whom you deal.

Fourth.—Be the most skilful in your calling, summoning to your aid to accomplish this end the knowledge of others which can be gained by reading, conversation, or observation ; remembering always that knowledge and its application with skill is the most profitable quality which you can possess, and that every new idea you acquire and use well, will be, without doubt, a dollar in your purse, gained or not lost, and possibly many more.

No one can fail in this country to make money who can gain employment and continues in it honestly and industriously. It is the easiest part of acquiring an independence or a fortune. The most difficult is the investing and saving, by which, what you do make shall be safely and surely set to work making more. As the reader will perceive, the moment he has money to invest and set at work he wants knowledge which he has not probably gained in his business. For how can the laborer, who has never seen the thing done or done it, be expected to know how ; or the carpenter, who has shoved his plane for years to know how to do that well, be supposed to know the business of a financier or banker, which takes a like apprenticeship and extensive knowledge to acquire. To know that you do not know how to do the business of a banker, if you have not been educated to it, *is the first and all-important idea in saving what you earn.* It is like the child who would be as apt to play with live coals as he would with his toys, if he had not been told they would burn him, or learned the lesson by experience.

The old and familiar adage, "Every one to his trade," applies in this case with astonishing force. And, reader, do not suppose for a moment that it applies simply to the laborer or mechanic. All, or nearly all who make, are ignorant of the trade of investing and making money with money. The intelligent merchant *may* know how, but, alas! how many failures do we see in this line of business; not failures to make money, for they universally make money, but the trouble lies not in that but in the values of what they invest it in after it is made or while they are making it.

Then, when the reader has been told to beware—look out, when he has made a dollar—and that his danger begins just here and nowhere else, he will have learned the most valuable lesson of his life in money-making. There is no fear of employment—there is no fear of getting business—selling goods or doing a money-making business in what you undertake; *all the danger and trouble lies in parting with your money or your valuables to increase and make more.* And if you read this book to gain knowledge of how to accumulate, stop right here, read the last page over and over and over again, and you will know where all the trouble lies why you have not made a fortune, if you have not; and you can put your finger on the very spot where you have failed or will fail, if you do. The remedy will be shown hereafter.

CHAPTER VII.

MANUAL LABOR.

Underlies all.—Great motor.—Value varies.—Good to make money. —Dollar a day.—Big result.—Calculate independence.—How much.—Laborer's interest.—Advancement.—Great banker.—Porter.—Sweep out —Use.—Shine somewhere.—Supply and demand.—Merchants' combination.—Brings competition.—Loss results.—Qualities vary.—Sell first —Sell next.—Trades-Union. —All labor same value.—Business stand-still.—High prices.—Complain of landlords.—Don't see it.—Values will tell.—People want work.—Will have it.—Trades-Union or no Trades-Union.—Labor threatens capital.—Capital replies.—Remedy.—Poor distressed.—Business leaving.—Find level.—Managers should see it.—Conflict coming.—Ground swell.—Land tremble.—Best get work.—Poor none.—Best win.—Poorest lose.—Who discharged. — Agreement.—Very nice. — Roped in.—They will see it.—Cunning plan.—Poor, poorer.—Rich, richer. —Rectify itself.—Capital must buy.—Conflict.—Capital live.—Labor yield.—Money made.—Good business.

THIS class of labor underlies the whole active structure of society—is the bone and sinew of the nation, and the foundation of its wealth. It feeds and clothes all—it builds our houses, works our lands, digs our canals, threads our railroads, makes our ships, moves on our factories, machine-shops, and commerce. It is the great manual motor which is to society what steam is to the engine. Like other kinds of labor, its value depends upon its quality, and that depends upon knowledge and skill. The laborer, no matter in what he may be employed, has the means of making money in two ways: first, by his labor, no matter what its quality ; second, by increasing the value of his labor by the application of knowledge and skill in his business. Though there is manual labor performed by every one in some shape or another, the term manual labor here is intended to apply to those who labor for wages.

As a means of making money, considering everything, it is quite as good as any other. The results may not be as great; but, on the other hand, the wants and necessities are not so great as in the more extravagant walks of life. It can be easily shown that the laborer by skill and a proper economy can have more money at fifty years of age than the average of merchants. But if the merchant would in a parallel way pursue the same course which the laborer would have to do to accomplish this, the merchant would have the most, undoubtedly.

Let the laborer look at the tables of earnings, and see what he will have if he makes just one dollar a day, and puts it in the savings bank, and it is improved at six per cent. for thirty years, or from the day he is twenty till he is fifty years of age. It would amount to $25,518, a very handsome fortune, and enough to support him handsomely the balance of his days without labor. But, suppose he would wish to work on till he obtained his independence from labor without wishing for more, how is he to find out that amount, and the way to do it? He must decide how much he requires a day for this end—say two dollars. Then he has to gain a sum that would, if placed at interest at six per cent. or more, give just this sum. Then how long would he have to work, at what rate must his savings be improved, and how much would he have to save per day to accomplish this interest of two dollars per day at six per cent.?

The amount to be saved would be $12,167; now, by

examining the tables of thirty years; by saving sixty cents a day you will have $12,770, if you have it improved at five per cent. If you had saved fifty cents a day, and improved it at six per cent., you would have $12,759. If you had saved forty cents a day, and improved it at seven per cent., you would have $12,302, and your independence would be accomplished at fifty years of age if you began working at twenty to this end. By the same means any laborer, male or female, can determine for themselves at what age they will say they will achieve their independence, and such will save accordingly; and if good health and strength attend them, they can accomplish it. If not, their little reserve of money under these circumstances will in all probability give them even more substantial comfort than the independence when gained.

A laborer, if he knows his own interest, has every incentive to make his labor most valuable by the acquisition of knowledge and skill, and then to perform it in the best way. By this means he will make money, and in the direct ratio of its positive value. Then, by pleasant ways and obliging manners, and by taking an interest in what he is doing, and letting his employer see that he is taking an interest in his interests, he will always procure the highest wages; remembering always that he or she has the same opportunity of advancement to higher positions in life, that others have. One of the largest bankers in New York, who amassed in his day one of the greatest fortunes, commenced as a porter, and for some years swept out the very banking-house which he afterwards managed with ability and grand success. The instances are not few, but many, where mere day-laborers have, by industry, perseverance, and skill, risen far above their former employers in wealth and position. In truth, it makes but little difference where the industrious, honest, frugal, and persevering start in life, they will shine out somewhere, their qualities will bring their reward sooner or later, and especially in this country, where all have an equal chance.

The price of labor varies like every other commodity, and has its market value. This depends upon the supply and demand. The best rule for a retail merchant is to work on low profits, as this will bring the largest result in the end. The same rule is a good one for the laborer; work at a fair, not an exorbitant price, and you will get constant employment, as the trader will get constant trade. If the traders combined and put up the price of their goods, and said they would not sell without they received a larger profit than competition would establish, it is plain to see the result! Other merchants would be found who would open stores, and sell when they could make a profit; and those in the combination would be compelled to keep their stores open and pay their own expenses and make nothing, while the others not in it would sell all the goods—make their own expenses, besides making a profit.

Thus, again, suppose they were all to combine to sell any one article at a given price, say hops, butter, pork, or any other article. As any one knows, these articles vary in quality; and the consequence would be that the merchant who had the best pork or the best butter would sell all the pork and all the butter, and the merchants who had nearly as good would sell none. In order, then, that all the merchants could sell alike they would all be compelled to keep just the same quality of goods. But every one knows, goods of the same kind vary *in quality*, and the undertaking would result in just this—the good would be sold *first*, the poor *next*, and possibly be left on hand to perish.

Demand and supply in labor must be governed by the same principles of prices as reign in every other department of usefulness ; and to endeavor to regulate by any other rule will lead to loss of money in the end. Trades-Union Societies have been formed in this country to regulate the price of labor in the various occupations by a set-up price for a day's labor, or for doing a certain amount of work. The result is, that prices of labor have been advanced to such an extent that capital does not find it profitable to employ it ; hence many of the mechanical interests in this country are at a stand-still. Few new buildings are being erected in New York, and the prices of rents are enormous. The very mechanics who have checked the erection of new buildings for their own accommodation, complain of the landlords for advancing rents to a point which makes it almost impossible, even with the high prices of their labor, to pay.

The moment one department of business, and especially such an important one as labor, is disturbed by a combination of price, every other dependent upon it will in like manner be disturbed temporarily. But as in the case of the combination among the merchants to advance the price of their goods, there will soon be found others who will come into the market to sell at a profit ; and when the merchant has found that he cannot sell at the higher price in competition with the new-comers, he is compelled to go back to the old mode. But when he attempts this he finds double the number of competitors ; and as just so much and no more goods can be sold, he discovers to his great detriment that he has a heavier competition than he ever had, and in order to sell, must cut under to get custom. This all requires time, but will as surely come as that people want goods.

The same with the high prices demanded by the trades-union. There are a great many people in this country who want labor, and will have it; and if they are not in the country now, there are thousands in neighboring countries who, being ground down in prices there by surplus population, are waiting an opportunity for employment at fair prices anywhere they can get them. They will rush to any point where employment can be had, trades-union or no trades-union; as necessity knows no law; they will earn where they can. There is any amount of work to be done at fair prices; but capital is a close calculator, and generally will not pay double price for anything, or more than he can find profit in doing. Labor may stand, and say to capital: "You can't do without me." Capital can say with more certainty: "You can't pursue your trade to a profit without me." And the spectacle in this country is just this now.

The remedy is simple, as it would be in the case of the combination of the merchants. Capital has simply to say to labor, we will buy you on the same terms as we buy other things; price being regulated by supply and demand, and at the market value. We will not patronize or buy of the merchant who combines with his neighbors to sell flour, or butter, or bread, at thrice its value, because it affects the poor as well as the rich. Nor will we have our work done *by any one who hires* a trades-union man, because he is combining with his neighbors to sell his labor for more than it is worth in the market, and thereby creating distress among the poor by locking up capital and preventing the circulation of money that otherwise all could use to advantage.

For these reasons, and others combined, our shipbuilding is leaving the country ; our building, and other improvements, are greatly checked, and our labor dependent upon these as collaterals is by no means in a healthy condition ; and as a result, the poor are made poorer and are distressed. This state of things will continue and grow worse, until things find their level in supply and demand upon equitable principles. There are many able men and strong minds guiding these trades-unions, and it is to be sincerely hoped that their better senses and good judgments will abandon in time these impracticable principles, and guide the minds of those whom they control to a just appreciation of their own interests and the interests of all concerned. A contest of strength between capital and labor in this country carried to a point that would be effective, would probably produce results little dreamed of by any. Though if this state of things continues, it will come with a certainty of the rising sun, not from capital itself, for it can live on other sources of profit, but it will come in a groundswell of the poor wanting bread, that will make the land tremble.

Combinations to regulate prices never have succeeded and never will. By peculiar circumstances combinations can be made temporarily successful ; but the laws of trade and of interchange are deeper laid than these, and as certain as effect follows cause these laws will remain for ever the same. No, sooner will the sun rise in the west or gravity act upwards, than that the great principle of supply and demand fixing prices will be overturned by combinations. Trials may be made to do it, but they will end, as all history teaches such attempts have ended, in failure.

As a mere money-making plan these trades-unions defeat their own object. The first-class mechanics are benefited by them, while those who are not first class are directly the losers. When there is work enough for all, and capital can make his profit, if the maximum wages are obtained by all, that is, the best mechanic gets as much as he could if there was no combination, then the lower grades get more than their labor is worth, while the best get just what theirs is worth. Now, somebody is wronged by paying more than he should, and common sense teaches that such a system cannot stand. But suppose capital finds that it cannot make— which it soon will find—by paying more than a thing is worth, what then? Some one must be discharged—will it be the best mechanic or the poorest? Certainly the poorest. But suppose capital finds still further that it cannot yet keep all at work profitably, what then? Why, the next poorest will be discharged, while the best will still retain work, and will retain it as long as any one is employed.

From this it will be seen that, under such an arrangement, the best mechanics *always* get employed, while the less skilful, or possibly the less favored, get it only when there is work enough for all, which seldom happens. The less skilful are gratified to have their services put on an equality in price with the most skilled, and hence they join, while in reality they are kept out of employment, because without capital is compelled to give more for their services than they are worth, they will not be employed at all. Nor can the less valuable, under such a combination, *compete at all* with the most valuable labor of the kind. The result is, that it is a *one-sided bargain* in the Trades-Union—the least skilled agreeing to keep out of employment and let the more skilled get the work, except there be work enough for all. This is all very well for the shrewd ones, but not so nice for those who are roped into it on the idea that one man is as good as another, and one man has as many friends among the bosses as another. But if all were allowed to enter the market and sell their labor for what they could get for it, the one who was one-quarter less valuable as a mechanic or laborer could get employment at that price as soon as the. best, while now he has to stand back and let the best have work at all times, and wait till a chance comes when there is more work than they can do, and then he gets employment.

It is a cunningly devised plan to lessen competition against the most skilful mechanics and laborers ; and be assured they will be found, if inquiry be made, to be those who were the getters-up of the plan, and who are now its strongest supporters. It crushes out the weak, and makes the strong, stronger. In other words, it makes the poor, poorer, and the rich, richer. Such things have been attempted before, but sooner or later the weak have found out the trap into which they have fallen, as they will do in this country, and the difficulty may rectify itself. On general principles, any combination that will undertake to make capital pay more for one man's labor by half or a quarter than it is worth, will simply prevent capital from buying. Nor is there power enough in labor by any combination to force capital to purchase ; and if the struggle ever comes to that, it will be found that capital will survive while labor must yield.

However, as a money-making business, it affords an

opportunity for all who can get employment to gain an independence. No matter what grade of skill the mechanic or laborer may possess, he can always gain employment at some price; and, generally, steady work at moderate prices will in the long run produce the most money. The tables of earnings will be useful for any laborer or mechanic to study, for they will show them how small earnings, properly cared for, will soon place them in independence, and, if continued, will lead to fortune.

CHAPTER VIII.

APPRENTICES.

Meaning. — How treated. — Knowledge acquired. — Intermediate steps. — Farming apprentices. — What kind of knowledge. — Study, land, and productions.—Use of tools.—How can I make ? Bound out.—Spends half.—Makes a farm.—Independent.—Can make a fortune.—Mechanical and manufacturing apprentices.—Good prospects.—Sought after.—Important principles.—To-day and to-morrow.—Good pay.—Object.—Disagreeable people.—No employment.—Manners make money.—Equal to trade—Never lose a friend.—Higher motives.—General character—Personal attention.—Makes money.—Reader may too.—Line upon line.—Work tires, but makes money.—Merchant apprentices.—Not bound out.—Higher pay.—Dress more costly.—Same labor same value.—Where doing best.—Too soon.—Too late.—Story.—Boy nailing box.—Prediction.—Richest in New York.—Straws show wind.—Wind moves straws.—Hands in pockets. — Leaning on goods. — Door post. — Conclusive. — Where begins, where ends.—Services and pay.—Pleasant manners.—Tricks in trade.—Carbuncles and cancers.— Sure discovered.— Character crystallizing. — Blemishes. — Mis-steps.— Widen. — Disagreeable partner. — Under man. — Deceitful. — Acrimony.—Taking advantage.—Better leave.—Yelping curs. — Refiners skimmer. — Honorable gentlemen .— Student apprentice.— Prospects in life.—Great strife.—In one hand, out the other.—Down-hill side of life.—Labor accumulated.

AN apprentice, in its strict meaning, is one who is bound by a covenant, to remain with another for a certain period, in order that he may obtain a knowledge of an art or trade. But the term, as used here, is intended to include all who are acquiring the knowledge of an art or trade, whether bound or not. In every department of industry they have different kinds of knowledge to acquire, and hence what would be useful to one, would be of no use in the other. The money compensation during the term of apprenticeship is very small; and generally no charge is made in advance, as is the case in some countries. There are two intermediate steps to the principals in mercantile business—the apprentice and the clerk; in the mechanical and manufacturing trades three—the apprentice, the journeyman, and the foreman; in the farming and growing two—the apprentice and the day-laborer; in the intellectual one—the student.

The farming and growing apprentice should have a good common-school education, that he may be able to read understandingly works on agriculture, and be able to find out the best implements used, the best grains known for profit, the composition of soils, what they require to raise various kinds of grain, that the proper manures may be applied. He should know the most marketable stock, study their natures, and the diseases to which they are liable, and be able to know what disease any animal has by inspection, and know the remedy. In truth, he should study and understand all that can be known about land and its productions, and about stock and their most profitable productions. Then if the land becomes unproductive he will know what remedy should be applied. He should also become acquainted with the use of tools, should in truth have a set, and use them, for he will find that by their use upon a farm he will save and make many a dollar. A farmer can find implements that he can make in weather when he cannot work outdoors, and the sum total of their value in the course of a few years will amount to a large sum. In fact, to be handy with tools upon a farm is about as necessary as to know how to work it, provided the farmer intends making the most money by his opportunity.

"But," says the farming apprentice, "I can make no money; what encouragement is there for me?"

If you are bound out to the farmer till you are twenty-one, there may not be much money to be made till after that time, though generally the apprentice has a small set-out at the end of his time. But there is no business which does not require knowledge and preparation to carry it on; and in this respect this business does not differ from any other. Although the apprentice is not making dollars in hand, he is accumulating a capital in knowledge and skill, which is the same thing in another form, and will bring him the money in time. In case, however, the apprentice is not bound, but receives compensation, he has an opportunity to make. If, then, he commences at fifteen years of age, and gets ten dollars a month on the average till he is twenty-one, he can make some money. With care he can clothe himself and have all the necessary comforts on half that sum, leaving $60 per annum as the net earning. This, accumulated and improved at seven per cent. for the six years, will amount to the neat little sum of $407; enough to make a handsome payment on a farm if he would wish to do so. If, however, he would wish to continue to hire out, and if he has done all he could to make his services valuable while an apprentice, he can get $20 per month, if not more; and if he spends half his wages he will have, if he continues to work till he is thirty-one years of age, at the same rate, $2,484, by improving his $407 at compound interest, and his earnings for the ten years at seven per cent.

This amount will buy a comfortable farm, and the

apprentice at the age of thirty-one is an independent man; for a man *is* independent who owns the farm he lives on. And it may be remarked here in comparison that not one in one hundred has this amount at command earned by themselves at that age. And if this young man should put this at interest at seven per cent., or into a farm that would yearly produce this amount, he will find the truth of the comparison; and even more than that, when compared with men at the age of say seventy-one years. For he will see by the tables of compound interest that this sum will be in forty years, that is when he becomes seventy-one years old, $37,185.48; and if in the meantime he had been able to earn *one dollar* a day off the farm as his profit, and improve it in like manner, he would make in cash in this time by that $65,621, which, added to the first sum, would make his total earning to that time $102,806.48. It is safe to say there is not one in a thousand who has this sum at that age. This example is given to show the farming apprentice that his occupation is well chosen when he *can* make more than nine hundred and ninety-nine in one thousand of the average business men, besides having an occupation highly reputable and respectable, and entirely independent. This branch of the subject is further continued under the chapter of " Farming and Growing."

The mechanical and manufacturing apprentice takes in a wide range of employment in those businesses. In these the system of binding boys out for a given term is more common than in the apprenticeship at farming. The compensation is very small, but the chances of learning a trade at which good wages can be had at the end of the apprenticeship, make such positions sought after as a means of getting a living, of making money, and of advancement, to become principals in the business. There is on this account competition to gain places as apprentices, for they are sure footholds for the future, as well as an immediate means of support.

There are some very important principles which apply equally to all apprentices. Each should understand that he has a future, and although he gets his living and a little more at the present, his hopes of higher pay and higher place lie solely in the future. They, in truth, work to-day for what they are to receive for to-morrow. In what way, then, are they to secure the most money? And this is the great question. They will see at once that if they learn nothing, they may reasonably expect to get no more than they do as an apprentice. If, on the other hand, they make themselves good tradesmen, they will get good tradesmen's pay; and as the tradesmen's pay varies according to quality, to be of the best quality is to get the most pay possible from the employment.

The object, then, of every apprentice should be to acquire the most knowledge and the most skill he can, and this will secure him the most money, provided he has other qualities which will not detract from his ability to get the price. There are some people so disagreeable in their manners, and make those around them so uncomfortable, that they do not get employment at all. Hence it will be seen that such qualities will lose the most skilled mechanic money, and the reverse if he possesses opposite qualities; they make money for him because they do not prevent his getting the real value of his services. The apprentice, then, should see to it that he does not destroy the value of his prospects by bad behavior, ill manners, or a churlish way; but on the contrary, to study manners, pleasant and agreeable ways, endeavoring to make *all* with whom he may come in contact friendly towards him and personally interested in him. *Depend upon it, he will make money as fast this way as by the knowledge and skill he is acquiring in his trade.*

As a means of doing this, he should read, study, and acquire general knowledge; make solid and good acquaintances, then cultivate them. Never lose a friend, if possible to avoid it; that very one may be able some day to throw a fortune in his way. Of course he must always have a higher motive than the mere dollar to do this, but remember that to neglect it may land him in the poor-house. He has certain ends to accomplish in life; he can do so by any honorable means. His general character, as he develops himself in life, has more to do with success than he may imagine. Spare no pains, young man, to make yourself beloved by your employer. You take many turns of the body and motions of the hands to do your day's work; take but a hundredth part as many to please him by little personal attentions, and be assured you will, in the end, make more money by that than by your labor. Do the same to every one with a good feeling, and you will make still more.

The repetition of this principle so often may tire the reader, but it matters not; it is of sufficient importance to be repeated on every page, nor even then would its full strength be told. He must have patience, even though the story be in "line upon line, precept upon precept, here a little and there a little." It may tire, so does work; but still work must be done, and work makes money.

The merchant apprentice has a wider field, with more

numerous opportunities of employment. They are seldom bound to their employer, but receive a small compensation at first, which is gradually increased as their services become more valuable. The compensation is higher than in either of the former named, because the expenses are in like manner higher from necessity. The business to be done is of a different nature, requiring a mode of living and dress more costly. As will be seen, it would scarce be a money-making operation for the merchant to place behind his counter a young man dressed appropriately as a mechanic or manufacturing apprentice; or as a farmer working the fields. The one kind of clothing is abstractly just as good as the other; there might be money made by the one kind of dress and lost by the other. It is on this account that any difference exists between the prices of labor in one department of trade and another, where knowledge, skill, and physical ability are the same in both.

An apprentice cannot be worth much to the merchant without he is incited to labor from a consideration of his own advantage, advancement, and the moral obligation he feels himself under to do his duty. If he takes no interest in the inside of the business he had better be outside altogether. If his thoughts and feelings are elsewhere, his employment had better be there too. In order that the apprentice shall make the most money for himself and his employer, his mind and thoughts should be concentrated upon his duties, and he will know when he is doing the best by experiencing a high pleasure in his occupation, in feeling that night comes too soon, and the time to resume in the morning comes too late. If he can bring about these feelings his success is certain.

There is, too, a certain something about the conduct

of the apprentice that foretells the final character. As an illustration: A man of great observation and a clear scrutinizer of character, was one day in a hardware store, and saw a lad trying to nail up a box of goods. He tugged away at it for a time, never minding what was passing around him. He had nearly completed nailing on the cover, when the nail that he was driving flew into a pile of hinges which lay on the floor close by. The boy stepped to the pile, looked for an instant, but not seeing the nail, stepped back, laid down his hammer, and deliberately went to work unpiling the hinges to get the nail. He succeeded, replaced the hinges, then drove the nail home to its place, muttering to himself as he did so, "Served me right; I shall be more careful next time." The gentleman remarked to himself, "That boy will be a rich man if he lives." In thirty years he was the richest man in his line of business in New York.

It was not so much the trifle of the nail, or of any of the attendant circumstances, that led the gentleman to conclude what he did. But "Straws show which way the wind blows," and as a converse to this proposition it might be added that the wind shows what way straws *will* go. The *manner* in which a thing is done will reveal to an observing eye the train of mind which guides it. And if an apprentice is seen standing around in a store, where there are always a hundred-and-one things that can be done to advantage, with his hands in his pockets, or listlessly leaning upon a pile of goods, or braced up against a door-post, he may be at once set down as having no special thought on his business. The straw shows which way the wind blows with him. If, on the other hand, he is restrained from universal usefulness and holds back from doing something because others in the same establishment do not do it, he is a *straw*, and the wind will show which way he will go. Others of more mature age and higher position, would do well to reflect whether they show which way the wind blows, or by a different course, pointing which way the aerial current is running.

The custom in this country is such, in regard to mercantile apprentices, that it is difficult to say at what exact point this time ends and the clerk begins. But we must content ourselves by saying that the apprentice must be regarded as quite a youth, and before he has attained sufficient knowledge and skill to enter into the body of the business in the way of aid—that is, before he sells or takes an independent department, either at the books, or in receiving, or shipping, or the like. In order that the apprentice may know that what services he does perform will all be paid for sooner or later, he is referred to the case of the two salesmen cited in the chapter, Fountains of Wealth. He will see there a parallel to his own case; and if he does not get the value of his services this year, he is laying by in reserve his earnings for another. For depend upon it, the immutable law of value will stand in his case as it does in all others.

Cultivate pleasant manners—a frank, honest, open face, and let it extend to the heart. Endeavor to impress every man with whom you have dealings that you are fair and just. *Tricks in trade are carbuncles and cancers upon the face of your success.* Men will be as much afraid of you with such guide-boards and signs, as they would be of the things themselves. Nor flatter yourself that your tricks will not be found out. Whether they are or are not, they indicate the true character, and the character *will* show for itself. The character is just at this period crystallizing—see that no blemishes are imbedded in it for all to look at who touch you in after life. A misstep at this point, or a small dereliction from rectitude, widens, to be greater and greater the further in life you go.

If you are sufficiently unfortunate to fall in with some house who has a specially disagreeable partner, or an under-man who has the confidence of the principals because he is sufficiently deceitful to accomplish his object of a high salary, and has sufficient acrimony to make himself hated by every one else, be as cautious of *him* as you would be of a robber. If he judges or imagines that your talent may presently or remotely come in collision with his, you are measurably ruined. You would do well to leave at once. He will curdle and turn to gall in the mind of your employer every act you may do, no matter how well done. If he finds he cannot oust you in any other way he will personally insult you, relying upon your position and his strength to accomplish his end. If you remain, he will increase his efforts till he will destroy, by annoyances untold, your taste for business and your desire to please.

Leave at once; there are gentlemen enough to serve. Such yelping curs are the ignorant, the scum which comes up from below, to flourish upon the solidities of others because it is their nature. These characters, after a while, become known, and the refiner's skimmer consigns them to their proper element. But they have lived long enough, possibly, to damage you. But be on your guard for such obstacles in the way of your success, and let no considerations tempt you to intrust your future fortunes and the formation of your mercantile character to such a deformity. Look well to the character of those with whom you are to associate yourself, and be not over anxious to get a place if you cannot do so among honorable merchants and high-minded gentlemen. There are very few cases such as has been named, and many which are everything to be desired.

The student apprentice, like all the others named, is laboring to acquire skill and knowledge of his intended profession for like purposes. What has been said of other young men of your age under this head, in many respects, will also apply to your own case and to your prospects in life. Every day brings its opportunity to acquire knowledge, and when the day is gone that opportunity is gone also. If the young could only be placed at the stand-point of experience in after life, and look back upon the space now under treatment, how differently they would view their opportunities. All are striving for a living, and more; and while they commence life with strife, and end it generally in like manner, the object for which they are all laboring is caught in one hand and cast away by the other, in ninety-nine cases in a hundred. Is it not then worth while for the young apprentice to obtain some knowledge, among his other acquirements, how he can do better in the world than one in a hundred? He studies everything to know how to get money; in other words, how to get the knowledge by which he can get money. Has he ever studied how to get the most with the knowledge he has acquired, and the nature of the thing itself—the reasons why it will not stay with him, and why, after doing all that intellect and perseverance could accomplish, he is still left on the down-hill side of life, with just these in full action, and cannot point to a single day's labor accumulated as the evidence of what he has done?

CHAPTER IX.

CLERKS.

Important class.—How regarded.—Compared.—His latitude and longitude.—Large chance.—Solid question.—Rule for success.—Always a market.—Examples.—Spending don't increase value.—Habits.—Bad loses money.—Good makes.—Confidence gained.—Reputation.—Character.—Not trustworthy.—Loose life, loose morals.—Blocks advancement.—Money loss.—Choice of cashier.—Good habits make money.—Justice cited.—Splendid honors.—Selection of position.—Reasoning à priori.—Nothing saved as clerk, nothing as principal.—Makes profit and can again.—Double way of making money.—Associates, friends, or enemies.—Too expensive.—Conventionalities of life.—Who helps you.—Who clings a dead weight.—Who will you please.—Singular infatuation.—Money spent to please others.—Great point.—Choose for yourself.—Consider chances.—Two means.—Polite, affable, pleasant.—Great question.—Which offers most.—Calculation.—Clerk makes $251,318.—Compared.—Ambition.—Business for himself.—Close calculations.—Be modest.—Mind your business.—Make friends.—Pleasant smiles.—Agreeable news.—Costs nothing.—Makes money.

CLERKS form an important class auxiliary to the carrying on the various departments of business. Some make it a profession for life, aspire to nothing further than the pecuniary value of their services, and are satisfied with what that may yield; others regard it as a species of servitude out of which they hope to emerge to be principals, in the hope of securing larger remuneration. Such ambition is laudable, and is well in itself; but it is quite certain that clerkships can be so managed financially as to result in an independence to every one and a fortune to some, while the management of a business on their own account in nineteen cases out of twenty, if not a larger proportion, will result in neither. One has but to look at the statistics of success in mercantile business to prove this; though all the statistics in the world would not prevent the ambitious young man from making the usual effort to acquire a sudden fortune. This being human nature we must take it as it is, and endeavor to show such the means of making the most money while clerks, and the way to accomplish their ambition by the safest path, and then to point out the hidden rocks in their channel of life discovered by previous wrecked mariners, freighted alike with ambitions and hopes, which have long since sunk into poverty and distress.

But let any clerk on a fair salary, take his latitude and longitude in life, and refer himself to the co-ordinates of comfort and happiness enjoyed by principals, or even men of fortune. If the reference be made candidly, soberly, and with common-sense judgment, he will discover that his individuality is perfect, and that his chance of making an independence is greater than that of the average of business men who operate on their own account, if not greater than theirs, in time, to make a fortune. Not only that, but in the meantime he will, if he is philosophic, take as much comfort in life, if not more, than those who are in the way of making largely, with the constant danger before them of losing all.

So that clerking, if rightly considered, is not only respectable, but, considered in all the relations of life, honorable and profitable. Then the solid question arises, How can the most money be made out of the situation? The answer to this question can easily be given, and it only remains for such individual to make practical use of the information, which may or may not be new to him.

Your business, then, being to assist others to carry forward their plans and operations for a certain amount of compensation, two consequences result: " What amount of assistance am I to give for the compensation?" and, " Will the compensation be equal to what I do?"

Every business man who pays the market value for the commodities he purchases, will in like manner find that he will be compelled to pay for the value of these services by the same rule; if he does not, some one else will; and hence follows the rule, which is inevitable: *That services, like any other commodity, command in market their true value;* so that the clerk has but one principle to act on—to get the most money out of his situation. This constitutes the whole range of his business life, so far as getting money is concerned, if he determines to remain a clerk.

Many in this line do not know in what consists such value, and if they do, neglect to use the information for their own benefit, and possibly do not know how to proceed to accomplish the object if they know the fact. But one thing may be assumed as true, that there is so much demand for such valuable services, that the moment they can be ascertained they always find a ready purchaser. One example of this kind is cited on page 29 to explain that in this lies the fountain of wealth to the clerk. As will be seen by that case, the one was doing no more than the other apparently, and each receiving the same amount of money; the value of the services of the one became nearly twice as valuable as the other; although one spent all his income while the other spent only one-third. From this it will be seen that spending money does not necessarily secure increased income, but on the contrary almost certainly decreases it proportionately with those who are saving. Here, then, is a good lesson how to make saving valuable; and this brings us to a very important feature in this matter.

Habits of living, as well as habits of life, generally have a strong bearing upon the appreciation in which the clerk is held by the employer, and the confidence he can feel in him, and the security of trusting important matters to his care. So that the more loose habits a clerk has the less he will be trusted, and his services will of course be less valuable; the fewer he has, the more as a general rule he can be trusted, and the more valuable will be his services. It may seem of little or no consequence to a young man who is a clerk to be seen indulging in drink, in cigars, in billiards, or in debauching of any kind, but the point is not as to the particular drink, cigar, game of billiards, or a given debauch; these will probably not hurt him, nor may it lose him more money than the simple cost, which may be a trifle, but it is the *character* which the repetition of doing such things implants upon the clerk, making him liable, if he is human, to do worse.

No wise man in business would intrust such a clerk with his heavy interests, although there are thousands who do just these things that are as honest as the sun to rise, and could be trusted with untold millions. No one will deny that a loose course of life makes loose morals, and no one can say when the effects will take place. Nor is it intended here to preach a sermon on morals, but to open the eyes of some who complain of fortune, when they themselves have blocked her wheels by such as they supposed innocent and comparatively inexpensive amusements. They may never have cast a thought that these things have retarded promotion, advancement, or high salaries, but probably have blamed their employers for being mean and close-fisted, and even unjust, by giving to others what they supposed belonged to them.

There is a positive money-loss in all these things, and it is not alone confined to the clerk. If, then, the question be brought home to the clerk himself, he will see the force and truth of the position. You are the president of a bank, or a large private banker, or a large wholesale or retail dealer, and if you wanted a cashier with a salary say of $5,000 per annum, would you select one with the habits named? Though he might be as quick as lightning, smart as the smartest, and as accurate as a multiplication table, it is easy to tell what you would do if you were a man of sense, though you might have just those habits yourself.

An instance can be cited. A young man now in business (1867) was a clerk, and he had decided to enter business on his own account. He had never tasted a glass of liquor, smoked a cigar, or been addicted to the ordinary habits of young men. He had been in business but a short time when a friend of his had a son whom he wished to place in business; and such was his confidence in this young man, from his general character, that he gave his son $350,000 in cash, as capital, to join the young man, and the concern is to-day doing a splendid business on strictly business principles. Whether the young man is any better or more capable than others addicted to such habits is not the question to be decided here; the only question is whether *such a character* inspires more confidence than the other, and whether it would command more money, out of which to make money, than the other all other things being equal.

If these propositions are true, and it is believed they cannot be denied, then high moral character, free from what is called bad habits, is worth money to the possessor, and hence money is made through such means, and directly too.

There is another question which bears very strongly on the ability of a clerk to either become a partner of the house he is in, or be selected as the managing man for capital in a new one, or which will affect his credit starting on his own account. If he has spent all his salary as a clerk, why would he change from spending all his profits when in business on his own account? Reasoning *à priori* he would. Will such a reputation secure him what he wants and needs? Probably not. But if, on the other hand, he has shown himself competent to manage his little mercantile affairs as a clerk to advantage, that is to a profit, and has saved, is it not good reasoning to suppose he would do a larger business well also?

In other words, would you select one to make profit who never had done it? Would you give as much for a man to help you make profits who had never made a dollar of profit in his life, as you would to the one who had made profit by business, although the business was small? The proposition is self-evident; and hence deduce that the clerk who has saved of his earnings is worth more, and will bring a higher price in the market than he who has not. For if a clerk cannot take care and nurse his own, he is certainly not so well calculated to take care of another's as he who can and does.

This course of economy and saving is a double way of making money. First you make it out of your own little business as clerk, and then you increase the value of your services by showing your capability to do just that which is the object of all business, namely, to make profit by business. How, then, can the clerk expect advancement, either to become a principal or have his pay increased, without these things are studied and attended to. Can we not see in this principle why so many merchants fail in business?

These habits and failings to save are mainly attributable to what you call your friends and associates. If you will examine yourself, you will find that naturally you are averse to almost everything you do in this way, or if not now, there was a time when you were. Who has given you a taste for them, or if not a taste, who has induced you to indulge in them? The answer is simple— your associates. Then, is it not worth your while to consider whether such associates, although they are agreeable and pleasant, are not too expensive to you? In other words, can you afford so much money for just the pleasure of this society, or rather the difference between such society and that which might be equally agreeable but not so expensive?

The great trouble in all these matters, arises from the constraints which the conventionalities of life throw around the rising generation. They must do as everybody else does, or they will be pointed at. This pointing will do no harm to any one, not even to his own feelings, if he looks at it in the right light. Will it reduce the salary of the clerk, or will it tend to increase it? Will it prevent his advancement, or will it accelerate it? It will not rob him of a cent, but will put dollars in his pocket. What motive, then, has he to please those who are thus sapping the very foundations of his wealth and future advancement? Will they pay your bills? Will they give you a dollar? Can they?

No; they are powerless to be a benefit to you, and cling a dead weight upon your prosperity.

Then, who are your friends, and who your real enemies? Those who do not point at you, but approve of your simple habits and saving ways; can and will aid you with money to make money, and with advancement; while those who do point will do neither for you, and will be well satisfied if they can hold you up to ridicule. Will you, then, please your friends or your enemies? This is the great question, and in its answer lie success and happiness, or failure, want, poverty, and distress.

There is a singular infatuation about doing as others do, but the philosophy of the thing is seldom thought of. *Money is generally spent more to please others than ourselves.* Those then who have the independence to make themselves the standard, instead of bowing to the standard of another, have achieved a great point in money-making, in being respectable, in being comfortable, happy, and prosperous. Assuming, then, that the clerk has sufficient independence to choose his associates, to live to gratify himself instead of others, to make money instead of squandering where nothing substantial is returned, to cater for his own advancement instead of for those who are a dead-lock in his way, has one of two things to choose for himself—whether he will make clerking his aim in life, or whether he will use that position as a stepping-stone for entering business on his own account.

By reference to the tables of earning, and an intelligent consideration of the chances of success in mercantile life from the statistics which have been given heretofore, the clerk can determine as to his future destiny, or rather, which he will choose.

If you determine the first course, you have only to make your services of the greatest possible value. This is accomplished by two means:

First. By a thorough knowledge of your business.

Second. By establishing a character for honesty and trustworthiness.

You will then be able to procure what your services are worth by being affable, polite, pleasant, agreeable, social, and attractive to all with whom you come in contact. Under all the circumstances of comfort, taking a solid view of life, and the chances of that terrible condition of want after plenty, which so many merchants and principals in other businesses experience as a reward for years of toil, it is doubtful whether the clerkship does not present more attraction in the long run than entering business as a principal. Let us examine the matter a little. Suppose we assume an instance of one who receives the following rates till he is sixty years of age, and see what the result is, compared with the average of success by merchants:

From 15 to 20 years, average,	$500.
From 20 to 25 " "	$1,200.
From 25 to 30 " "	$1,800.
From 30 to 40 " "	$2,500.
From 40 to 50 " "	$3,500.
From 50 to 60 " "	$5,000.

Now suppose he spends one-half of his salary each year. By the tables he will have at sixty years of age $251,318, compounding and improving savings at seven per cent. How many large merchants have this at that age, and how many have less, and how many have nothing!

If, however, the clerk is determined to try his luck in

business on his own account, he can have no surer guarantee of success than by first making his own capital at clerking. This is achieved by making his services valuable, and then saving till he may have sufficient to start on. A small capital, well managed, will make more money than more, on which you are bound to pay interest. To decide this question of advantage a series of close calculations is to be entered into of the expenses of your concern, such as store-rent, clerk-hire, losses, and other current expenses, and good judgment required to see what will make the most according to all the chances. Then to accomplish your object dress neatly, so as not to be remarked either way. Be modest, unassuming, never boast of what you are doing, of your profits, or your business, or what you intend to do. Mind your own affairs, and let others alone. Make friends with all by your pleasant smiles and agreeable words; they cost nothing, and make much money.

CHAPTER X.

FARMING AND GROWING.

Good business.—Steady increase.—Large or small scale.—Different names.—Ordinary farming.—How to pay for a farm.—Small daily earnings.—Buy and work.—Your capital.—Keep accounts.—Inventories.—Earnings and loss.—One hundred dollars profit.—Big result.—Very fine.—Get a wife.—Common sense.—No nabob.—Prince of the realm.—Imitate me.—Man of independence.—First cut.—Value your property.—Making or losing.—Questions.—What kind of things.—Simple merchant. —Everything should pay.—Losing money.—Earn their living.— Produce must.—Others', not your own taste.—Routine farming.—Stocks in fashion compared.—Costs same to keep poor as good.—Example.—Great gain in good.—Make largely by good stock.—Sell, and buy half.—Increase good stock.—Sell poorest, keep best.—Breed from best.—Poor grade.—Damage to implements.—Large sum in time.—They pay for farm.—Stitch in time.—Illustration.—Little thing great damage.—Expense a moth.—Rats in granary.—Pick up.—Hang up.—Like retail merchandizing.—Relative comparison.—Tables of earnings.— Calculate and understand.—Inducements.—Independence.— Happiness.

WITH good health and bodily strength no employment gives a more sure result for a comfortable living than that of the farmer or grower. Like the capitalist with his money at interest, growth and increase march steadily on through day and night. The grain, the grass, the herds, and the fruits, respond to the toil of the husbandman, and furnish a rich reward for his industry. On the large or small scale in which these are carried forward depend the results, whether much or little.

But whatever the scale may be, under ordinary circumstances a profitable harvest is gathered.

Farming, by which term is meant the working of from sixty to two hundred acres of land to produce the ordinary crops of the country, is carried on in about one style, and varies but little in its general features. There are, however, grazing farms, as they are called, of larger size; and in the western and southern portions of the country, still larger bodies of land under one control, where, in some cases, universal crops are raised, while in others, sugar, cotton, and rice are produced. These latter are called plantations. They are all, however, farms, and the terms used are more to indicate the kind of farming than for any other object.

We will speak first of the most numerous and the most important branch—that of the ordinary farming. The amount of money to be made from this is more fixed in amount, and the profit depends mainly upon the economy with which it is conducted. As every one knows, there is no such thing as making a princely fortune from an ordinary farm. But with proper management and a just economy, money can be made here as well as in any other branch of business. From farming at large all the national wealth proceeds, directly or indirectly.

The independence of the farmer consists in having his farm paid for and being out of debt, for with this a living can always be had, and a good one, too. How is this to be accomplished? The quickest way, is to make the most money off the land in the least possible time. Suppose your farm is to cost $2,000, how much have you to make each working day to pay for it? If you make a payment each six months, you will do the same as improving your earnings at seven per cent., as most farms are bought and sold on interest. Look at the tables of earnings and you will see that if you make $5 per day for one year, you will have $1,992.39. If you make $1 a day for five years, you will have $1,835.96. If you make 50 cents a day for ten years, you will have $2,212.89. If you make 25 cents a day for fifteen years, you will have $2,018, and so on. Now, what does this show? That the small earning of twenty-five cents a day, for three hundred and thirteen working days, will make $78.25 per annum to be saved to pay for your farm, besides the interest on the first amount or sum agreed to be paid. It then becomes a serious and close question for any one wishing to purchase a farm, if he has not the money, to decide upon the best way to procure it.

Let us look at this matter. If you conclude to make the effort in five years, you will have to make yearly, on your farm, $453 clear. Forty-five cents per day for interest, and $1 a day, or $313 in savings, that is, $1.45 per day for the first year. The interest would be $21.91 less the second year, and so on to the last. Now, if you work without the farm, at any other business, you will have to make $313 per year, and improve the earnings each six months at seven per cent. So it will be seen that your farm costs you, by laboring on it instead of working at another business to pay for it, forty-five cents per day. But it must be remembered that there are expenses for tools, etc., in addition; but these are accumulated capital, are valuable; and such may be considered so much additional earnings.

It is clear, from this statement, that if you intend to have a farm, you should buy one, and work on it, instead of working at another business, to make money to pay for it. For it is plain to see that your farm is cheap, under your own supervision, at forty-five cents per day. Then, if you have the money to pay for the farm, and do pay for it, see that it not only does as much for you as it did for the former owner; that is, that it should first pay you the interest on the capital, $140, but that it pays you as much, in addition, as you would have paid down yearly, if you had paid in that way, besides getting your living off of it. If this is not done, depend upon it, there is a screw loose somewhere, and you are losing instead of making money. In other words, you must have at the end of the year $453 in valuable property, more than you had at the beginning of it, or you are not doing as well as you would be working to pay for it otherwise.

The natural question which the farmer would ask, is, How is this to be ascertained? For, generally, a farmer keeps no accounts, and only knows what his debts are. No farmer knows whether he is making money or not if he does not keep an *accurate account* of everything, and, like the merchant, take an inventory on the first of January of each year, of what he has got and what he owes. The way the business is generally done, the only wonder is that he makes at all. As far as can be judged, there is no business so loosely carried on as that of farmers, from the fact that they are generally ignorant of the close, drawn-up way in which all business accounts should be kept; that they run on from year to year not really knowing whether they have made or not.

An example of inventories is given on next page. From these inventories it is seen that the farmer made in the year 1864 the sum of $835.97—that is, he made by *his farm*, over and above his interest on capital, and services in any other business, the sum of $282.97. In 1865 he made $759.95—that is, the sum of $144.95 more

We give a formula of account by which a farmer can tell whether he is making or losing money.

INVENTORY FOR 1863.		INVENTORY FOR 1864.		INVENTORY FOR 1865.		INVENTORY FOR 1866.	
Interest on Capital $2000	$140 00	Interest on Capital $2000	$140 00	Interest on Capital $2000	$140 00	Interest on Capital $2000	$140 00
My services	318 00	My services	318 00	My services and Son's	475 00	My services and Son's	500 00
Owed to me	75 13	Owed to me	101 25	Owed to me	100 00	Owed to me	10 00
3 Horses	150 00	3 Horses	220 00	4 Horses	300 00	4 Horses	325 00
4 Cows	175 00	5 Cows	250 00	6 Cows	295 00	6 Cows	280 00
4 Calves	40 00	20 Sheep	50 00	20 Sheep	75 00	50 Sheep	80 00
10 Sheep	30 00	50 Hens	35 00	50 Hens	35 00	50 Hens	35 00
25 Hens	15 00	6 Hogs	250 00	6 Hogs	275 00	6 Hogs	286 00
3 Hogs	60 00	15 Pigs	30 00	10 Pigs	25 00	10 Pigs	20 00
10 Pigs	20 00	10 Turkeys	10 00	15 Turkeys	15 00	20 Turkeys	20 00
8 Turkeys	8 00	200 Bushels Apples	100 00	180 Bushels Apples	90 00	125 Bushels Apples	62 50
100 Bushels Apples	50 00	5 Barrels Cider	100 00	6 Barrels Cider	120 00	5 Barrels Cider	100 00
3 Barrels Cider	60 00	350 Bushels Wheat	700 00	400 Bushels Wheat	800 00	450 Bushels Wheat	900 00
200 Bushels Wheat	300 00	200 Bushels Oats	250 00	300 Bushels Oats	125 00	300 Bushels Oats	150 00
100 Bushels Oats	50 00	500 Bushels Barley	500 00	600 Bushels Barley	600 00	500 Bushels Barley	500 00
400 Bushels Barley	400 00	5 Ploughs	35 00	4 Ploughs	33 00	4 Ploughs	30 00
4 Ploughs	32 00	1 Horse Rakes	25 00	1 Horse Rakes	20 00	1 Horse Rakes	15 00
1 Horse Rake	10 00	1 Dray	15 00	1 Dray	12 00	1 Dray	10 00
1 Dray	15 00	2 Wagons	140 00	2 Wagons	120 00	2 Wagons	100 00
2 Wagons	150 00	2 Sets Harness	60 00	2 Sets Harness	50 00	2 Sets Harness	40 00
2 Sets Harness	75 00	1 Mowing Machine	100 00	1 Mowing Machine	90 00	1 Mowing Machine	80 00
1 Mowing Machine	120 00	6 Hoes	2 50	6 Hoes	2 00	6 Hoes	1 50
5 Hoes	2 00	Cash on hand	25 00	Cash on hand	200 00	Cash on hand	600 00
	$2,340 13		$3,311 25		$3,996 00		$4,278 50
I owe	240 05	I owe	375 20	I owe	300 00	I owe	100 00
	$2,100 08		$2,936 05		$3,696 00		$4,178 50

than the interest on capital, $140, and $475, the services of himself and son; or, in other words, he made by his *farm*, $144.95. In 1866 he made $482.50, and fell short $132.50 of making the value of his own services and that of his son's, and the interest on his capital. His farm did not pay for itself that year by $7.50, and no profit was made from it. Such bad years will occur on any farm, or in any other business, no matter what it may be.

Let us suppose, then, that he averages from his farm alone $200 per annum; that he makes his interest, $140, and his own services, $313; if he does, he is doing a splendid business, for his income is then, in total, $653. Now look at the table of earnings; at this rate he is earning $2.09 per working day. This sum, accumulated at seven per cent., will yield in five years $3,837.17; in ten years, $9,250.86; in fifteen years, $16,887; in twenty years, $27,655; in twenty-five years, $42,847; in thirty years, $64,277; in forty years, $137,148; in fifty years, $282,126! Can a farmer make money?

"Well," says the farmer, "this is all very nice; very fine; but how can this be done?" We propose to tell you, and if you have average crops, and follow directions, you will not only do this, but more. We will tell you, too, under the head of "How to make money make money, and how to keep it," how to invest it, so that the results stated shall be obtained. But first of all you must have a wife, and both of you must have what is called "good common sense," and know what you are about. If you are not up to this standard, you had better get your living the best way you can, and be satisfied with what you can get. But if you have strength of mind enough to know that you are a farmer, that you must dress, spend, and act like a farmer, you have made a good start. That you will not dress, spend, and act like or play the nabob till you have the money to play it on, is one more step in the right direction. If you will say to yourself, "I am a prince of the realm, and hold in my hands the elements of our nation's wealth; so let others imitate me, if they wish, not I them," you have said true words, and have a just appreciation of your position.

The farmer owning his own land, and out of debt, is the true man of independence. No one can say to him, go here, or go there. He eats the first cut, the country at large is served to the second; he walks upon his acres, and no man can dispute; he sleeps the sweet repose of contentment upon his own downy pillow, and greets the rising sun with a smile. The business of the farmer *being to produce*, everything of clothing or tools should never be bought of others, if it be possible to make them himself, or within his own family. Make your inventory *every year*, putting everything in that you could *sell for money*, even to the most trifling thing. Take off each year for depreciation and wear as much as will make its cash value, if sold. This inventory should only contain the articles *on hand* each first of January, as stated in the former examples given. You will then be able to know just how you stand, and whether you are making or losing.

Now, for the mode of accomplishment. In the first place, what crops do you raise? Have you ever kept an account whether one kind of grain has done better than another? or whether one field has done better than another, or whether one field is better adapted to a particular kind of crop than to another? If you have not, you are just doing what a merchant would who has started a store, or, possibly, two stores, and has never calculated whether they are making money or not. You would, undoubtedly, say this was simple in him, but, like all human nature, we can discover defects in others while we are ignorant we possess the same ourselves. Every field, every piece of wood, every horse, cow, ox, hog, pig, turkey, hen, or fruit-tree, should be responsible to you for an increase, for they must all be fed and cared for ; and, if they cannot show a clear gain to you, of what use are they. You are losing money in their feed, and the labor bestowed upon them.

The first great principle, then, is to look at every field, animal, and tree, upon your farm, and *see to it that they earn their living by increase.* Crowd on, to every single thing, all your energies to make them work to advantage for you, and never take a business step that does not point in this direction. The great principle, in raising or growing, is to select such grains, fruits, or animals, as will produce the *greatest value with the least expenditure of labor.* Following this principle out with care, requires extensive information ; for how can a farmer know without reading and inquiring, whether he has that which will bring the most money? The grower must remember that, if he wishes to thrive, he is not raising articles to suit his *own* fancy, but the fancy and tastes of *others ;* and, hence, whatever may be his judgment as to their intrinsic value, their only value to him is what others will give for them.

Generally, farming is carried on by a rotation of crops from year to year, without inquiry as to whether the land is more suitable for other crops, or whether the stock or fruits are such as are in fashion, and will produce the most money. A farmer may consume his substance by supporting a dwarfy unsalable stock, from a want of knowledge of the requirements of the market. He may think that the cattle that he and his father before him raised, are just as good as any other stock. In one sense they may be, for the pound of beef in the one may be just as good as any one of the three or four pounds in the other; or the quart of milk from the one may be just as good as any one of the three or four quarts from the other. But he will find out, by sad experience, that the tastes and fancies of consumers change, as well as the ability of two cows on the same food to give equal quantities of milk, or to produce the same amount of beef.

It costs as much to keep a good horse as a poor one, or a good animal of any kind as a poor one; and it costs as much to keep an unsalable and an unproductive stock as it does to keep a salable one or a productive one. Let us examine this point, and, for an illustration, suppose an old-fashioned farmer had thirty head of stock, worth, on an average, $40 the head, making in value $1,200. Another farmer, who has paid attention to the demand for fancy stock, had the same number of head, worth, or would bring in the market, $90 per head, in value $2,700. Now, we will suppose, too, though that would be unequal in fact, as against the higher priced, that in produce of milk and butter, and increase, the total profit upon each lot was twenty-five per cent. per annum. The profit on the first lot would be $300, and the profit on the second would be $675. In addition to this, they would each be compelled to sell a portion each year; say they each sold one-eighth of the whole amount. The first would sell $150, and the second would sell

$337.50. The first would then receive from his stock $450, while the second would receive $1,012.50, the difference being $562.50. In other words, the one that had the fancy stock would receive $562.50 per annum more than the other; or the difference, in three years, would make up the difference between the poor and the good stocks on these amounts.

Now this amount of difference per annum would be $1.79 per day for 313 working days; and this improved at 7 per cent. for five years gives, by tables, $3,286; for ten years, gives $7,923; for fifteen years, gives $14,461; for twenty years, gives $23,685; for twenty-five years, gives $36,696; for thirty years, gives $55,051; for forty years, gives $117,472; for fifty years, gives $141,637. Now, Mr. Farmer, is it worth while to look to the kind of stock you raise? The first cost is nothing. If you cannot afford to get it, sell what you have and get half or quarter, so you will not be compelled at the least to keep the poor stock. Not only should the farmer and grower have the stock which would command the most money, but they should also consider the means of increasing it to be the best. They may attend closely to obtaining good stock, but this is not all that is required to keep it the best. The best males and the best females should be bred from. Instead, then, as is generally the case, of *selling the best fillies, the best male colts, the best bull calves, or the best heifers, keep the best to breed from and sell the poorest.* If the stock-grower wishes to make the most money, he will accomplish his end in this way. If he fails to do this, he will find in a few years that instead of having good stock *all the while to sell*, he will fall back on a very poor grade of stock, or, at best, he will have the poorest of its kind.

These figures show a difference in stock alone, while the same and more could be said about hogs, poultry, and fruit-trees. A great source of loss, and by no means an unimportant one, is that in agricultural implements, caused by exposure to the weather while they should be under cover, out of the rain and sunshine. This source of loss alone to a farmer, in twenty or twenty-five years, if not watched, will doubly pay for his farm. Implements made of wood, such as wagons, drays, ploughs, rakes, mowing and reaping machines, hand-rakes, forks, etc., will not last half as long by exposure as they will under cover; and the farmer, if he has any amount of them which he neglects in this manner, will lose more than he imagines.

An old but true adage, "A stitch in time saves nine," is one of which all should realize the force. A little thing out of order may produce serious results. If any one of your agricultural implements requires repairs, do not wait till you want it, but have it done at once and put in its place. An illustration given by Mr. Say, the political economist, will show the importance of care in little matters:

"Being in the country, I had an example of one of those small losses which a family is exposed to through negligence. From the want of a latch of small value, the wicket of a barnyard, looking to the field, was left open. Every one who went through, drew the door to; but having no means to fasten it, it reopened. One day a fine pig got out and ran into the woods, and immediately all the world was after it. The gardener, the cook, dairy-maid, all ran to recover the swine. The gardener got sight of him first, and jumping over a ditch to stop him, he sprained his ankle, and was confined a fortnight to the house. The cook, on her return, found all the linen she had left to dry by the fire, burned ; and the dairy-maid, having ran off before she tied the cows, one of them broke the leg of a colt in the stable. The gardener's lost time was worth twenty crowns, valuing his pains at nothing. The linen burned and the colt spoiled were worth as much more. Here is a loss of forty crowns, and much pain and trouble, vexation and inconvenience, for the want of a latch, which would have cost three pence ; and the loss, through careless neglect, falls on a family little able to support it."

Expenses is the moth that eats away earnings. They are like rats and mice, or other vermin, in your granary. They consume your hard earnings invisibly, and all you know is that they are gone. Scrutinize well, then, every expenditure, and weigh its necessity. Thought costs nothing, and hence it is not expensive to think. But to think, and think to advantage, saves you many a dollar, and brings many more to your pocket.

Pick up—hang up.—Your land is your best friend—treat it well.

Pick up—hang up.—Your extremities are your heart—let it be active.

Pick-up—hang up.—Knowledge is a good land-dresser.

Pick up—hang up.—Care, a good granary.

Pick up—hang up.—Carelessness, a rat-hole.

Pick up—hang up.—Daybreak dews, farmer's diamonds.

Pick up—hang up.—Sow when you should—reap when you can.

Pick up—hang up.—Quick market—empty fields.

Pick up—hang up.—Go away slow—come back quick

Pick up—hang up.—Good master—good horse.
Pick up—hang up.—Much care—much money.

This subject is by no means exhausted; but enough has been said to illustrate the subject as far as space will admit. The farmer can, however, read to his advantage what is said under the head of retail merchandizing, as his business partakes very largely of that character.

To the larger class of farmers and growers, the same general principles apply. The figures, in any relative comparison, will be correspondingly great; so much so, that the results will be astonishing. A careful study of the use of the tables for earnings, will give an idea how to make the proper substitutions in any supposable case. Enough has been shown, however, that the reader may see how important it is to the farmer, to calculate and understand as well and as thoroughly as the merchant, the market value of what he is raising, and what will bring the most money with the least expense; and he will see, too, that this branch of industry presents as many inducements to the money-maker as any, besides giving him a life of independence, and, if he chooses to make it such, of happiness.

CHAPTER XI.

MECHANICAL BUSINESS.

Mechanical produce.—Bonds.—Strong arm.—Higher grade.—Genius and hammer.—Wonderful results.—Revolving tongue.—Two heads.—Which makes most.—Dollar a day.—Large result.—Can make.—Do make.—Can rise.—New beginner.—Golden opportunity.—Impressions made.—Reverse.—Man you want to see.—Be a gentleman.—Sunshiny heart.—Out of one pocket into another.—Praise.—Strict honesty.—Otherwise dead loss.—Example.—Tailor's trick.—Shoddy.—Don't offend.—Customer considers.—Another shop.—Loss and gain.—Important principle.—Another example.—Somebody lost money.—Extortion.—Smoke-stacks.—Plumber.—Defective joint.—Carpenter.—No screws.—Flare up.—Revelation.—Complained of before.—Loss of work.—Hard times.—Plumber disabled.—Builds largely.—Honest mason.—Replaces bad work.—How much won and lost.—Pennyworth.—Great results.—Robbers.—Overcharged.—Who lost most?—Employed most, employer least.—Guarantees of success.—Effects from reaching.—Discredit spreads.—Journeyman's neglect.—Interest in business.—Why abuse it.—Judging of credits.—Mechanics not bankers.—Different branch.—Consult engineer.—Reject credits.—Sure dollar.—Principle holds.—Another head.—Paradox.—Ride or walk.

MECHANICAL produce, as a means of money-making, ranks among the surest methods known, with the same amount of capital, both for the principals and the operatives. It takes rank in usefulness and necessity with the products of the farmer. As has been seen before, the two are bound together by bonds almost, if not altogether, inseparable. The hammer of the mechanic is as often raised in the land as the farming implement. They are alike producers—the one using land combined with labor, the other using the products of the land combined with labor, to produce required results. These important members of society constitute a strong arm in the body-politic.

The higher grades of mechanism require great scientific acquirements and extensive practical knowledge. Mind and genius mark out the works for the mechanic's hand. By such means pyramids have been raised; walled cities made impregnable; water highways coursed through desert lands; antipodes communicate with each other; iron ships plough the sea without sail and against contending elements; monsters with their iron heels stride over the land with burdens of produce inconceivable; and finally, the climax exists in a revolving tongue, which tattles to every man in the land at the same moment. Genius has moulded all these things within her crystal brain, and mechanism has hammered out the picture into the animated structure.

As a money-making employment, the produce resolves itself into two heads; completed results, and the manual labor to produce them. The money from the results goes to the employer, and the employed receives from the employer the money for his manual labor. It would be a difficult question, after careful investigation, taking everything into account, which can *really* accumulate the most money in certain cases—the employer or the individual employed. This will, undoubtedly, be looked upon as a startling proposition, as any one would suppose, at first thought, that the employer would make the most. A little investigation and calculation will determine this question, and put it in its true light.

As a general rule, good mechanics can furnish themselves and families with all the *necessaries* of life and make a dollar a day. They, of course, do not do this, because they spend uselessly their earnings. If they spend what they gain, and the employer did the same, they would both be making money equally fast; or rather, neither would make at all. But suppose the mechanic did make a dollar a day continuously for twenty-five years, and improved it every six months at seven per cent., how much would he have? The tables, for twenty-five years' earnings of one dollar a day, gives the sum of $20,501. Now the question arises, Does each boss mechanic on an average make this sum? By no means. Then the proposition is true, that a mechanic *can make* and accumulate more than the employers as a class *do make.*

There are as many opportunities for advancement in the mechanical as there are in the mercantile business. There are two great opportunities for distinction. A young man can rise from the hammer to the conducting of a large mechanical business; and if he acquires an education and gains knowledge, can shine in the intellectual class of engineers, inventors, architects, or sculptors.

This chapter will be mainly devoted to show how the employer can make the most money by his trade. The laborer and apprentice have been considered heretofore separably. Let us suppose, then, that the apprentice has been thoroughly grounded in a knowledge of his business, that he has passed through his allotted time, has been a successful journeyman, and finally taken his stand and solicits work on his own account. He has assumed to pay a certain amount of expenditure beyond that of his personal or family expenses. He then wants, nay, must have business. He has his sign up, his shop open, but no one comes. At last a customer enters, either out of curiosity or want, and makes an inquiry about something in the beginner's line of business.

Now is your golden opportunity, for you can, by management, make one business friend if not a customer, and possibly both if you never see another. You should contrive by your conversation and manner to make the following impressions upon him:

First.—That you understand your business.
Second.—That you understand his wants.
Third.—That you are honest and fair.
Fourth.—That you are obliging and in his interest.

If you succeed in accomplishing these ends, you have commenced business nearer success than half the world.

Many mechanics who did not understand their interest will make impressions something after this fashion:

First.—"It's none of his business what I know."
Second.—"I know near enough what he wants."
Third.—"I am honest enough to make a profit if I can."
Fourth.—"I am as obliging as I choose to be, and know my own interest."

These indications of thought might gratify the personal pride, and independence of mind of some, but would neither bring dollars into their pockets, nor suit a customer who could be of great pecuniary advantage. More than this, such a young beginner might be in the presence of the very man whom he had hoped while a journeyman might come along and lend him money to extend his business upon. Above all things, never assume an antagonism of interest with the customer you deal with, but the reverse, and you will be brought to see the dollars that flow from proximity and intermingling.

To be a perfect gentleman is quite easy, and very profitable in transactions. It is not half as difficult of learning and practising, as your trade with tools. The garb may be even assumed for interest's sake if you do not feel what you act. The grand idea is a sunshiny heart shown forth in the face, with pleasant, agreeable, and obliging words, with an air of interest in the cause of the customer. It takes coppers out of his pocket and puts them into yours, in a way as pleasant to both as the mannerism. You make twice by such means; you make the profit, and rivet a customer to your business. He talks about you; tells others what an honest, good fellow you are; how well you do your work; and above all, you are reliable.

You will soon find yourself surrounded by a lot of pleasant-faced customers with open pockets. They will finally come to you for many things they want done not in your line, and urge you to employ the men to do the work, and charge them what is right. Such is the certainty of success attached to such a course of trade, that it has come within our knowledge that a tinman was applied to to build a millionaire a house! Simply because the tinman was honest, and the millionaire vainly supposed that he, the tinman, could make any other mechanic in like manner honest and faithful, whom he employed.

There is no one quality so much needed, and which commands so high a price, as *strict honesty*. When a mechanic is found honest and capable, working for small or fair profits, doing his work for the interest of his employer, he at once becomes crowded with work, and an independence and a fortune stand waiting for him but to be gathered in. There is very little difference what your trade may be, money will roll in from all quarters to fill your purse. A trick, a dishonest job, or an exorbitant profit, is a dead loss. Better not do the job. This, no doubt, would be regarded by some tradesmen as an extravagance.

We will give an example to show its truth. The instance was a tailor, and the deception had been practised on a suit of clothes. The superior knowledge of the tailor had not been used for the benefit of his customer, but, as he supposed, for his own, by a little trick by which he would make an undue profit. The cloth sold to the customer for the suit *looked* just as well to the eye of an inexperienced person as though it had been a first-rate article. But the haberdasher had sold it at a bargain, and the tailor had bought it because a large profit could be made on it *sub rosa*.

Our victimized customer had his suit from this cloth, wore it but a short time, and found, to his amazement, that it was "shoddy." The gentleman could not harbor the thought that he had been intentionally shaved ; but having his own way of testing such matters, he went to the tailor, showed him the "shoddy," and asked an explanation. The tailor replied that "We are sometimes deceived in cloth ourselves, and this seems to be an instance. But," said he, "I have a cloth here," taking up a piece, "that is the best I ever saw. Let me make you a suit from this." Now, this gentleman, who had been deceived once by the tailor, was no fool in such matters. He reasoned by analogy, "I know one thing. I have been deceived by this man in one piece of cloth, and I knew nothing about that; why may I not be deceived again, as I know nothing about this ? Then, too, I have paid this man good money for what he acknowledges himself was a deception ; but he says nothing about making me another suit of clothes for nothing, nor allowing me anything in the way of compensation." All this he was revolving over in his mind while looking at the cloth, and the tailor was eloquent upon its merits.

Like a sensible man, he concluded that as he had got the worst of the last operation with the tailor, he would not expose himself again to the same thing, and quietly took his departure with the reflection, "that if this man has intentionally deceived me I want nothing more to do with him; and if he has bought this cloth through ignorance, he does not understand his business, and I will try some one else." The poor ignorant tailor, however, flattered himself that he would still continue to furnish him with his clothing.

The gentleman did not return, as the tailor supposed, but dropped into another establishment, called the attention of this tailor to the worthless suit, told him the story, but the man said nothing about the other tailor, which a little surprised the gentleman, and the fact made rather a favorable impression upon him. The new tailor began showing his goods, and remarked that "This cloth is showy and *looks* as good as this, but this is much the best and will wear twice as long as the other." The gentleman was pleased, and said to himself: "This man has the air of open-hearted honesty, and for aught I can see has equally good clothing at less prices."

The result was that he sold the gentleman his clothing for the year, amounting to $450, and also his three sons, who had purchased at the same place with the father; one bought $550, the other $400, and the third $375, making altogether a loss to the first tailor of sales amounting to $1,775, and a gain to the second of the same amount. It so happened that the father and three sons continued to buy on an average the same amount each year for twenty years, when the father died. Now let us see how this affair turned out in money made by one and lost by another. Tailor No. 2 made 30 per cent. on the amount sold on an average, or $532.50 per annum for twenty years, and tailor No. 1 lost that much by his little deception. That is, one tailor gained $1.41 per day, and the other lost that sum. By the table of earnings for twenty years, we find that this, improved at 7 per cent. for that time, would amount to $18,657. The tailor No. 1 tried to make some 10 or 12 dollars by deception, and it cost him $18,657. Is "honesty the best policy" or not in trade? This is a single instance of the ten thousand cases that occur daily through utter ignorance of the results which flow from such little "tricks in trade," as they are denominated. From this illustration some very important principles to mechanics may be deduced.

First.—Customers do not generally understand your trade, and do not know whether the goods are well made or work well done on inspection. You do; therefore be honest. If not, sooner or later you will be caught, and will lose money by it whether you are caught or not.

Second.—If a man has paid you good money, and you find out afterwards that he has not had value received in goods or work, you never can make as much money by any other means as by paying him back his honest dues. That money will quadruple to you in a year.

Third.—Never speak ill of a fellow-tradesman; you will lose money by it. Let every man's experience be his own schoolmaster; you can't afford to teach for nothing.

Fourth.—If you have been deceived yourself, whereby

you deceive another, make full restitution. Don't wait to have it cork-screwed out of you. You will make money by it.

These principles underlie permanent success in mechanical trades and business growing out of it. The tradesman, and the mechanic also, have great temptation laid before them, from the very nature of their business, to give the customer less than *honest value.* Very few understand the value of mechanical work, or know how much a mechanic ought to do in a given time, and hence over-charge and under-time lie alone with the tradesman and the mechanic. But though this may be true, the customer, by an instinct from observation, will find out he is unfairly dealt with, though he may not know *exactly why, or how.* It is quite a common idea among mechanics that they must not do the job too well, for it will spoil the trade; hence they will do the work to answer a temporary purpose, and expect another job to do it over in a short time, and so on.

An instance has occurred while this article was being written. A low chimney of a neighboring house, seen from my window, required, it was presumed, a smokestack; for, one morning, two mechanics appeared upon the roof with their tools, and under the arm of one was a smoke-pipe, about two feet long. The men laid down their tools, sat down upon the coping, quietly took out their pipes, filled and lit them, and took a good smoke. They seemed to be engaged in conversation, as they were looking about and pointing here and there. Finally, the ashes were knocked out of their pipes, they got up, stretched themselves, yawned, and walked towards the chimney. Here they stood, with their hands in their pockets, for a considerable time, and after spending an hour, if not more, took up their tools and went to work. It is needless to say that the forenoon was exhausted in putting up the two feet of pipe. The next day they came back with another, and it was put in a different flue in the same chimney, and the operation was substantially the same as the one the day before. These two stayed up two days, when the same men came and took them down, and carried them off. The next day they came with them again, lengthened to about five feet, and about the same amount of time was spent again. These two stayed up three or four days, but in the meantime they came and put up a galvanized iron one in the third flue, which was about twelve feet high from the top of the chimney. In a day or two the men came again, took down the five-feet pipes, carried them off, and the next day came with them again, lengthened to the height of the galvanized iron one, and put them up. Since then, some four days, they have not appeared on the roof.

Somebody lost money by this operation. The man may pay the bill, and the mechanic may have supposed he had done one more job to advantage. But the chances are he will lose money by it; for if he had not been ignorant of his business, he would have known that, on account of the height of the adjoining walls, twelve-feet smoke-stacks were necessary, and he would have made them and put them up in half a day. If he was dishonest, and wished to "run the job," he will sooner or later lose by it, for, at least, he has taught his hands a bad trick.

This course of business generally brings about the same result as in the case of the tailor, by the varieties of way in which it is practised. The loss to the extortioner is the same, whether the extortion be in the way of exorbitant, or the under value of the work done. We will examine a case a little more in point, where the results were seen directly. An application was made by a wealthy gentleman to his plumber, to have some trifling repair done to a weeping joint of pipe in his house. He at once dispatched his journeyman to make the repair. Having arrived at the house, he proceeded to the examination of what was to be done. The repair was in plain sight, but was a little *inconvenient*, on account of some wood-work, but nevertheless could have been done without its removal; but in order to have plenty of room he tore away the wood-work and was then ready to proceed. It took but a few moments to do the work, though half a day was consumed in talking with the servants, and general puttering about. The work was, however, completed; and as it turned out, the leak proved to result from a slight defect in the work of the same principal and same journeyman at the time the house was built.

The plumber made out his bill, and it was paid by the owner with the passing remark, that "work should be well done at first, and all such expenses and annoyances would be avoided." The owner sent for his carpenter and told him to replace the wood-work torn up by the journeyman plumber. The carpenter happened in like manner to have done the work after the plumber at first, and on proceeding to the place, found, to his amazement, the new work split to pieces, and entirely unfit for use again, for it had been nailed down instead of *screwed* down, as he had directed, and as he supposed had been done. He reported the state of the case to the owner, who directed that new work should be put up. It was completed, the bill presented, and paid by the owner, who remonstrated with the plumber because his journeyman had destroyed the wood-work, as the carpenter said, "unnecessarily, as the work *could* have been done without." The plumber, piqued at the carpenter's remark, told the owner that "If the work had been *screwed* down, as it should have been, instead of *nailed* down, as it was, there would have been no difficulty."

These transactions and conversations revealed to the owner some valuable information, from which he discovered the following facts:

First.—That the plumber had done his work imperfectly at first.

Second.—From this cause he had lost, and no restitution was made.

Third.—That the carpenter had done his work badly at first.

Fourth.—From this cause he had lost, and no restitution was made.

Like a wise man, he revolved over in his own mind the whole matter, not because of its importance in the present case, but its bearing upon the future, for he was a large landowner and built extensively. He made up his mind and kept his conclusions to himself. Almost any one will overlook an error, or a mistake, or an unavoidable accident in another; but few men will be satisfied with being compelled to pay for it.

On reflection, the plumber remembered that the same journeyman, considered one of the best he had, and receiving the highest wages, had been complained of twice before for similar neglect, and had caused him much trouble at those times. It so happened that soon after, work became slack, business dull, and the plumber was obliged to discharge some of his force. Much to the surprise of the journeyman and all in the place, when pay-day came around he was discharged.

The carpenter in the meantime finding out that the plumber had "let the cat out of the bag" with the owner, respecting the improper manner in which his work had been done, brought up the journeyman carpenter for an explanation, who excused his neglect because he had no fit screws, and supposed that it would make no difference in that one place, as all similar work in the other parts of the house had been screwed down and done properly. A few days after the carpenter saw a journeyman from one of the neighboring carpenter-shops enter the house of his former profitable customer, with his tool-box on his shoulder. He well knew what that meant; and, incensed at the loss of such a man's work by the neglect of his journeyman to step out and procure what screws he wanted, not a hundred feet distant, discharged him on the very next pay-day.

Times being hard, and work dull, neither the journeyman plumber nor carpenter could get anything to do. They had each laid up a little, but it was fast going when all was expense and no income. They were willing to work for less wages than they had received, but no one seemed to want them; for all asked where they had worked, and why they had left. Having nothing to do, the plumber went into the country (for he was employed in New York), where he remained some time; and finally fell from a tree, while gathering some nuts, broke his wrist, and was disabled for life. The journeyman carpenter took sick, after being out of business for some time, was bed-ridden for a year, and died.

The rich man, out of whose work all this trouble had arisen from an imperfect joint of the plumber, soon built

largely to improve some vacant property which he had
The materials were all purchased, and his carpenter-work
done by the day, which was supposed would amount to
$53,000. The plumbing bill, done in like manner, was
estimated at $11,000. The mason who had done this
gentleman's work for a long time, was a very worthy,
honest man; but a little circumstance happened about
this time which won the gentleman's confidence completely.
The mason had done the work of a brown-stone
front house but a short time before, and the foundation to
the front stoop had been either carelessly laid, or from
some other cause, a settlement had taken place and
cracked one of the steps; and, although it did not detract
much from the value of the house, it was an eye-sore,
and was evidence of poor work somewhere. The mason
happened to pass the house one day, and his eye at once
caught the defect. He stopped, looked at it for a
moment, and then went on; but the thing kept troubling
him, and he finally said to himself, "This is not right; I
got my money for good work, and my work is not good;
the breaking of that step is the fault of the mason who
set the stoop, and I don't want that to remain as my sign-
board, even though I may not be legally bound to replace it."

He applied to the owner for permission to replace the
stone, much to his surprise; and it was done. When the
owner had determined to build this large amount of work
just spoken of, and when the mason's bill alone was estimated at $84,000, there were no questions asked, but
simply the plans were handed to him with directions to
do the work by the day, and purchase the materials as
cheaply as he could, keeping the owner advised of every
large bill. The mason was much surprised to hear that

his old friends, the carpenter and plumber, were not to be employed, which led to various inquiries what could be the matter. "Were they insolvent?" said one. Or, "Are they wrong in some way?" No one could find out why they were not employed, as they had been, by this large owner of property, and who was known to be, by every one, a very upright, honest, fair man, and one who was noted for employing one set of mechanics.

These buildings were finally completed, the amounts of the various bills exceeding the first calculation, mainly because more work became necessary. The plumbing bill amounted to $12,722; the carpenter's bill was $59,432; the mason's bill was $91,200. On inquiry, the plumber made $1,300, a little over ten per cent.; the carpenter made $4,350, and the mason made $8,120. Five years afterwards, the same owner built a new lot of houses and stores, the entire cost of which was: for plumbing bill done by the same plumber, $13,100, the carpenter's work $75,000, and the mason's work $104,210.

Now, let us see for an instant what the plumber lost by the careless hand, and his failure to make good defective work without being driven to it; what the carpenter lost in like manner, and what the other plumber and carpenter gained by their loss. The first great loss to the plumber was $1,300, and the jobbing work of this owner, which was worth in profit $100 per year for the five years to the second large job. $1,300 will amount at interest in five years to $1,820, and $100 for five years added and improved would amount to $588; add profits on the plumbing job, $13,100—$1,400, making the sum lost to first plumber and gained by second, $3,808.

If, then, the plumber had been thirty at the date of the making the imperfect joint, or of the first large amount of work done, he would have had when he was 60, $20,677. He lost, then, at the age of 60, $20,677, as the result of his journeyman having made a bad joint at 30. The carpenter, in like manner, lost the amount of the full bill of profit, $4,350, and the owner's jobbing for five years, equal to $350 per year, and the profit on the second large job, amounting to $7,422, which being computed as in the case of the plumber, amounts in the five years to $15,550, to say nothing of any other business transactions or profits after the expiration of five years. Now if the carpenter was 30 years of age when the first large job was lost, he would have lost, at the age of 45, $31,100; at the age of 55, $62,200; and at the age of 65, $124,400, for the want of 6 cents' worth of screws, or a failure to make good without charge the damage which the want of such screws occasioned.

These are the incidents growing out of the business of mechanical life. The trades here selected are samples of all others, and the losses occasioned in them can be traced to similar sources. Nor are mechanical trades alone affected by such little things. A man may fail to be elected President by one vote, and that vote lost by a neglect to speak pleasantly to an acquaintance in the street. Small matters sometimes guide great events; nor can the wisest tell what may result from a mere trifle. A nut carelessly or imperfectly finished in the boiler of a magnificent steamship may be the penny value that will send hurling into fragments her proud form, and hurry into eternity her human freight. Upon the hammer of the mechanic may hang the life or death of many human beings. There can be no end to the vast list of things that could and do occur by the wrongs of the journeymen. As has been seen, they can wrench from the pockets of their employers money at their will But, is it less than robbery, or are they not likewise robbers ? Is there any real difference between the man who does it slyly one way and the man who does it slyly under cover of darkness ? Is there any difference in principle whether a man is robbed by collusion of mechanics, by overcharges, or by bad work—or by robbers, or by passing any false token or counterfeit money ?

The fraud is the same in both instances, and the only reason why they are not so regarded generally in the community is that the one is quite common, the other comparatively rare. The mechanic whose bill or demand is a wrong, may wrench from the customer the money which he demands, and the payer may "stand and deliver," because it is the cheapest mode to get off. But, in all such cases, there are two who lose ; the one, however, much more than the other. In the case of the man victimized by the tailor, who lost the most then ? The losses could scarce be compared, and they fell, too, upon the one who could afford it least. In the case of the journeyman plumber who caused the loss of a small bill to the rich man, who lost the most, the plumber himself or the rich man ? and who was the best able to afford it ; he who paid for the half-day's work and materials, or the one who received the money ? In the case, too, of the journeyman carpenter, who lost the most ; he who failed to put in the screws where he should, or the rich man who had to pay for the blunder, or the carpenter himself, who received pay for repairing his own wrong, or the man who paid the money ?

Let us examine. The journeyman plumber had been out of employment just three months, when he fell from the tree and broke his wrist, which would not in all probability have happened if he had remained at work. He was receiving $2 per day, for this was some time ago. Up to the time of the accident, he had lost $164. Add to this his doctor's bill, $26; and two months' time in which he could do nothing, at 75 cents per day, after his wrist was broken, $42; and his board in the meantime, $12, and his account stands thus:

Three months' lost time, 84 days, at $2....	$168 00
Twelve weeks' board, $2.50 per week....	30 00
Doctor's bill.........................	26 00
Three months' lost time, 56 days, at 75 cts.	42 00
Four weeks' board, $2.50 per week......	10 00
	$276 00

He was just twenty years of age when he received employment at 75 cents per day. He lost, then, $1,25 a day on his former wages; and no matter what wages generally might be at any time, he would lose this much a day as the difference. Now let us look at all the losses in this transaction, with reference to the future, at 50 years of age. The journeyman plumber's loss may be set down at $1.25 per day till he was 50, or for 30 years; and also $276 compounded at 7 per cent., as we do the whole: Journeyman's absolute loss, at 50 years of age, $2,104.36.

If it would be just to estimate his loss of $1,25 per day on account of hurting his wrist, he would lose altogether, in that time, $40,548.78. The boss plumber lost $1,300 in the first job of the rich man, and $100 a year on his repairs for 5 years, making for the 5 years a loss of $2,408. He then lost $1,400 on the second job, by not getting it, which, added to $2,408, makes $3,808; improved for 25 years at 7 per cent., gives his relative loss with the journeyman, $20,677. The boss carpenter lost by profits on first job, by not getting it, and on repairs for 5 years, alike computed, $8,128; and adding the profits on second job, not got, of $7,422, makes $15,550, which, improved at 7 per cent. for 25 years, relatively with journeyman plumber and boss, gives $84,436.

Now, what did the rich man lose by the same operation, presuming he got his work done just as well, and no better, by those whom he employed? He paid the plumber $4.50 for what he did, and that, improved to the same date of all three, at 7 per cent., gives $32.24. He paid the boss carpenter $30 for what he did, which, in like manner, makes $228.30.

It is seen by this that the journeyman lost, by making the bad joint, absolutely $64 to the owner's $1; and if the accident was taken into account, he lost $1,229 to the owner's $1. The boss plumber lost $646 to the owner's $1; and the boss carpenter lost $370 to the owner's $1, on the works respectively. Who, then, loses the most money by bad work, the employed or the employer? But it must be remembered that these are not all the jobs which the boss carpenter and plumber lost from this one customer, for he still continued to build; and if the whole profit which these two men could have made was estimated, it would reach a large fortune if it had been saved and improved at interest.

As a consequence, the following may be assumed as a sure guarantee of success:

First.—Know well your trade, and do it well.
Second.—Be civil, polite, and obliging to all.
Third.—Be just, honest, and trustworthy.
Fourth.—Never buy till you know the value.
Fifth.—Stick close to your trade, and improve.

Sixth.—Get the money for what you do, and pay prompt.

If these are lived up to, success in money-making is guaranteed.

There is no mechanical trade that is not injured by just such cases as have been cited. It would be useless to prolong them further. Their effects are very far-reaching, and the reason why they are not more readily felt, is the fact of their distance, and not their uncertainty. Morals, however, being entirely set aside, the interest of the mechanic, in dollars and cents, is directly at stake. Then, too, when a boss mechanic discharges his journeyman it is a public stigma upon him, as a general thing; and a shrewd one, who hears of the fact, concludes there is something wrong somewhere. For a man's discredit spreads like falling quicksilver on a marble slab.

To the journeymen who performs the labor, a word may not prove unprofitable. Your neglect may cause great pecuniary loss to yourself and to your employers, as you have seen. No better evidence of ignorance of your own interest can be found than a boast, often indulged in, of independence of your employer. He is the journeyman's best friend, because through him he gets his money, and upon the same principle that the land is the farmer's best friend. To slight work is to lose money, because you may lose your employment. Look at the business as your own, only managed by the employer as a means of bringing you money. You, then, become interested in its good credit, thereby insuring your share in its results. You are in fact a partner in it, drawing profits, but paying no losses, expenses, or running any risks. Your pay comes whether the business in general is successful or not. In one sense you are the principal, the business your subordinate. If the business is not worth nursing, saving, or caring for on account of the principal, it is worth it as your bank which pays you a daily dividend. Why abuse it? Why go out and do that which will waste its credit and squander its money? Why by your carelessness drive custom from its doors, when your bread, your meat, and your money, depend upon its support?

In this business, as in most others, there is no trouble in making money; the trouble lies in keeping what is made. It differs in some respects, however, for work is sometimes done for those who do not pay, and hence money may not be made. At this point of the business a new principle enters, and that is the judging of credits as a means of making money. If the mechanic has read the article on Banking and Insurance, he must have perceived that the judging of credits is strictly speaking a banking business, whether it be done by one or by another, and requires skill and experience, as in any other trade. How many mechanics, however, do this thing, and risk their all upon the accomplishment of that on which they have never spent a moment of time, and possibly never turned a thought before, the very point that may lose them the money value of their long worked-for trade. *To judge of the value of credit is the most intricate and difficult branch* of business, requiring *practice, experience, and knowledge.* A mechanic who gives credit, goes into a banking business; and he knows himself, probably by sad experience, whether he is a banker or not. Let him ask himself whether he is competent to take charge of a bank, and he will appreciate his own position in doing the same thing for himself.

Suppose the mechanic wanted a journeyman, would he

hire the president of a bank, who had never raised a hammer? If you wanted to know the value of leather, would you go to the ironmonger to inquire? Or if you wanted to know the value of iron, would you inquire of the leather-dresser or shoemaker? If, then, your customer wants credit, go to his bank and find out if they will take his note, and whether they consider it good or valuable, or whether you could sell it anywhere without your own name. If you can get enough for the note, in this way, to pay you, go on and do the work; and if not, you had better let it alone, and make a sure dollar somewhere else in the meantime. Whenever you trust, take as much time to consider the value of the security as it would take you to earn that much money, and you will be pretty safe. A note may be good that would be rejected by a bank, because they might not know all about it; but the principle nevertheless holds, that a mechanic would do better not to touch credits that would be rejected by a bank, unless he can convert it into cash, or value, in some other way. All these various propositions are of but little consequence in gaining an independence, or a fortune; there is still something more to do, which will be explained under another head.

An inordinate desire to make is the cause of loss, because people take risks of values of credits, in the hope that they will get their pay; and a paradox results, that will be useful to the money-maker:

>He who makes money the slowest, makes it the fastest;
>He who makes it the fastest, makes it the slowest.

And another, quite as certain:

>He who walks early, will ride late;
>He who rides early, will walk late.

CHAPTER XII.

RETAIL MERCHANDIZING.

Moral certainty.—No credit.—Small losses.—Purchase well.—Sentinels.—One price.—Catalogue of qualities.—General behavior.—Pleasant manners.—Repulsive manners.—Example in Boston.—Influence of acts.—Two cheated.—Advertisemens.— Expert salesman.—What he wants.—Defects explained.— Trifling attentions.—Draw custom.—No excuse for failure.— Bargains.—Divide.—Small store.—Profits per day.—Results.— Money in business.—Taken out to speculate.—Loss dead certainty.—Causes of failure.—General principles.—Be polite.— Please everybody.—Everybody your friend.—Walking advertisement.—Brings dollars.—At all hazards.—Old adage.—True philosophy.—Failing don't pay.

THERE is no department of trade in which there is a moral certainty of success, except in the retail trade, if properly and judiciously carried on. The wholesaler is more or less compelled to credit, while the retailer can always sell for cash. He may, to be sure, have unsalable and unseasonable goods left over, on which there may be a small percentage of loss; but this amounts to nothing when compared with the loss of a bill or note of hand by the wholesaler. While the wholesaler has to look out as well for purchases as for sales, the retailer has but one great care, and that is to *purchase well*. For it is a quaint saying "that goods well bought are half sold." While the one, to make, has to stand sentinel over his credits, the other has to stand sentinel over his purchases.

The extent to which this is well done in both instances will determine the loss or gain to both parties.

A retailer should have but one price, and if the goods will not sell at that, mark them down till they do. This gives dignity to his establishment and confidence in the buyers, as many are not acquainted with prices, and if they see they are fixed, presume that the marked profit is a fair one. A skilful retailer must possess a catalogue of qualities which are not necessary for the wholesaler. The intercourse with customers is extensive and varied; he has to deal with every grade of intellect, knowledge, fairness and honesty. More generally depends on his behavior and manner than on the quality of his goods. There is no one quality that commands custom and brings profit so quick to a retail store, and so certainly, as *pleasant manners*. It is the magnet which points to fortune. It is more valuable than paid-for advertisements, and quite as attractive as low-priced or cheap goods.

There is a mannerism assumed by some, of repulsiveness and indifference, by which they fancy the customer will be made to take hold more sharply. It may prove successful at times; but such rash experiments will not bring back the customer who finds afterwards that somehow he was impelled, if not forced, into buying. The bargain may have been saved, but the customer is lost. Nothing can be more destructive to the interests of an establishment than such time-serving operations. A lady in Boston gave the following account of the bad manners of some retailers in that city:

"Some stores in —— street are noted and avoided, for the impertinently familiar manner which the **clerks** think proper to adopt towards their lady customers. When a lady goes into the store in search of some article that she is in want of, as soon as the gentleman sees her, he comes forward, makes a grimace, pulls up his shirt collar, runs his fingers through his hair, and assumes an air of easy familiarity that is quite refreshing to look upon. It is true he may not have much sense, but then he has a wealth of smiles; indeed, to listen to his conversation with his victimized customer, a bystander might come to the conclusion that he was proprietor of the establishment, and the lady had made the article in question a mere excuse for a morning call; this is annoying, but in this case one can leave the article, and walk out. But there is one retail store in this city that is a perfect trap—once in, it is impossible to get out; if the article does not suit you, you are worried and talked at; if you attempt to move towards the door, you are run after and brought back; if you tax your genius to give a most unmistakably minute description of what you *do* want, the reply is, 'Oh, yes, madam, in the back store; if you will walk back, we have exactly the article you describe.' And so they get you further in; after looking about on the shelves, they profess to have found the object of their search, and down comes the very opposite of anything you ever wished to possess. After making half-a-dozen fruitless attempts to reach the street door, and being each time perseveringly caught and brought back, you give it up, and become submissive and willing to buy anything they wish you to, making at the same time a firm resolve—as you see your money going for things you don't know what to do with—that if you live to be as old as Methuselah, you will never enter that store again."

It is quite too common among this class of traders to act as though the sale or operation in hand was to have no influence beyond the moment. This is a fatal error. It is not uncommon in other walks of life, but is more common in the interchange of articles. Such, laugh and chuckle at the ignorance of the purchaser, and commend themselves for having sold a poor article at the price of a good one. There are two cheated in every such operation— the purchaser and the seller; the one of his money and the other of a portion of his trade. Nor does the cheat stop with the simple loss of the trade of the individual, but he becomes a walking and talking advertisement of the trader's bad character, and deters others from hazarding what he has lost.

To be an expert and popular salesman requires study and careful drilling both in language and in manners. To be too verbose or persuasive beyond bounds will disgust. The main point is to impress the customer that you are endeavoring to sell him what it is his interest to buy, for that is the interest of the seller. By this means you can approach his feelings more nearly, and he will have confidence in your recommendation and in your opinion, for he well understands the seller knows more about the value of goods than he does, or possibly can know. If there are defects or imperfections in them, tell him frankly of them, for if he finds them out afterwards, you are sure to lose more than you may have gained in the particular operation. Trifling attentions, which might seem of no importance in themselves, please the customer, and though it may not bring the dollar then, it is sure to do so sooner or later. Money is made in this way by every action and word that interests the customer in you and your establishment.

With these general suggestions carefully alluded to, there is *no excuse* for failure in the retail trade, supposing always that the buyer for the establishment fully understands the business and does not buy more stock than his capital warrants. Rapid sales with small profits will soon tell. If you are lucky, and by chance get bargains in purchasing, divide with your customers, for you must always bear in mind that their interests are your interests; and if your business is known to be conducted on this plan, they will be constantly flocking to your store to see if you have had good luck in this way, for they are as anxious to pick up bargains as you possibly can be. By this means you will sell other goods.

It could be shown by facts, that the *kind* of business is of very little importance; one is about as good as another, though some can be more extended than others. A small beginning is better than a large one, on the same principle that it is always better to have too small a store to do your business in than too large a one. Let us look a little at the profits and the results, so that you can know when you are doing well. If you make on the start *sure*, every day, *three* dollars, for 313 working days, over and above all losses by depreciations and expenses, you are making more than the average of wholesale merchants; that is, if you make it and keep it. This small sum, if increased to six dollars the second, to nine dollars the third, to twelve dollars the fourth year, and so on, will make in ten years, if improved in your own business at 8 per cent., a large sum of money. If the daily earnings should be three dollars per day, gives $13,980. If six dollars, gives $27,961. If twelve dollars, gives $55,922. If twenty dollars, gives $93,205. If the money was kept in the business, and the business well managed, it would, in all probability, increase faster than 8 per cent. per annum, and in order to secure the earnings and make them work to the best advantage, this course would be the proper one to pursue.

But the same trouble generally attends this as it does other businesses. Tradesmen are apt to take money out of their business and invest it in other modes of money-making. If they do, they encounter the risk of doing that which they do not understand, and loss results, to a dead certainty. Just here is all the trouble. If, however, the retailer has more money in his business than he wants, if he can buy all the stock he wants for cash and still have cash over, it must be set at work to earn. The mode of doing this will be explained hereafter.

Causes of failure may be stated to be generally:

First.—Want of knowledge of the suitableness and value of the goods purchased.

Second.—Too much expense for the amount of business done.

Third.—Want of care; to know how everything stands.

The general principles which insure success are:

Be polite.—Work at clerking till you save enough to start on.

Be polite.—Owe no man a dollar.

Be polite.—Trust nothing, because you can sell without.

Be polite.—Rise early and work late.

Be polite.—Know the market value of what you buy and its demand.

Be polite.—Keep slow goods moving.

Be polite.—Be honest, economical, and industrious.

Be polite.—Take care of that which needs care.

Be polite.—Cheap bought, easy sold.

Be polite.—Keep insured.

Be polite.—Turn all your keys yourself, if possible.

Be polite.—Make your customers' interest your own.

Be polite.—Keep expenses down; make your profits rise.

Be polite.—Catch the passing penny, then hold it.

Be polite.—Keep your glass, your stock, and your conscience clean.

Be polite.—Buy slow; sell quick.

Be polite.—Beware of your friends, but not your customers.

Be polite.—Mind your own business; you cannot afford to attend to another's without pay.

Be polite.—When you buy, keep one eye on the goods, the other on the seller.

Be polite.—When you sell, keep both eyes on the buyer.

Be polite.—Few words and many pennies; time is money.

Be polite.—A failure, if honest, is capital by experience; start anew, don't lose it.

By the use of these general principles, it is very easy to get business; and this is all that is necessary to make money. Remember, that to make every one who enters your place of business friendly to you, and interested in you, is to have a walking-advertisement that will bring you untold dollars. The sum you make on a sale is of not the slightest consequence in proportion to this. Save your customer, and his interest, *at all hazards*, and never let him go away dissatisfied, no matter what it costs; you will make money by the operation. The old adage of "Throw a sprat to catch a mackerel," should be studied in its true philosophy; and no matter what the business may be, as in fishing, the principle pays well in money. If you are after that, your feelings should never be allowed to stand between you and your object.

There are many principles found in the other parts of this book, that apply equally to this trade as they do to others; and although what has been said under this head may be of advantage, there are many others that could be said equally so.

CHAPTER XIII.

MANUFACTURING BUSINESS.

Important stand.—Phases of labor.—Imperfect arrangements.—Sinks capital.—As a rule successful.—Two name credits.—Guarantee.—Himself judging credits.—Not so much made.—Combination of qualities.—A maximum outlay.—Fortunes expended.—All things to correspond.—Comfort and ease.—Slave to business.—Manufacturers and merchants laugh.—Large results.—What becomes of it.—Profit and loss account.—Might be avoided.—Such financiering. — Robin is alive.—Power of individual judgment.—Pile of gold or bank bills.—Reputed credit is taken.—Snug business.—Under control.—Happiness and most money.—Calculations of expenditures.—Talent and judgment ahead.—Back-door leak.—Wrong end first.—Cause of failure.—Grand pitfall.—All general principles applicable.—What paper to take.—Wonder why they do not thrive.—Leak in the bottom.—Male and female operatives.—Principals and operatives compared.—One as much chance as the other.—Operative best chance for independence.

By the course of events, this branch has assumed a very important stand among other businesses, and large amounts of money are made by it, both by the employer and the employed. It gives great scope for genius in labor-saving machinery, and to the skilful mechanic in their construction. It is, also, one of the means of making money work to advantage, by its use as capital, and generally may be regarded, in all its phases of labor or its products, as a money-maker. The causes of failure in this business are the same, generally, as the causes of failure in other departments of credit, or interchanging of products. The trouble does not lie in the ability to produce or obtain a market for the products. Failures, or losses from such causes, are rare. The manufacturer frequently sinks capital, in the first outlay in buildings and machinery, from the want of knowledge of what he does require for his purposes. But if he understands just what he requires to accomplish his ends, the business, as a general rule, is successful, and the results in money gained are generally successful also.

The general results to the owner are more complete than in most other business; more successful, as a rule, than wholesale merchandizing, or the mechanical trader, where these two latter depend upon their own judgment of credits for their sales. The reason of this is apparent. Manufacturing is generally carried on at a remote or inconvenient place for sale, and the manufacturer is compelled to employ a commission-house to accomplish this. The commission-house charges a commission on sales, and guarantee for credits given. In this way the manufacturer has *two* names, instead of one, as is the general case with the wholesale merchant and mechanic. Fewer losses result to him, as the commission-merchant, who generally charges $2\frac{1}{2}$ per cent. for guarantee, is more cautious in his credits, for so small a profit, than the wholesale merchant or mechanic, who makes his fifteen or twenty per cent.

When the manufacturer, however, undertakes to make his own sales, and assumes to judge of the value of his credits, he stands about the same chances of success that others do who pursue the same course; without he is in the market constantly, himself, and sees to the standing of his customers, and is, in every sense, a stirring business man, he has but little opportunity of gaining, and an almost certain chance of loss. But it not unfrequently occurs that the business is of such a nature that it requires the establishment of an exclusive house for the sale of the commodities manufactured. In such a case, it becomes a combined manufactory and mercantile business, and if conducted with skill, is almost uniformly successful.

To make the most money out of it, requires a peculiar combination of qualities in the management, and the widest range of special requirements, namely : The highest grade of mechanical skill, to adapt proper machinery ; a superior knowledge of the wants to be supplied ; a concentrated and vigorous action throughout the manufacturing department, and in the selling department ; mercantile skill as a wholesale or retail dealer, as the nature of the business may require. It would, therefore, seem to combine almost all other trades and businesses within itself; demanding, also, that they should work harmoniously and perfectly together.

It is apparent, then, that it is a business requiring the utmost care to be successful ; that is, to make the largest success possible. Nor are there many men who take the trouble, when they are about entering into or establishing a manufactory, to investigate the matter, and know just what they may be able to do as their maximum, and make their machinery accordingly; but they start by degrees, putting up one thing one year, and pulling it down the next, because not large enough ; and again pull it down the next, and put up something still larger ; and so go on, from year to year, till at length they get a maximum machine that will do the maximum work.

How many instances can every reader call to his

mind of this kind, where even the buildings themselves are abandoned and new ones built, because a proper foundation was not laid for increasing wants at the beginning. It may be safely stated that fortunes are thus expended in the course of a few years by just such want of forecast. Few men, if any, strike high enough; and in knowing just where to strike the most money is made.

As a general rule, they commence moderate, and as the business increases they tear down and build over, and thus go on increasing and increasing till it becomes too large for profit or too unwieldy for success, and some unforeseen event leads to embarrassment or failure. Commence with a view to a fair business as a maximum, make all things to correspond to it, and when it is attained be satisfied and reap the benefits in a thrifty and steady business always under control. When you get money enough pay all your bills in cash, and if there is a surplus, invest. Comfort and ease will attend you, and prosperity and an early fortune will be the reward.

Business should be looked at as an occupation and a means of support first, and an independence or a fortune afterwards. You may as well be a slave in another way as be one to your business. Nor is the large business the sure road to fortune; it is the most insecure route. The sure road, with comfort, is to make slow and sure, and always be your own master; and you have but to look at the tables of earnings to see how moderate the income requires to be to accomplish with ease what you desire. A large manufacturer would probably laugh, as the wholesale merchant would, that fifty dollars a day saved and improved is a very heavy amount, and more than one in ten makes in the long run. Even this small amount in twenty years of business, improved at 6 per cent., would be $590,015; if at 7 per cent., $661,606. How many large manufacturers do this? In truth, how few make their $5,000 per annum? For this income yearly improved in like manner reaches respectively $188,450—$211,318—only $15.97 per day. What manufacturer of any note could not make this, and have it clear at the end of twenty years?

These are large figures for the ordinary run of manufacturers, who suppose themselves worth that, or even more any day in the year, but how many come out after twenty years of business with this amount of clear cash, besides their operating gear and traps? Very few; and why not more? Any manufacturer pretending to do business would sneer at the idea of making but $16 per day, with a manufactory, tools, and men. So they might, and they do make more; but what becomes of it—that is the question? Lost in bad debts; spent in extensions; lost in side operations; lost by indorsing; lost by lending; and lost or spent in a hundred-and-one ways.

Let any manufacturing concern in the country that has run 10 or 20 years but look back upon its books and examine the profit and loss account, and the owner will be satisfied. Then let him examine closely, and see if all these losses and expenditures *might not* have been avoided; if not all, at least most of them. He would be taught a lesson which, if he improved, would make him a rich man, if he was not, in ten, rather than twenty years. Without he was a prodigy in his business, he would find that his judgment upon credits alone had cost him a fortune. That on this one item, instead of selling for short paper and a good indorser at a less profit, he had been unwise in parting with his substance for single name paper, which every one in trade knows the value of sooner or later. Such financiering to make money is like the child's game of lighting a splinter of wood and passing it from hand to hand, saying:

> "Robin is alive, and live like to be,
> If he dies in my hand you may saddle-bag me."

In other words, most business men take risks of credit because others do the same, and it requires a well trained determination not to be influenced by such action. More money has been lost, or not made, by assuming credits than from any other cause. In fact, a business man may be sure he is liable to error in this respect when he does not *lay out all the power of his own individual judgment*. As has been remarked before, he is never safe in making a credit until he has considered how much labor has been spent to obtain the amount he proposes to risk, and if the profit be the temptation, he may be morally sure he is going to make a mistake. It is a good rule to pile up the amount in gold, or in bank bills, upon a table, having first obtained all the information upon the value of the credit that can be obtained by any possible means, and then make a decision. In about seven or eight cases in ten, he will conclude to take the risk, otherwise he will probably take twelve out of every fifteen, and probably more.

Nothing is so profitable in the long run as a snug, well managed cash, or close credit business. If the goods made are always good, they will be always salable, either for cash or good indorsed paper, or paper about which there is little or no risk. The manufacturer has less labor to perform to make the same amount of money. He is happy and comfortable in his business and in his home; buys to better advantage and sells to better advantage; is strong wherever he is felt, and when sales are dull in the market he can accumulate stock without weakening or cramping himself. It is always better to have your goods inquired for, and sometimes not be found, than to have them always found when inquired for You will make more money.

There is, too, money made by considering every expenditure, and seeing whether it can be lessened or avoided. Things are often replaced by new ones when the old ones will do, though possibly not quite so well; and it must be the subject of close calculation to see when that moment arrives. Where the new are necessary for profit, what is done for show or display is generally a dead loss; the same amount taken off the profit on your goods will insure sales for cash or first rate values on credit.

In truth, it may be said that vigorous action and close attention will make money in this department of business *fast*. There is no difficulty in managing this part of the business, and *all the talent and judgment in the concern will do best and make the most money for it, not here, but in close attention as to what is got for the goods when made and sold.*

As most trading is now or has been carried on, the talent manages to get, and pay, while the goods slip out the back-door in charge of subordinates. If the matter be just *reversed*, success will follow. For if there is any one principle well established in trading it is this, that almost all failures are attributable to losses by those to whom valuables or goods are sold; not by store expenses, not by depreciation of goods, not by buying goods, not by having too much on hand. Isolated cases there may be, where failures result from some one or other of these causes, but they are so rare that they are not worth noticing, whereas the other is the grand pitfall into which traders plunge themselves.

All the general principles of banking, wholesale merchandizing, retail merchandizing, and of mechanical business, in the previous chapters, are more or less applicable to this business. In that of banking may be found a valuable lesson for any manufacturer to follow. If he goes to a bank to get money on his note he can answer whether he can get it without an indorser. If he can he is lucky, and is in good credit. Are the goods you sell less valuable than their money? If they are as valuable then sell them for as good paper as your own, if the bank will take it without indorsement; but if they will not, then sell them for as good paper as you give the bank, and, rely upon it, you are nearer being rich suddenly than you ever were before.

Of course there are a few in every department of trade who do conduct their business upon such principles, and who are successful; but those that do not, wonder why they are not equally thrifty. They work hard, think they are industrious and enterprising, and they are so in reality; but while they pour the dollars into their coffers rapidly, they about as rapidly disappear. They keep watch of the top, but pay little attention to the bottom, where the real leak occurs.

This business affords employment to a large portion of our population, male and female, giving them an opportunity to gain an early independence, or if their industry and savings are continued, a fortune. If they procure constant employment and good wages, small savings well improved, will soon give a large amount. All the principles laid down as the best means of increasing the value of their labor given heretofore, should be carefully attended to, if they would accomplish the end they desire. And if general results are looked at, the principals have no greater opportunity of making money than the operatives, for we will show an example by which this can be judged of.

A manufacturer goes into business with a cash capital of $25,000; the operative with none. The principal has to make, before he realizes any profit, his entire expenses and the interest on his capital, before he is on an equal footing with the operative. All this, of course, requires many expenditures, and he probably has much more interest to pay, over and above his capital. But all such matters must come out of the profits; the interest on the capital, and the capital itself, must only be taken as a comparison. The interest on $25,000 is $1,750, yearly. Then the manufacturer has to make, in 20 years, $73,968, simply to get 7 per cent. on his capital. Suppose the operative laid by $2 per day for the same time, he would have, by tables of earnings, $26,464. The manufacturer would have to make, in the same time, $100,432, to have made, over and above his interest on capital, the *same amount as the operative.*

When it is considered that the manufacturer may lose his whole capital, and make nothing into the bargain; and if he does, his money is in property, generally, and not in cash, as it is in the case of the operative, there would seem to be a large balance in favor of the operative, over principals with small manufacturing capitals. The operative gains steadily and securely, with no risks except that of getting employment, and that depends upon himself, while the principal may lose all.

CHAPTER XIV.

WHOLESALE MERCHANDIZING.

Nothing saved.—Startling proposition.—Millions made.—Capital lost on average.—Elements of calculation.—Banking and merchandizing compared.—Merchants don't make 7 per cent.—Banks succeed, merchants fail.—Capitals compared.—Results.—More profit more loss.—Secret of failures.—Profits over 7 per cent.—Manner of doing it.—Auctioneers most successful.—Reason.—Double name paper or cash.—Since 1860 great earnings.—Cause.—Change, probably.—Old story.—Examination of credits.—Made able to pay.—Shave customer, shave yourself.—Short indorsed paper.—Mode of crediting.—References.—Mercantile agencies.—Called reliable.—Good as an auxiliary.—Not relied on alone.—Every item.—Mercantile clerks.—Jobbing merchants.—Where the trouble lies.—Ability in the wrong place.—Without recourse.—Make money fast.—Make one thousand dollars.—Rich in ten years.—Example.—Small per diem earnings.—Suggestions.—Failure paid for.—Give all to creditors.—Pay for blunder commendable.—Good treatment.—Makes money.

It is asserted here that up to the year 1862 nothing, comparatively, has been made in this branch of trade in the three large cities, New York, Philadelphia, and Boston. Rather a startling proposition, but nevertheless true, as to realized profits. That is, the amount of capital invested has no more than been withdrawn as a total result, if it has that. While millions upon millions have been made, nothing has been saved in the aggregate. Few have been fortunate enough to retire at high tide and take with them round little fortunes. Now, suppose we take the average capital of wholesale houses during that time to be $50,000, and see what that would amount to improved at compound interest at 7 per cent. for an average term of 25 years in business. By the table, we find it to be $271,500. So that in order to make anything, they must come out with more money than this sum being their capital improved for twenty-five years, if they continue in business so long. If the whole or the average do this, with this sum, they have simply made expenses. This, however, is *far above* the average. For, as has been seen by the statistics, not 5 per cent. but what fail entirely.

The cause of such failure becomes a matter of consideration in the calculation for success. What are the elements of this calculation, and where are we to look for the remedy? This is the grand point. Now, why do these merchants fail? Is it owing to want of capital? Not at all; for those who have large capitals, even as much or more than successful banks, generally fail. Now, let us look what a bank makes, and compare it with what a mercantile house makes on the same capital. A bank stands in good credit, is considered safe, and its stock sought after, which year after year pays 7 per cent. A mercantile house, with the same capital, would be considered as doing business to no advantage if they did no more than divide the interest on their capital at the end of the year. Here, then, is a paradox. Why is the mercantile house, which deals in the same thing as the bank, expected to make more? The bank has 12 to 14 experienced business men, selected on account of their success, to do their business, while the mercantile firm has one, two, or three. The odds on making even 7 per cent. seem to be against the mercantile house.

The banks, too, generally succeed, while the mercantile houses generally fail, which shows that they do not make as much as banks. This is true. Now, let us suppose a bank with $200,000 capital, and that they divide $14,000 to the stockholders, after paying all expenses. Suppose, also, we have a mercantile firm with the same capital, and that it should turn its capital over three times a year; that is, should sell $600,000. To do as well as the bank, they would have to divide $14,000, the balance to go for expenses, or about 2¼ per cent. on sales. If there were three partners doing the business, each with families, as a safe rule, their united expenses would be $15,000, and store expenses, at least $10,000, making the grand total to be made on sale of $600,000—$39,000, or 6½ per cent. Now, if the firm lost nothing, they would, on this statement, just clear the interest on their capital, and if they did lose, so much would have to be deducted.

But such an amount of sales, without loss, on the present system of doing business, is impossible; so that one of two things must take place—either they would not make the interest on their capital, or they would have to make more profit in order to do it, to cover losses. Now the settled principle in business is, *the more profit the more loss;* and as a general rule, the profit over the settled rate of interest will be absorbed by loss. Close around this principle, then, lies the great secret of mercantile failures. To ascertain just where it is, and what it is, is the great desideratum.

As goods are sold, every one acquainted with business of this kind knows, that the average profit on sales amounting to $600,000 is more than $39,000, and that at a low calculation it reaches from $60,000 to $90,000. This result would be eminently satisfactory if there were no losses; for the net profit after paying expenses and interest on money, on the supposition we have made, would amount to from $21,000 to $51,000, say take the average $36,000 If the firm did this business for 20 years, we should have by the table of earnings the sum of $1,521,826; if the earnings were improved at 7 per cent., or if continued for 25 years, the sum of $2,357,838; in like manner, if for 30 years, the sum of $3,417,993; if for 40 years, $7,547,062; or, if for 50 years, $15,526,069. It must be remembered that this is over and above the interest on the capital, $200,000, and over and above what a bank would make in the same time, profits improved at 7 per cent. on the same capital, if it divided 7 per cent. as its profits.

Now, is there no way that the merchant can secure a part, if not the whole of this difference? It is believed that there is, and that will entirely depend upon the *manner* in which the business is done. If he made no losses the thing could be accomplished, for there is no difficulty in making the sum of profits by sales. Then the whole difficulty lies in the *losses incurred*. How can these be prevented? In the answer to this question lies the success or failure.

The most successful merchants, as a class, are the auctioneers. Why? Because they do their business nearer the principles of banking than other merchants. They sell on shorter credits and for indorsed paper, or for cash. Their commissions are small compared with the merchant's profits, and they *demand and get* security accordingly. From these facts, and a general consideration of the subject, cash sales or sales for short and indorsed paper, will give the required results, provided due care is taken in the selection.

Since 1860, mercantile business has been done more for cash and short credit, and the result is apparent to any one. There never has been a time in this country when merchants have been in a more prosperous and healthy condition. This will not in all probability remain so long. The inordinate desires, and the necessity, from expenses, to make more, will induce longer credits, and hence larger profits, thereby giving the buyer a chance to use the proceeds of goods in side operations, or cripple himself by the increased price of goods, till the same old story is re-enacted for the thousandth time —loss all around.

The general impression is among merchants, that if they can secure a customer and sell him at a large profit and get his note, and *it is said* to be good, here the matter ends. As the very foundation of the security of the note, the merchant should see that his customer not only got his goods of him at a price that he could make ready sale of *them*, but that he bought of other good houses doing business upon the same principles—know all that he buys, and of whom, and when due. In other words, see to it that your customer is *made able to pay* by a judicious and careful selection of his *whole* stock. To shave a customer is but to shave yourself. Look at the prospects, the profits of your customer, as though they were your own; for they will turn out so in the end, whether you attend to it or not.

This is one, and the surest way, to make your note good and have it paid; but if the customer feels that this is more than he wishes to communicate, sell him, if you can, for good indorsed paper, on short time, or for cash, by taking off a liberal per cent. You will probably lose by selling him otherwise. These seem to be stringent terms, but it is easy to show from statistics and experience that it will make most in the end.

The usual mode of giving credits by mercantile firms is to drum in any stranger that can be found at any hotel, and sell him a bill of goods, making the most profit that can be stuck on. After this is done he is asked for his references, and the salesman, a clerk, and sometimes the porter, is started off to make the inquiries. Of course they are all, as a general rule, satisfactory; for the buyer would not send you to any one who would not speak well of him. Generally they are merchants, who are selling the same individual, and their interest lies in your selling him, too.

Then resort is had to a mercantile agency—to be sure the best place where you can get what is *called reliable information*, and they are usually valuable on the higher grades of credit. But if you take their recommendations you look to the amount of your own sale as compared with his capital or business ability, *but know nothing* of how much he is buying on his capital, at the time, of others; so that he may be good for a small purchase made of you, but if you knew he was purchasing at the same time $50,000 on a capital of $5,000, you would probably not sell him. So that such information is *not reliable* as a means of giving credits. It may be an auxiliary, *but should never be relied on alone.* No intelligent opinion can be arrived at in giving credits on single-name paper when you are not in possession of *every item* of the individual's business. And to accomplish this end (if it was practicable) houses might club together who sold the various articles on credit to country merchants, whereby they could control the subject on single-name paper.

These remarks are more particularly directed to the interest of the jobbing merchant, but his credit in like manner is dependent upon the same general principles; and the merchant who sells him must, in like manner, scrutinize the elements of his business. For it must be borne in mind that upon dealing for cash or short indorsed paper, or any single-name credit, and upon its careful selection, depends the success of the merchant or his failure. That while toil, anxiety, hard labor, saving and accumulating, are not the act of a day or an hour, how frequently do we see all this hazarded by a credit decided upon in a few moments, and that, too, not by the intelligent action of the owner, but generally by youth, inexperience, and by him who had *no interest* in the result. Is it then a wonder that merchants fail? or if not, lose largely by such inattention at the *very working-point, requiring all the judgment, tact, skill, and knowledge*, that can by any conceivable means be brought to bear.

It is a safe rule in crediting, when you can dispose of the paper without recourse. If this be adopted as a settled rule of a mercantile house, and they pursue it (and it can be done), they *will certainly make money and make it fast*. There is no trouble in doing it in individual cases, but if that should be adopted as a rule generally it would become impracticable. There is no fear, however, that merchants will suddenly become so wise and keen. Any one may undertake it with impunity and be sure to make an early fortune.

The merchant who starts in business with the determination to make *one thousand dollars* a year for the first year over and above his expenses, and determines to owe no man a dollar at the end of the year, and to have the money in bank, or in good salable property, will, if that course be pursued, be a rich man at the end of *ten years*. This is more than the average of mercantile houses make, as will be seen by looking at the statistics given in a former chapter. Let us examine this case. The second year he will undoubtedly make this $1,000 $2,000, and in the third year $3,000, and so on—increase $1,000 every year till the end of ten years. He will, then, have made, keeping the money working in his business, say an average of $5,000 per year, and by using it in cash purchases will improve it equal to 8 per cent. per annum. This will be on an average $16 per day. Look at the table of earnings for 10 years, and we find the earnings of $10, $5, and $1, added together, give the neat little sum of $74,564.31. If he only made $1,000 per annum for 25 years, and improved it at 8 per cent. in his business, he would have $74,342, being $3.13 per day improved at 8 per cent.

What merchant, however, with ordinary means, selling for cash or passing paper without recourse, cannot make $25 per day? This in 10 years would, improved at 7 per cent., be $111,144; in 25 years, $512,549; in 30 years, $768,865; in 40 years, $1,640,525; in 50 years, $3,374,939. How many accomplish these sums? and how few who do not make this sum per day, and even more. It is no great sum to make, but a *very large sum to keep*. From this it will be seen how much of the energies and attention of the merchant should be turned in this direction. It is, in fact, the whole matter of money-making. The getting of the small daily sums will comparatively take care of itself.

The following suggestions may not be out of place.

Look to your credits.—Owe no man a dollar if you can avoid it.

Look to your credits.—Credit no more than you can afford to lose, but no credit will make more money.

Look to your credits.—Have a general extended knowledge of all things you deal in.

Look to your credits.—Go into business on your own account late rather than too early in life.

Look to your credits.—Get into an old firm rather than establish a new one.

Look to your credits.—Avoid large sales to individuals.

Look to your credits.—When you buy, take care ; when you sell, take quadruple care.

Look to your credits.—Make no useless expenditures while you owe others.

Look to your credits.—Make a little and make it sure ; then look at it.

Look to your credits.—Keep your property well insured ; you cannot afford to lose while you are trying to make.

Look to your credits.—Be honest, economical, agreeable, and pleasant.

Look to your credits.—Keep your expenses low and your profits high.

Look to your credits.—Look out when your credit is too good.

Look to your credits.—Take little credit and have much money.

Look to your credits.—Have a small house and large capital.

Look to your credits.—Be modest, but feel your strength.

Look to your credits.—Let fashion alone, or it will not let you alone.

Look to your credits.—Marry early a good wife ; a poor one is better than none.

Look to your credits.—Mrs. Grundy will not pay your bills ; therefore don't let your wife spend too much to please her.

Look to your credits.—Have an eye to all that may damage by neglect.

Look to your credits.—If you fail, give up all to your creditors and start anew.

Failure is one of the things paid for by the purchaser in the price of his goods, and, therefore, he has the moral right to fail. But when he does fail, he is morally bound to give up what he has to his creditors, for that is presupposed in the sale. Failure as a rule is disgraceful, because it indicates inability and want of skill and knowledge, and hence affects the individual for life. The seller charges a guarantee on the sale to cover loss by failure, and the individual is bound by no rule of honesty to pay more than what he has on hand at the time of failure. To do so afterwards, and pay in full for his own blunder, is commendable.

No one can properly estimate the money benefit that arises in treating those whom you employ justly and fairly. Kind, gentle, and proper treatment to those who work for you or manage your affairs, will put untold dollars in your pocket. The reverse will lose you as much, if not more.

CHAPTER XV.

BROKERAGE AND COMMISSION.

Kinds of brokerage.—Skill and fidelity.—Knowledge and activity.—Know everything.—Trusted.—Ultimate success.—Broker and owner same time.—Will leak out.—Confidence lost—Little costs much.—Legitimate brokerage.—Solely as agent.—No risks.—Speculators in stocks.—Best way poor enough.—Gambling table.—Reasons why all lose.—Same in stocks.—Buys and sells without rule.—Mathematical chances.—When to sell, when to buy.—Must do as others do.—Then land where others do.—Nothing new.—Stand to principles.—Commission business safe.—Simple commission.—Credit sales.—Your main trouble.—Guarantee and bank notes compared.—Rightly done, profitable.—Five per cent. large results.—Example.—Energy and honesty.—Acceptance without property.—Danger.—Violating business rule.—No risk pays best.—Capital.—Business qualities.—Owners scrutinize every point.—Capable and reliable.—Satisfactory results.

BROKERAGE is a percentage paid for selling or procuring property of various kinds, procuring insurance, or labor, or money. The percentage is sometimes paid by the person receiving, and sometimes by the parties parting with property, labor, or money, or the insured or insurer. There are other kinds of brokerage, but those noted are the most important classes. The first, brokerage for selling or parting with property, is made by the purchase, or sale of stocks, merchandize, vessels, real estate, and the like ; the second, procuring fire, marine, inland, or life insurance ; the third, shipping seamen, hiring servants, or laborers, and the like ; the fourth procuring money on bonds and mortgages, loans on securities, on notes of hand, and the like.

The value of these various services to all parties depends upon the skill and fidelity with which the trust is fulfilled. The ability of the broker to fulfil the trust to advantage to himself and his principal, depends upon his knowledge and activity. Then, to make the most money by his business, he must *act for the interest of his employer and be perfectly reliable and honest, skilful and active.* He must know *everything* about the matters in hand, both in value, supply, and demand. He stands to his employer in the light of a trustee. The manner in which he performs this duty will either make him or lose him money. It may not in a particular instance, for he will get his brokerage whether the work be well or ill done; but how will it be with the next operation, and with his reputation to get more business?

His ultimate success will depend upon the above, mainly, but there is still another, and that is, whether he confines himself *strictly to his legitimate business.* A broker cannot be a broker and at the same time buyer and seller on his own account, without losing money by the combination. He cannot be a buyer and seller extensively, or he will lose the character of a broker altogether. He will have to buy and sell on the sly, if he does it at all, and *be assured it will leak out.* The buyer then will not know whether he is buying of the owner, or of the owner through a broker, or whether he is selling to his broker, or through his broker to another. All confidence is at once lost, and the broker loses the most.

The little money he might make on a side operation, will be largely overbalanced by loss of his regular business. If a broker wants to buy, employ another broker to buy for him, or proclaim the purchase to be for investment. *Never speculate in the articles you buy and sell for others ; you will lose more than you will make.*

The most money, if the business is legitimately carried on, is in brokerage on the sale and purchase of stock, but the temptation to brokers is so great in this business to speculate in them on their own account, that few men have the strength of mind and ability to resist; and hence few start with a fixed determination to act only as agents that do not soon find themselves in the almost universally confused vortex of broker and speculator, and the result of such combination is generally *failure in the end.* Whereas a strict adherence to a simple brokerage, taking no risks, and acting *solely as agent,* will roll up a fortune in a short time. It requires only to be known that by *no peradventure* money in your hands *could be lost,* and dollars will roll in on such a concern from every quarter of the country. To this end never sign your name to a responsibility or assume one. Take the proceeds of each day's business and set it to work at interest, and you have only to look at the tables of earnings and put your finger on the year when you will have a fortune.

You may have customers and probably will, who speculate in stocks, and if you cannot refrain from doing so yourself, it is well enough to know the best way it can be done ; but the *best way is poor enough* in all conscience, as the experience of all will certify. If any one has nothing to lose and everything to gain, this sort of business is as good to him as any other ; but not otherwise. There are certain rules of the gambling table that apply in stock speculation. As a rule, one would naturally suppose that it was an even chance to win or lose ; but there is not one chance in one hundred of winning in the long run, when there are ninety-nine that you will lose. The reason why the gambling table is so fatal is not because there is not as much chance of winning as losing on a single cast, for there is just as much, less the percentage in favor of the table to pay current expenses. But the trouble and fatality lie in this, that the game is usually continued when the *table is the largest loser*, and the game *stops* when the better is the *largest loser*, and has no more money to go on with. These fluctuations being very great, the bank always goes on because of its capital, while the better, not having an equal capital, is bound to stop—he is broke.

It is just so in stock speculations, except that there is a still more fatal element in that than in gambling. A man buys a stock to rise, and he will hardly ever strike the highest point or sell to an advantage. Why? Because he will either be afraid that it will not go higher and sell at a small rise, or wait for it to go still higher and then not sell till it gets lower. If it begins to fall, however, he will not sell at the first fall, for he believes it will recover; and it still goes down and down till he will, usually, like the gambler, stop at the lowest point.

The only hope of making money by speculating in stocks is to determine a rule of chance mathematically, and adhere to it strictly. Then suppose a stock is twenty per cent. below its average value, buy what you can hold and determine that you *will* sell at ten per cent. advance. The chances are in favor of your making the ten per cent. If the stock is above its value *never* sell short, as you may not be able to get the stock by reason of a corner, and hence will lose largely. Notwithstanding this is the true rule to work upon for safety, the experience of speculators is, that the most money has been made in selling "short," as it is called; for generally when stocks begin to tumble, failures occur which bring more of them into the market, and hence prices fall still further, and reach an unnatural depreciation. If the stock is so large as to warrant the belief that a "corner" cannot he had under any combination, it is probably a reasonably safe way to speculate. But to the solid money-maker nothing of the sort should be resorted to, as money *always* is lost in the end by it.

As a general rule, if an eight per cent. paying stock is below par, buy; if a six per cent. paying stock is above par, sell; if a seven per cent. paying stock is par, hold—buy or sell if above or below. Good stocks, if they pay eight per cent., or over, will do to hold to make money; but if they pay no more than seven per cent., bond and mortgage at seven per cent. is better; though the stocks are frequently held in order to have convertible securities; but if they are not so held, bond and mortgage is the safest and the best, because all stocks are liable to accident. Bond and mortgage is not, when proper care is taken.

A great deal more could be said on this branch of business, but the limits of this work will not allow. The general principles laid down are all that are required to *insure positive success.* But one point must not only be remembered but carried to its fullest extent—*take no risk.* If your principal wants you to buy, do it in his name as agent. But, says the broker, "I could do no business—if I do business, I must do it as others do it." All that can be said to such a one is, *then do it,* and land just where the whole of them land in the long run.

But you *can* do otherwise. Though it may go what might be called slow at first, the moment it becomes known that you are *positive*, everybody who wants a legitimate, honest, reliable, and trustworthy broker, will go to you, and will leave the half broker and speculator, for all experience has shown that they are not safe. You will be a rich man, and see them drop down one after another by your side. " There is nothing new under the sun," and "what has been will be again." So that for a time you will probably see prosperity, fortunes, and millions, roll up by the side of your comparatively small earnings; but the result will be the same as the result of the race between the fox and the tortoise. You have but to *stand by your principles and your determination*, and you will equal the most prosperous and far outstrip the crowd. All other principles given under the preceding chapters as applicable to other businesses must be observed also in this.

The commission business is also a safe and money-making business. There are two main points in it, however, in one of which lies all the danger of loss. Goods sold purely on commission is of the character of a brokerage, but the per cent. is higher, and this portion of it is safe, and with energy and care, combined with business tact, can always be made profitable and especially safe, as no risk is run, the principal assuming all. But when sales are made on credit, and the commission merchant guarantees the sales and charges a percentage for it, the danger in this business begins. The commission is very small, and amounts guaranteed very large; and to make the business at all successful, those conducting it must do it on at least as careful judgment in value of credits as banks take their paper, if not better, for the guarantee ordinarily is $2\frac{1}{2}$ per cent. on six months' paper, while the banks get $3\frac{1}{2}$ per cent. for the same length of credit paid once in the mean time, for they do not take as a general rule over ninety-days' commercial paper.

Commission business, when it guarantees credit sales, is a very close business; but without, it is one of the safest, and sometimes the most profitable business, that is done, especially when a house gets 5 per cent. on sales and makes no guarantee. It is not a difficult task for a good house to sell $500,000, and some go as high as $1,000,000, and higher. Examine the case of one making this amount of sales, $50,000, less expenses of $20,000, leaving a clear profit of $30,000 per annum. Let this be done for twenty years, and we have, if improved at 7 per cent., the amount of $1,267,196. In ten years this would make $425,126.

But upon any basis where there are no losses, a commission business put to work on these principles will soon realize a splendid amount to the merchant. If business can be procured, there is none so safe as this, nor so certain of realizing an independence, provided the credit sales are not guaranteed. The success, however, depends entirely upon the amount that can be obtained to be done; but if there *is energy and entire honesty* to back it, the goods and property will come, possibly slowly at first, but success is certain with perseverance. The great feature on such small profits is to run no risk, and the danger lies in accepting while the property or goods are in transitu, or on the promise of their coming to hand. Better not do the business than break over a rule; if you do, you will lose money by it, if not in the transaction itself, by the loss of your credit as a man of business having a rule of business action, and violating it yourself.

Nothing pays a merchant so well in this line of business, as the well known fact that he takes no risk, and therefore what property is sent to him is safe. If you guarantee, in order to get property, you must have a large capital to back your credit; if you do not, little or no capital is required, and you can substitute therefor personal qualities; and if they are substituted, a man must know that they are as good as money. This is credit, and without that is founded on capital, the personal qualifications must be of the highest order and more dependable even than money.

And finally, every quality that should belong to every business man, he should possess in an eminent degree, for if he is successful in obtaining property to manage and sell, it will be in large amounts, and from owners who will, if they are business men, scrutinize every point, to be sure that their property is in capable and reliable hands. Once a character is established and your rules of action known, there will be no trouble A good living, an independence, and a fortune, await you in time.

CHAPTER XVI.

INTELLECTUAL LABOR.—LAWYERS.

Large class.—A type.—All profit, no risk.—Minds below mediocrity.—Foist services.—Preliminary education.—Copperless youth.—Business, Independence, fortune, fame, follow success.—Hidden values.—Stir about.—It will come.—Golden opportunity.—Friend, or business enemy.—Plant an anchor.—Supposition of gain or loss.—Office behavior.—Lawyer polite.—Office for business.—Parlor for pleasure.—Made money by impressions.—Reverse.—Cigars, smoke, spittle, and high heels.—Intended client quits.—Another instance.—Too much to do.—Do nothing well.—Clients meet.—A little Lawyer.—Made him rich.—Mammon offended.—Desire to be thought great.—Great man itch.—Lawyer failed to make money.—General reputation injured.—Engagements.—Time lost, no restitution.—Trespass and money.—Reason.—So common.—High charges.—Effect.—Just charge.—Ideas of clients.—Important suggestions.—Mind that regulates, assumes.—Human nature displayed.—Money lost.—Clouds of sunshine.—Everybody obliges.—When arguments fail.—Haggard countenance.—Iron look.—Gimlet eyes.—Disprove existence.—Compared.—Elements of success.

This division of labor comprehends a large class of the money-making community, and like all other labor has its value, which is greater or less just in proportion to the knowledge and skill displayed in it. It is not intended to speak of all the divisions of this kind of labor, but to give one or two examples which may be taken as types of the whole. Nor is the lawyer cited because of any special individuality, but as a large and important division which will cover as many points as any other. As a general rule intellectual labor presents as many opportunities to the money-maker as any other branch of industry, and probably more than any other to make an independence. For what they gain they have, and cannot lose their capital. They are in the position of getting all the profits, and none of the risks of loss of what they put into their business—referring simply to the intellectual. It cannot from its nature take the wide range of manual labor, because its success requires mental ability, which all do not possess. It frequently happens, however, that minds absolutely below mediocrity succeed in making professions profitable, by possessing personal qualities by which they can foist off their services at some price. This being so, money sometimes flows into them quite as fast as to the abler minds, which trust alone to their value for a market.

The profession of the law may be considered under all circumstances a safe and certain way to make money. It requires generally some capital to pay for the preliminary education, and to live upon while business is being made, though there are many cases of high success which have grown out of the copperless youth, and when they do come up in that way, they come up strong and vigorous. Numberless cases could be named where the raw boy entered the lawyer's office to run errands and sweep out, for just enough to keep soul and body together; and by sleeping where he could, with now and then a nice bit to do away with the monotony of crackers and water, he steadily pushed on, reading when he could, till, finally, a legal education was acquired, and he admitted to practice. Then in came business—an independence—a fortune—fame—and high position.

A wise man will not only argue analogically, but if he sees a fact, and the mode by which it is attained is simple, he will not try another. So it should be with the law apprentice and with the practical lawyer. If he sees one man in his profession making money, watch him and see what he does, if you wish to do what you are not doing. There are, to be sure, various roads leading to the same place, but if you do not know the way yourself, is it not wise to follow the teamster that has driven the way, and who is just in front of you on the road? Then do as the successful man does, and your chances are as good as his, all other things being equal.

If a lawyer had the concentrated ability and knowledge of ten eminent, successful ones, his capital would lie as dormant and worthless as gold and silver in the earth, without use. Till he gets a start, he must stir himself about among men of business, if he has not already done so while a student; become acquainted with people; make personal friends, and personal interest; for although you do not get your dollar every time you do this, and for every hour you spend in profitable and agreeable conversation with a friend, or even a stranger, there is a dollar in it, and if you have done your part and made the favorable impression, you may get it shortly. *It will come.*

As in the case of the mechanic—your first case is *your golden opportunity.* You must look well to what you say, what you do, and what impression you make upon your client, to make the most money by your opportunity; whether you will make him a permanent client, and one who will sing your praises wherever he goes, or become a business enemy. The manner, the interest, the promptness with which you attend to his case, and the interest you manifest in his interest, will decide a great point in the money history of your life. Remember that in every step of your profession, and in every move you make, there lies your dollar if you choose to get it. If you fail to plant an anchor of interest in your first client, you lose largely, for you have to make a new start. The difference in the final result to you is the same difference that there would be to you in dollars, whether you placed the amount you received of him at compound interest, or whether you did the same, adding each year the same amount to it.

Suppose that you received for your first case $200, and you displease the client, this compounded at interest, 7 per cent. for twenty years, would amount to $774. If you pleased him, and added through his business and what he would recommend to you each year, $200, and improved it in like manner, you would have $8,468,—a difference of $7,694 on your scale of fortune, for pleasing or displeasing your first client. This would seem to be worth a little care on your part, and worth working for. Such apparently little and unimportant matters are worth considering by the lawyer who is striving to make the most money by his profession.

Generally, then, if a client or a man on business enters your office, speak *pleasantly* to him. If you are writing, or busy, rest for an instant, till you ascertain whether he has called to ask you a simple question, or wishes to see you on business for a length of time. He will either proceed with his inquiry, or speak of some other disconnected subject, or tell you he wishes to speak to you on matters of business. If he merely asks a question, and his manner indicates haste, answer him at once and let him depart. If he speaks on general matters, and has not called on business, ask him pleasantly to sit down in either case, for you cannot tell what may come out of his call and your politeness.

When the ceremony has been gone through with, if

really engaged, you can say—" My friend, or my dear sir, you must excuse me for a few moments; call at my house at 8 o'clock any evening when I am at home, and we will talk over the little pleasant matter you speak of." Or if he is on business: " Please excuse me just now, as I am very busy; call again at 2 o'clock, I shall be disengaged, and will see you." You have made money in three ways, by these civil and gentlemanly answers.

First.—You have improved your general character in the community—a point essential to your success.

Second.—You have shown to your client that you are a gentleman and systematic in your business, and he will have confidence in you, and will personally respect you; and if nothing happens will give you other business if he has it, or will recommend you.

Third.—You have shown to your friend that business hours and the office are not intended for social intercourse—that your house and your parlor are. He respects you more highly, and will think you a business man, will recommend you as such, and give you his business if he has any.

The reverse, however, of this, is too frequently the case. On entering such an office, you may see a young man with a book in one hand, a cigar in the other, his chair on its two hind legs, his feet on the mantel, about level with his shoulders or above, a pool of tobacco spittle on the floor, the besprinkled evidences of previous hydraulics of like stamp, and an atmosphere of cigar smoke.

The caller was a business man, who had heard through a friend that such a young man highly promising had begun business just where he found this individual. A call was enough; he made some casual inquiry and he regained the street as soon as possible, lest he might meet the very friend who had sent him there. That cigar was the cause of his failing to make the costs in the suit—about two hundred and thirty dollars—and the failure to get a good client.

Another instance of a young lawyer who had a propensity of trying to impress everybody with the idea that he had so much to do he could not find time to do anything. He made a great fuss about business when any one of his clients came to his office, starting the clerks off in every direction at the same moment, and making a great fuss generally. It so happened one day, that one of his clients was on his way to the lawyer's office, where he had already been several times to get a moment's conversation with him on the subject of a case about to be argued. Every time the client went he was compelled to go some four miles, there and back, and each time the lawyer made the excuse that he had not a moment to spare and could not say a word to him on the subject. It also happened, too, that new faces came in during the client's stay, and did talk with the lawyer as long a time as the client wished to talk to him.

But as he was on his way thither as above stated, with great anxiety about a point in the case which he supposed the lawyer might have overlooked, he was joined by a large dry-goods dealer, who commenced relating an incident which had just happened to him. It was evident the man was somewhat excited, and he began thus: "A little puppet of a lawyer," said he, "whom I have made rich by the business I have given him, has worried my life out of me by making me call at his place time and again, about a matter that would not take him two minutes to do. Several times I have called and he has quietly kept his seat, as though I was some errand-boy, and said, 'I will see you about that matter to-morrow, I am engaged just now—won't you call again?' I have just called for the last time, and can you tell me of a good honest gentlemanly man—one who is a gentleman —and knows how to treat people, and especially an old man like myself?"

The man said in reply: "I know of several lawyers who have such a desire to be thought great men, that they assume an immense amount of importance at times, and it is more particularly the case with the young and those who have not in truth much bottom to go upon. My lawyer is a middle-aged man, a good honest fellow, and rather smart; but he has of late caught the great man itch, and he treats me now just about as you complain of being treated, though my time is not as valuable as yours, and I don't mind it as much."

Some other conversation ensued, and the parties separated—one to go where the client had an important case, and, therefore, was compelled to submit in a measure to bad treatment; the other, to procure one to whom he might transfer his business. Both these lawyers failed to make money, not because they were not well read, nor that they were incapable, nor because they had failed to do what they did do well; but they lost money, or failed to make it, because of a little foolish mannerism. Neither meant to be rude or unobliging or disagreeable. They might have each supposed they were too much engaged to attend to their clients, and it was just as easy for them to come again. They both lost time, too, for neither of their clients would have detained them in the aggregate as long as they were talking in excusing themselves.

The lawyer of the dry-goods merchant lost money, or

failed to make more out of his client, amounting at least to seven hundred and fifty dollars. He lost the client of the other lawyer just named by reason of a want of favorable recommendation of the dry-goods merchant, for that individual had determined to leave as soon as his case was through. The business of this last man amounted in ten years to about one thousand dollars.

Both injured their general reputations, and some individuals were deterred from patronizing them as soon as they heard the opinions expressed and their peculiarities commented upon. It would have been quite as cheap and more gentlemanly if they had dispatched the business at once with each of their clients. There are but few instances of such extremes in the legal profession; but few or many, they should be referred to in a work of this nature to indicate whereby money is not made, and also wherein money is lost. There is an equity in all matters of life. If you make an engagement with a person to have a paper drawn up ready at a given time, and the party to whom it has been promised appears and it is not ready—though you, as a lawyer, charge for your time in drawing the paper—you do not feel like paying the man for his loss of time, when he is compelled to come again, and very likely lose double or three times as much time as you have consumed in drawing the document.

This very important principle applies to every department of life, and is a trespass and wrong done to an individual's time, which, in justice, should be discharged by an equivalent. A mechanic, in like manner, agrees to finish an article for you, and compels you to call once or twice for it at the great sacrifice of time and inconvenience; but when you come to pay for the article he would be annoyed that you should charge for your lost time. The reason of this is that custom has allowed these people to commit this wrong so long without holding them responsible that they claim the wrong now as their vested right. They, however, lose money by it, whether they know it or not. But this does not excuse a man of intelligence acting under such universal wrong.

There are other means of attracting business and keeping it peculiar to the legal profession. High charges, although they bring immediate money to the pocket, are not the most profitable in the end. If a client thinks he is overtaxed, he may not, from motives of delicacy, say anything about it; but the thing hangs on his feelings, and if he has occasion for a lawyer a second time he hesitates, looks about, and is in many instances guided by his feelings, and not by his judgment. A just charge is the best, for it makes money the fastest.

A good lawyer will never undervalue the ideas of his client, especially if he be a man of some intelligence. In truth, the client has but the one case to think of, while the lawyer has many, and the chances are very good that the client himself may suggest very important points in the case. A wise man will hear all that is said, cull the good and reject the chaff. To be popular with clients and to be on the best of terms with them is money made. You thereby form yourself into a pleasant tone of feeling which makes you frank, free, open, and apparently honest, before judges, juries, and clients. It is human nature, however, for the mind that apparently regulates to assume superiority. The wholesaler has a natural repugnance to be on social terms with the retailer to whom he sells goods. The importer lords it over the wholesaler even to whom *he* sells The banker looks askance at his customer.

The feeling is natural, and no one is to blame for entertaining it; but it is not a money-making operation to display it in any of the businesses just named. Nor is it policy or advantageous to merge it in the relations of lawyer and client. No lawyer can estimate the value of an open, frank, honest face, the exponent of clouds of sunshine in the heart. He has an advantage before the community little dreamed of. Business is easier carried on, persons will oblige him, clients will oblige him, the court feels more willing to oblige him, will give weight to his sayings and sympathize with his pleasant talk unintentionally. Juries are prejudiced in his favor, and his honest manner and kind words win when arguments would fail.

But in a long course of legal practice now and then we see grey-haired, haggard countenances, the controlling elements of which are shrewdness and cunning. No pleasant, pleasurable emotions seem to float on their hearts. They have a fixed iron look, with eyes like gimlets to bore you through at a glance. When they come before a jury their very looks put the jury on their guard lest talent and ability should disprove existence or transform them to idiots. Such a character, even with the advantages of great legal acquirement, fails in money-making before the well-balanced and good-natured man of equal attainments.

Pleasant manners, a neat office, close attention, good legal acquirements, small expenses and perseverance, will insure to any member of the bar the means of making money. The amount made will depend entirely upon the care and attention given to it.

CHAPTER XVII.

INTELLECTUAL LABOR.—PHYSICIANS.

Profession eminently useful.—Various branches.—Different qualities —Range of demand.—Money matters.—Melancholy examples —Professionals and misers compared.—Duties.—Elements of success.—Opposites compared.—Directly or indirectly.—Example.—Dress and manners.—Lad sent for doctor.—Reception. —Sharp lecture.—Lad's answer.—Time rolled on.—Doctor lost money.—Trifle important.—Can look back.—Married life. —Another independence.—Means will come.—Life insurance. —The two cases cited.—No more examples necessary.—Specific charges.—General rule.—Cardinal principle.—Extensive success.

THIS is another branch of intellectual labor. In this, as in all other classes, there are degrees of usefulness and of necessity, skill and education, while the profession is eminently intellectual, useful, and necessary, in its higher development, to the comforts of man. It affords the means, at the same time, of making an independence or of increasing it to a fortune. The main profession is subdivided into various branches, some more and some less intellectual; some more and some less mechanical; though all profess the controlling element in execution which binds them to this division of labor. The object here is not to show what constitutes a good or an indifferent practitioner, what is skill, or what is the reverse, in the profession. Each individual is taken as he is, and then shown how he can make the most with the knowledge that he possesses, presupposing that the more knowledge and the more skill he displays, the wider will be the range of his demand, and the greater the pecuniary profits resulting.

It is often remarked that professional men pay but little attention to their money matters, and that they are generally poor because they think money is of little consequence. There are a few such melancholy examples of humanity. Their *real* wants are few, and easily satisfied. So long as they have clothing to wear, food to eat, and books to read, their money wants are just equal to their expenditures. They will not undertake the care of money to the exclusion of their natural tastes. They see no pleasure in a heap of gold, which requires sleepless nights and watching days to guard, when that will give no more than they possess. The pleasure of acquiring knowledge, with them, is like the pleasure of acquisition with the miser. The miser would take no heed of the professional man's occupation; it would be irksome to him, while the professional man would be disgusted with the miser's joy.

Notwithstanding such views, every professional man has his moral and political duty to perform, and he should do it. He should strive for his independence, and for the independence of those dependent upon him, as his first great duty, and then to his tastes afterwards. There are several ways in which this can be accomplished, which will be referred to hereafter. The public, however, has no demand that he labor beyond this point, while it has, till he shall obtain that end.

The first great elements of success in this profession are knowledge and skill; and next to these is pleasant, winning, mild, and gentle demeanor. No one can estimate such manners, for as much as they will make in money for the possessor, and especially in a physician who has to deal with human nature in its most nervous and excitable state. The very presence of such an angel of mercy at such a time, seems to soothe and allay disease without medicine. The effect on some is truly marvellous; and if it has no other result on others, it makes his presence in the chamber of the sick a ray of sunshine that revives and vivifies the drooping system. The opposite quality, on the contrary, chafes and excites, producing a repulsiveness which operates unfavorably upon his finances and future employment. Cases could be cited where such qualities, combined with ordinary skill, produced more money than the opposite supported by the highest talent, with greatly superior knowledge and skill. But the proposition is almost self-evident, and needs no further illustration than the mere mention of the fact.

Civil treatment to all, however, is absolutely necessary for the physician to be able to procure the most for his talents and skill. He may carry the opposite to such an extreme as to almost entirely neutralize all his ability, and only be able to procure business in very extreme cases. It requires no argument to show that he loses money by such a course, and that he would make it by a different one. In truth, any element of intercourse with men and society that has been referred to in this book, heretofore, applies directly or indirectly to the physician. We will cite an instance of uncivil treatment, and its consequences.

A certain physician, and, by-the-by, a very eminent one, being in a small place in the State of New York, had his office and his sleeping apartment in the same building, and connected on the same floor. The front room was used as his office and consulting room, and the rear one as his sleeping apartment. He was a pompous, conceited man, wore a white vest, and white cravat, and dressed otherwise in keeping. A lad of about twelve years old, brought up on a farm, arrived in the place accompanied by his father and mother, on a visit to his brother who lived there. It so happened that the father fell sick, and as this physician was the family physician of the brother, of course he must be sent for to attend the father. There happened to be no one immediately about to send. The lad of twelve, who had just arrived, was determined on to do the errand; so after a full explanation of where the doctor could be found, and of his room and its location, the boy started off. From his knowledge of such things in the country where he came from, to go for the doctor was to go to an apothecary's shop, and not to the private rooms of an aristocratic doctor in white cravat and vest. Being rather an energetic lad, he soon found the place, and waiting for no ceremony while his father wanted the doctor's services, bolted right into the presence of the august doctor without knocking. The doctor looked up amazed at the boy, and the boy, having but one object, was about to ask the doctor if he was the man he wanted, when the doctor rose and in a very imperative way spoke to the boy: "How dared you enter my office without knocking?" The boy replied, "Isn't this the doctor's shop?" "Who are you?" sharply asked the doctor. "Well, my brother lives over here, and my father is sick." An explanation took place, and the doctor having discovered who the boy was and his business, read him a sharp lecture on manners, to which the boy replied: "They don't knock at doctor's shops where I came from." Though the boy was a rough, country lad, he knew that he had done no harm intentionally, and remembered long afterwards what he thought was the eccentricity of a crabbed doctor.

Time rolled on, and the boy grew to be a man of influence and wealth, finally, in the very same place, which had in the meantime grown immensely. The insulted boy never forgot it in his manhood, nor did the doctor, who still practised, ever get a cent from him or from any one that he could influence, for the doctor had by this little unnecessary incivility made an enemy for life. So that it is plain to see that the doctor lost more in the end than he made by the visit to the sick father that resulted. More money is lost to individuals by just such little trifles, than is lost by credits or bad debts. The professional man who sometimes badly feels the want of money, may look back and see when he could have made instead of lost through this means.

It is the general belief that a physician will make more money in his profession married than single. We are of the same opinion. But a serious question arises in such an arrangement. "I have," says he, "but one to support now; I shall have two, then." If you make more money you will have more means to pay the additional expense. All experience proves that the married couple get on better than the single bachelor, for somehow or another the means come along, though it may look a little doubtful to look forward to it. Much, however, depends upon the choice of the wife; but if she has the right views and right intentions there will be no trouble; the living will come with industry and perseverance. The only trouble will be in the scale of expenditure and style of life adopted.

There is, too, another independence to look out for in

case of accident. A small item a year, which can be economized, will secure a life assurance, say to fall in at the end of ten years, by which you can make money and have it at that time if you live, and if you do not, your family is provided for. This will be fully discussed hereafter. The two cases of intellectual labor cited here, the lawyer and physician, are all that the space will allow. What has been said under the first head in almost every particular applies equally to the second. It would therefore be useless to repeat them here. Nor would it be instructive to give more examples of the same kind of labor; that is, intellectual labor, which receives its reward in specific charges made for specific services. There is the same general principle in such charges as there is in merchandizing. Excessive profits drive customers from them, and excessive charges will in like manner drive customers from it. To charge reasonably, but justly, is a great element in making the most money by the opportunity. This cardinal principle should never be lost sight of by those who seek extensive success, not only in this department of labor, but in every other.

CHAPTER XVIII.

INTELLECTUAL LABOR.—PROFESSIONAL SALARIED PERSONS.

Learned of the land.—Noble objects.—Idiosyncrasies.—Day of adversity.—Sphere of action.—How can I ?—Trifle bagatelle.—Results compared.—Scale of equalities.—Can and do.—No credits needed.—Nothing to detract.—Friends and influence.—Limits of expenditure.—Style of life.—Profits always due.—Most from services.—Personal qualities.—Spending part.—Ten per cent. not your own.—Fifteen per cent. reserve.—Contingencies.—Bad luck.—Helter-skelter.—Independence and courage.—First-rate business.—Results.—Life insured.—Increase style of life.—Formula.—Life becomes a fixity.—Wants relation.—One quarter less.—No difference.—All beautiful.—How can I do it ?—Answer.—Spend your profit.—Fail sure.—Simple plain story.—Stand like a man.—Take your choice.

THESE form a large class of the most intelligent and learned of our land. For what they contribute in various ways they are the least rewarded for their positive usefullness in mere money. This, however, is not all they strive for; it is a means, generally, of maintaining a livelihood for higher and nobler objects. As a general thing, they are too indifferent about money, or what it will bring, further than to accomplish their peculiar ends. From enumeration of cases where devotion to learning absorbs all thought to the exclusion of such matters, criticism will hold in saying or expressing a regret of such idiosyncrasies. Whatever such a one may care of, or for himself, he has a special duty to perform as a citizen which nothing should be allowed to crowd out of its legitimate place. Health, vigor, and intellect may not always be left to produce what life and necessities demand. Knowing, then, this fact, no one can insure himself by simply providing for the wants of the hour and doing nothing for the day of adversity or the uncertain future. The life and health may be spared, opportunities and employments are not always open to him who will take.

There would seem to be no class whose duty is apparently so imperative as this, to provide an independence for themselves and those dependent upon them, for there is none so helpless out of their particular sphere of action. They know, of necessity, but little about the business of life, from the fact that the whole course of it is exclusion from the world, except so far as their specialties bring them in contact with a small portion of it. If accident of employment, or of health arises, they are at once at a loss, not being competent to turn their hand to collateral employments, as others generally can do who are educated to other businesses. This duty, then, of providing an independence, would seem to extend further than a mere moral and political one, with this class.

The direct question is then put by the professional salaried person: "How can I make money?" The reason why this question is so often propounded is, that the salary seems but a mere trifle, a bagatelle, alongside of the talked-of incomes of the immensely wealthy, the merchant, manufacturer, or the high-grade mechanic. The only way one class can measure itself with another on the successful money scale, is to compare results. For, as is well known, it is easy to talk or boast, and believe at the same time what you are saying; but in money matters belief don't make dollars or fortunes. Results are the only sure criterion of the positive profitableness of a calling or profession, and here is where the professional man must look to see whether in the great scale of equalities in this respect, he has a chance; whether the money results of his calling fall below or rise above the average of other businesses.

There can be no dispute as to one point, and that is that the salaried person, if he obtain fair remuneration, *can* accomplish more in that way than the average of merchants *do*. To satisfy himself on that head, he has but to look at the statistics of mercantile life given in the chapter on "How to make Money," and he will at once see that at least such results can be avoided. Nor is it believed that any other of the main branches of trade that make or undertake to make by giving credits, have risen much higher in the scale of final money-making than the mercantile. In the class under consideration, however, no credits need be given to obtain what is received, and hence it more nearly approaches the certainty of the retailer to a success.

In this class, as in every other department of labor, their services are valuable and will command a high price, just in proportion to the knowledge and skill possessed, provided no other qualities detract from preventing the individual obtaining it. In order, however, to obtain it, even under such circumstances, as a general rule it requires standing, influence, and personal friends to secure positions, and sometimes to retain them after they have been obtained. But this depends more upon the individual himself than upon others, as a general thing. Permanency, industry, and close attention to business, will insure the greatest amount of income, and the largest results in the end.

Professional men are measurably confined within certain limits as to their expenditures, even though they decide upon a course of retrenchment as a sinking fund. Their positions and professions require a certain style of life consistent with their calling; and sometimes this unfortunately absorbs, or nearly absorbs, their entire income. But there are certain principles which regulate salaries, as there are which regulate the price of manual labor, or any other kind of business. In a particular instance the price may be too low, and if so, it must be raised, so that an average corresponding with others will be obtained. No one will work for simply enough to pay for necessaries; there must be a margin for profit, or the business would run out. No one would be found to do less.

So that the professions are of sufficient consequence, and the results flowing are of sufficient value to pay not only for the necessaries of those who conduct them, but a profit beyond; and in this fact lies the security that such services will be properly rewarded. There can be no general rule laid down as to what this profit should be, or what it is. But one thing is certainly known, that there is scarcely a salary paid for *valuable* services that will not support the laborer and leave a handsome profit over. So far as that matter goes, however, the object in hand is to show *how* the most can be got by given services; in other words, how to get the most over necessaries, and then what to do with it.

As has been said before, the most knowledge and skill will entitle the salaried person to the most money, abstractly, for his services. But there might be such a thing as the most undeserving receiving more than the most deserving. But these are exceptions, and in the end will regulate themselves. The rule will hold good in the long run, if the individual has no personal quality to stultify his merits. And here many of the general principles hold good that are laid down for the clerk, and need not be repeated. It may then be assumed that the professional salaried person is in the due receipt of his income, and what can be said to aid him in making money?

You can make a profit by not spending all that you receive. In other words, make up your mind, on a careful consideration of all things, how much you can live on, and then do it. Never be too grasping, and put your profits too high; if you do, you will share the same fate of the merchant—fail in your undertaking. But a safe rule, from our knowledge of salaries, would be a saving, or rather not using, twenty-five per cent. of receipts; but if this be too high, twenty, fifteen, or ten. You would probably make most, and carry out what designs you do make, by calling it ten per cent., and laying aside the fifteen as a reserve to help out of any accident. Thus, if your salary was $4,000, you say to yourself, "My style of life and expenses shall be $3,000; four hundred dollars is not mine, because I have constituted myself a trustee for myself and family, and this is to be invested *anyhow*, for their benefit. This I have no *right* to touch, to spend. I have $600—fifteen per cent.—that I can improve at interest, if nothing happens, in the same way, but some unforseen accident may occur that my expenses *may* exceed $3,000. I will hold this as a reserve for such contingency."

Now, this is a safe platform for a salaried person, and nothing but *extraordinary* bad luck can make him fail in his undertaking. With the $400 you can take a ten-year endowment policy, which will insure your life in the meantime. This will be explained under Life Insurance. The $600 should be deposited in a savings bank, at interest, where it will be under control at any moment for use. Buy nothing beyond what you have cash in hand to do, and all will go well and prosperity will be your lot, with many comforts never dreamed of in a helter-skelter way of doing things where you have never known how or where you stand.

If you can have the independence and courage to live up to this, and spend $3,000 when you have an income of $4,000, you will be doing a much better money-making business than the average of wholesale commercial houses, and without comparison a *first-rate* business. Just look at the result and you will see. Your endowment policy, besides insuring your life in the meantime, will accumulate at 6 per cent., and your $600 at the same, that is, $1,000 a year, at 6 per cent., which in ten years will give you $13,246.42; in twenty years $37,643; in thirty years $80,403; in forty years $160,436. This result can be obtained besides keeping your life insured for the whole time, and in case of death your family gets the amount of the policy. As you gain knowledge and skill in your profession you will, in all probability, be enabled to obtain an increase of salary, which increase can be used towards current expenses, and thereby increase your style of life, if you have no other calls for increase of current expenses.

This formula will answer for any conceivable amount of salary. The life-policy will not be the same; it may be smaller or greater in proportion to the receipts. By such a platform for life, you are not constantly endeavoring and always failing to decrease your expenditures, for such efforts make you unsettled and unhappy without attaining the object for which you strive. But when you have a fixed sum to spend there is the end of the whole matter, and you at once become satisfied and contented with what you do spend, and with the result. Make the *want* the ability to supply it, and life and living become a fixity.

You will accomplish nothing more if you spend all in pandering to wants, for they are relative ideas; and by supplying all, you will in the end be no better satisfied, or accomplish more, than by supplying three-quarters of them, and denying yourself the other quarter. For if you had no fixed principle of living, the probabilities are you might spend all your income, and satisfy one want in a hundred. The salaried person may say to himself: "This is all beautiful in theory, and it is very well; and I can see plainly that it is my duty to provide against accident or a rainy day, but I try my best now, and can hardly make both ends meet; how can I do this thing and make it work practically?"

The answer is just here; that you receive a certain amount of salary, which by usage, and from the demand of your special kind of labor, is sufficient to pay your expenses in a style of life commensurate with your occupation, and twenty-five per cent. of profit. If you spend all your profit, you are doing just what the unsuccessful merchant is doing, and your condition will be the same as his when your employment ceases, and you and your family, if you cannot get something to do, will be thrown upon public or private charity. This is the simple, plain story, plainly told. Then, as an intelligent man, will you do what you *can* to avert this end, or will you do what your intelligence teaches you you should do, and be independent of both, and stand like a man before your friends and the community. Take your choice; the responsibility lies with you, and the information, too.

SPECIAL REMARKS.

---o---

THE reader must not conclude that the trades or occupations *not herein named* are neglected or forgotten. Space will not admit that each one should be specifically referred to. Those which have been treated must be considered as types, and have been selected on account of their importance, and the large class of individuals they contain. Nor must each suppose that what is said under each head contain all the principles applicable to it.

The contrary is the fact. There is no principle in the one that does not apply generally to *each;* and further than that, *those principles apply to every known occupation not specifically named herein.* It will therefore be seen that to name every occupation, and recite the principles of money-making applicable to it, would be a series of repetition, cumberous in their extent, and wearisome to the reader. Nor is it supposed that *every* principle governing this important subject is displayed here, but enough has been, and will be said, to illustrate the most important. Whether the ideas set forth will be advantageous or not, will rest entirely with each individual. The main idea intended to be urged is the high moral and political duty each one is under to secure for themselves, and those dependent upon them, a *monetary independence from charity.*

CHAPTER XIX.

INVESTMENTS.

Distinct branch.—To know how.—Great idea.—Whole against one.—Banks for savings.—Life insurance.—Bond and mortgage.—Swiftest.—Why?—Lawyer and security.—Bank stocks.—Investigate.—Paid a dividend.—Subscription.—Government bonds.—Railroad stocks and bonds.—Good.—Manufacturing stocks.—Some speculative.—Fire insurance stocks.—Good and bad.—Money stocks.—Some pay.—Class not good.—Petroleum.—Gas stocks.—Profitable.—Monopolies.—Life insurance stocks.—Mutual cash.—Large dividends.—Other stocks.—Collaterals.—Movable property.—Largest fortunes.—Real estate.—Richest men.—Location.—Double increase.—Vacant lots.—Little trouble or danger of loss.—Changes.—Skill in judgment.—One of the means.—Appropriate building.—Some gifted.—Not worth a snap.—Indulging principle.—How to approach an investment.—Money will command security.—Can't get it afterwards.

THE reader must understand, what is not generally supposed, that he now enters upon a *distinct branch* of money-making. Though labor and money have necessarily been combined, in many of the preceding chapters, to make money; yet the purely making money, with money, is a distinct trade; and the failure of many to know this fact, has led to great losses. The man who has made his dollar, and wishes to make it earn, or work, has arrived at a point, where, to do it to advantage, he must *know how*, or his dollar will very soon take its departure into the pocket of some one who understands the trade, and is keener and shrewder than himself.

No one can be safe in the possession of money, for investment, who does not *come up fully to appreciate this idea*. Toil, labor, saving, and self-denial, are often sacrificed through this ignorance; wealth and comfort are swept away, and poverty and distress take their places; and such people wonder why their lot is so hard in the world. But when they will reflect, for a moment, that the *whole world* are after just what they have got; and every device that cunning and ingenuity can devise are brought to bear to obtain it, is it strange that *one* cannot resist the *whole?* There is no trade so intricate as the investing of money safely; but like the mechanic art, when once learned, how easy, and how simple!

No one, then, having money to invest, should undertake to do so, without knowing the *exact value* of the thing taken in exchange for money. The most simple, however, is the Savings Institution, where the depositor has only to inquire the general standing of the bank, and then make the deposit, and the money will draw an interest, if at dates less than six months, of five per cent.; and if allowed to remain longer, six per cent. per annum. Another mode, equally simple, is to take a ten-year endowment policy, in the best mutual cash company, in which you will be entitled to a share of the profits, which will aid in payment of premiums. You will get your six per cent. per annum, and have your life insured at the same time. This is preferable to the savings bank, if you have capital to go into it, and be sure of making your payments. See chapter, Life Insurance.

These two modes are within the reach of the smaller amounts of money. To those having larger sums, bond and mortgage on real estate, at seven per cent., is the *very best* means of investing money for those who are not *skilled* in financering; and it is believed to be the *swiftest means ever yet put upon any money-making course.* The legal rate of interest in some States is higher, and in some lower, than seven per cent. The legal rate of interest in any, on bond and mortgage, is the surest way to accumulate. The reason for this is apparent on reflection, and the result is secured by a principle that is *all-important* in money-making.

If the amount loaned is properly apportioned to the value of the property, the *security is perfect;* this, however depends upon the lawyer engaged to supply the deficiency of knowledge in the lender, to examine *every particular* of the security offered, to see if any *flaw* exists or intervenes. Now let every one who has money to invest stop just here, and glean a lesson *never to be forgotten.* If the lender intends to invest in any *other security*, take the same pains to get an opinion of its value by one *skilled* in that knowledge. You can yourself determine what would be the value of your security if you are not a lawyer, and undertook to loan your money on bond and mortgage, which is, taking the borrower's note with the land as collateral security, if you could not ascertain *positively* that you had the land as security or no.

The next simplest and most secure investment is in dividend-paying bank stocks. This again requires investigation, though how many there are who simply buy such stocks without one step taken to investigate their value, or making a single inquiry of any one skilled in such knowledge! The books of a bank are always open for inspection, and he who has got into his brain the value of money will look to see for himself, or engage some one to do so, as to the whole state of its affairs, before putting his money into the stock of such an institution. Especially should the character of the officers be looked to, and their style of conducting the business be scrutinized closely. Do not presume, because they have an imposing banking-house, and a large number of employés, that this is the base of security, and will furnish sure dividends for your money. Investigate—investigate, and take advice.

Never invest in any stock till it has paid a dividend. As well might you entrust your money in the hands of a man calling himself a merchant, and setting up his sign to trade, who has never in his life yet made a dollar. He may, perchance, succeed, and so may the stock divide, but the surest way is to let others take such risks; those that can afford to lose; but those who have limited means ought not to run such chances. Their little is their all, and certainty and positive security should hang around every dollar.

On the other hand, no one who thus invests, even the capitalist, expects to lose; and regular subscriptions to bank stocks, as means of investment when the character of the officers to manage them is well known, may not be regarded as unsafe; and, too, there is sometimes an advantage in being among the first subscribers to such stocks, for the subscriptions are at par, and when once filled up, the stock cannot be got, except at an advance. Such cases of investment are proper subjects for advice of skilled financiers.

Government bonds and government securities, are regarded by financiers as safe and good investments without inquiry, though the rate of interest, till quite lately, has been low in comparison with other equally good securities. But they are more in demand by large than by small capitalists. Being as safe as any security, they take rank as among the best of the land. State bonds, of various issues, are sought after in like manner. These securities, however, by the manipulations of politics, generally are below par, and some are quite low in the market.

Dividend-paying railroad stocks and bonds are good securities, and form a large class of profitable investments. They have a good prospective value, also, from the fact that business is constantly on the increase, and greater experience in construction and in running reduces yearly their expenditures. From necessity, too, they are compelled to hold large amounts of real estate, which increases in value. Such stock and bonds judiciously purchased, cannot fail to be productive of income, and the basis is constantly growing more and more valuable.

Manufacturing stocks have been the source of large fortunes, and also of heavy losses. There are, however, certain manufacturing stocks which pay not only well, but exorbitantly. From the nature of things, such large profits engender competition, and, in the long-run, it is doubtful whether they are more profitable than bond and mortgage or bank stocks, which pay less dividends, but are more sure. The general rule of business applies to them, *the more profit the greater risk of loss.* In certain sections of the country they are favorite investments, and the inducement of heavy gains will always render them active as investments to the more speculative class of minds. Still there are manufacturing stocks, founded on the making of staple articles, under careful and economical management, which always pay a remunerative dividend, with a certain amount of safety and security to those investing.

Fire insurance stocks have been favorite investments. When they do pay they pay largely, but as a class of investments they have proved speculative, and under certain circumstances total loss has been the result. There are periodical times when goods are falling and trade dull, when those holding such securities would do well to sell and reinvest, if they desire, when goods are on the rise and trade brisk. Marine and inland insurance has generally been good paying stocks, but for the past five years severe losses have occurred. Though not so risky as fire stocks, they neither pay as high dividends, nor are they subject to such danger of total destruction.

Mining stocks form a very large class of securities, such as they are. It is doubtful whether as a class they have ever paid a profit. While fortunes have resulted in gold, silver, and lead mines, thousands have lost every cent thus invested. Coal has been the most successful of any, as its consumption is based in necessity, and hence has in most cases, when judiciously entered into and carried on with honesty and economy, been paying. A safe rule in mining stocks is never to invest till a dividend has been seen. This if followed would have saved many a man a fortune, and the ground being rooted up in vain in search of hidden treasure. Petroleum stocks need no praise or censure.

Gas stocks have been very remunerative, and always will be as long as the present system is followed. They are monopolies both as to price and quality of the article furnished. The result is, they make just such *quality of gas* as they please, and sell it for *just what price they choose* to charge, and hence, is there any wonder why they should not make large dividends and heavy profits?

Life insurance stocks, on the cash principle, have been

profitable investments, and would so continue if business could be procured; but its profitableness has brought up mutual cash-paying premium companies, which are securing all the business by giving to the insured the benefit of the profit to help pay their annual premiums. In this department the Mutual Life is then a good investment for the insured, as the dividends in the most successful company now in operation averages about forty per cent. upon the annual premiums falling due.

There are many other stocks, too numerous to mention particularly, which are good investments, but those named are the principal. Every stock, however, before being taken should be thoroughly investigated, and the principle laid down heretofore is really the only safe one in stock investment, that they should *first show a dividend*. There are so many combinations and varieties of money making or money losing, that no more definite rule can be given to guide those investing.

Stocks and bonds form but a small portion of investments for money-making. Notes of hand are both bought and held as collateral security for money. This should not be done by any who are not thoroughly acquainted with the business: otherwise an almost certain chance of loss results. Loans are made on stocks and bonds in like manner; but when the value of the stocks or bonds are known, the risk is not so great, and can be done with comparative safety by those not skilled in judging of credits.

Investments are also made in all kinds of movable goods, with a view to sale or use, for a profit. They can hardly be considered investments, in the strict sense of the word, but as money is parted with for them, it is necessary to point out the chances of loss or gain by the purchase. Here the greatest care must be taken that the value given shall not be above the regular market value, and as much below as the circumstance of the case will allow In that event, no loss will accrue, but a gain by the sale. To do this, requires knowledge and skil· of a peculiar kind, only attained by experience and practice.

The largest fortunes made in this country have been by investments in real estate. But, like others, they must be made with sound judgment, and forecast of utility, or loss may result in some few instances, but as a general rule, all are more or less successful. The richest men in New York have made the bulk of their huge fortunes by real estate, though some have made by merchandize in conjunction. Every part of the country has, in like manner, had its smaller results in this way, but the large cities have been the most shining examples.

The investment in real estate is certain if it be located upon any of the leading streets ; first, for an income equal if not greater than can be had by any other equal security ; and second, by a continuous percentage added thereto yearly for increase in value. How long or how far this will continue no one can tell ; but it has continued and promises still to continue. Thus, within twenty years, real estate which sold then, now sells for one thousand dollars for one invested. Many think that such opportunities never will occur again. This is a mistake. The same chances now exist of making investments in this way that ever have been.

There are to-day plenty of vacant lots, and even improved property that will largely increase over regular interest, but not possibly in the time named—one thousand to one. Vacant lots will, if in proper localities, pay a very large interest over seven per cent. It is, too, the cleanest and snuggest investment, requiring no attention, and giving a certain return. The improved pays a regular interest, and if in the right lines will pay immensely by increase in value.

Vacant lots can always have some light improvement which will part pay interest on first cost, if not the whole, leaving the yearly increase in value a splendid dividend on the investment. Then there is no anxiety about honest cashiers, or the vicissitudes which attach to almost every other kind of property. The tenant may fail to pay a month, or a quarter's rent, but your capital is there intact. Real estate investments resemble more nearly the accumulations of the savings institutions, because your compound interest is added from time to time in the regular march of increase in value, while if the increase is applied to the purchase of other real estate the increase is rapid and immense.

There is no other investment that is not in danger, though it may be remote, of total loss of interest and principal. It is, therefore, considered the very best and safest of all means of improving money. But to those who are so situated that they cannot give attention to such business, the bond and mortgage at seven per cent. stands next. To invest, however, to advantage, the opinion of men skilled in value of real estate and the best locations should always be obtained. But when once invested, do not sell without business should show indications of leaving the location; then sell and reinvest in the direction of the change.

By watching the drift of things an experienced dealer can always foretell by certain signs when a new state of things will spring up, and when property, which has remained dormant for some time, will suddenly be brought in market at greatly advanced rates. But generally speaking any real estate is a good investment that will pay current expenses and seven per cent. on cost, as the progress of the country will of a certainty cause it to increase in value.

One of the means of judging the value of parts of lots as compared with the whole, may be stated as follows : the first twenty-five feet from front of a hundred foot lot is worth one-half of the whole; the first fifty feet is worth three-quarters of the whole ; the first seventy-five feet is worth ninety per cent. of the whole. This rule will apply generally on any important street ; when the street is not a business one, but one for private residences only, the front decreases somewhat in value in proportion to the rear.

As a general rule for the improvement of real estate, too much value in building in proportion to the value of the lot may prove a loss. There should be a judicious apportionment of the one to the other, but a little show on the front will always pay well. There is, however, no species of investment that requires more sound judgment and peculiar tact to hit just right always, both as to price and location, than this, and any one investing can well afford to pay a skilful judge a round commission to locate him right. There are many extensively engaged in the business whose opinions are not worth a snap, while there are others who will never make a mistake.

Some are gifted in this way, while others with ever so much practice seem unable to get hold of the true underlying principle. Some men are naturally money-makers in merchandize, while others are blunderers forever. Much more could be said on investments, but space will not permit. Let any one who has money and wishes to make it make more money, consider what he has in hand, and let him approach an investment as he would his bitterest personal enemy, looking out at every step for an assault. No matter what you invest in, hold your money till you get its *full equivalent in value*, and that, too, made as secure as security will make it ; remembering that while you hold the money it *can* and *will* command *any* security you ask. When you have parted with it you cannot get more than you have.

CHAPTER XX.

HOW MONEY IS LOST.

Endorsing paper.—Lending money.—Object.—Inquiry.—Lose friend and money.—Take and give security.—Loss on notes of hand. —Credits.—How avoided.—No change probable.—Loss to a dead certainty.—Reasons for crediting.—Profit the bait.— Short notes remedy.—Small and large transactions.—Don't save under forty.—Why?—Reason.—Paper moonshine.—Loss. Reasoning.—Others controlled.—Million of moonshine.—Now he controls.—Plenty of dollars.—Safe rule.—New enterprises. Schemers.—Crafty individuals.—Seductive talk.—See dividends first.—Petroleum and 7 per cent.—Entanglements.—Responsibility.—Good rules.—Pay lawyer to keep out rather than get out.—Stock speculations.—Stock investments.—Follow same course.—Injudicious investments.—Same old story repeated.— Gold mine in the sun.—Petroleum well.—Millions preceded.

To those who have had experience in this way no explanation is necessary, and few, probably, will be benefited by telling it to them. But the object of this book would not be accomplished without a rehearsal of what every one who has handled money or valuables knows One prolific source of loss is endorsing paper not your own, and in which you have no interest in the profits or results flowing from it. Why do you do it then? Probably to aid a friend or assist another to get what he cannot obtain without your aid. You lend him then *your* capital, without interest generally, and without receiving any benefit, except possibly a return of the favor. If, for a return of the favor, you run a double risk to make one profit, which is poor financiering at best If to oblige a friend you are helping him to do what he cannot do himself, thereby overstraining his ability, and helping him probably to a loss.

You are, then, not doing him a friendly act; but one by which, if not successful, you will lose your friend and your money too. If your friend has placed himself where he *must* have aid, it is certainly better that he should suffer the consequences, than an innocent party who has had no hand in the matter. By refusing to endorse, you keep but your own, which no man could complain of, and if your friend be worth keeping, you will retain him also. The same can be said of lending money. But if you do either, remember that your money is as good to you, as theirs to a Bank, and the Bank would require security. Therefore take security if you endorse or lend, and give it in case you require either yourself. No one can complain if you adopt that as a rule of action.

The largest source of loss is the parting with money or valuables for notes of hand, or credits without notes. On this subject much has already been said. In this lies most of the causes of failure of merchants or traders of any grade. But says the reader, "How can this be avoided? Goods must be sold, and they cannot be sold to any extent without crediting, and if you do credit endorsers cannot always be had?" True; the way things are done generally, the propositions are correct, and what are the results? Failure or loss? The results of statistics in mercantile life proves the fact most conclusively; and, as long as the same system is pursued, the same results will follow. Then we say yes; go on and credit, if you please, and reap the almost universal penalty in failure and poverty in after years.

There may be some, however, who will do differently, and desire to make a change from this certain road of destruction. To these the pointing out the causes of failure may be interesting, instructive, and may do good. If the merchant will look at his goods as so much money, why will he part with them on any less security than the banker or financier, who is generally successful? *Until the operator can ground this principle in his credits, failure is almost certain;* if not hopeless failure, loss of profits and money follows, to a *dead certainty*.

The reason why men give credits in this way is, that they are allured by the profit, and lose sight of the absolute money engaged; for, let any one investigate the matter, and he will see that if no profit was in the transaction, or very little, the credit would not be so readily given, if given at all. Then the principle results *that money is lost in an overstrained desire for profit,* as a general rule, though it may be lost occasionally where this principle does not enter. Nor need the merchant say that business cannot be done without excessive crediting.

If the purchaser cannot give, or will not give, endorsed paper or security, if he is worthy of credit, let him give what he would be compelled to give to a Bank—thirty, sixty, or ninety day notes. Nor should these be taken without the utmost scrutiny; for if such merchants will *realize* that the acceptance of such a note might be the cause of his failure, he would be very cautious. Experience has shown, too, that there is not as much danger in loss on *small*, as on *large* transactions. Men generally lose on big amounts, and such would be the philosophical reasoning, if experience had not taught the fact. No one will be likely to go wrong in taking paper, who will adopt the banking principle of time and responsibility.

That some losses will occur, even under such a severe rule of credit, no one will deny; but such is the most perfect plan in the giving of credits for merchandise, or other valuables.

Very few men—a mere fraction of the whole—keep money that is made before they are thirty-five or forty years of age, in general trading business. Why? Simply because men will not profit by the experience of others. Hence the same routine for one and all; and if they are successful, and escape the rule, it is good luck if not good management. They have such overweaning confidence in their own judgments, that they can see what others can't, and only discover that they are human when their money is gone.

A merchant who had made a very handsome fortune in *paper moonshine*, came forward with it to breast the storm of the commercial crisis of 1836. The result was, that with the bankrupt act which followed, and the crash of the time, his fortune had dwindled to a mere song. Being a young man, with an anological mind, he set himself about an investigation of the whole matter, to see wherein he had made the grand mistake that lost him his years of labor. The conclusion was, that he had put his fortune and money into the hands, and *under the control of others, whose interest, upon general principles, was to keep it, rather than return it.* He saw his blunder, and from that day commenced a new financial life, upon the principle that he would never put a dollar of his money *under the control of another man.* He has lived up to the principle to this day; for, as he says, he has at this time, on the 1836 investment, in interest and principal, about one million of dollars in the hands of others, which is as much as one man ought to have out at a time. This principle, carried out, has led to investment in bond and mortgage, and real estate, and the result in dollars can be easily imagined.

It is a safe rule to adopt in any business, and will in the end lead to the most money. It brings the trader to sell for cash, and the capitalist to avoid dishonest bank officers and scheming men who control moneyed institutions. It avoids nearly all the risks of losing, and brings money directly under the control and supervision of the one who takes the greatest interest in its preservation. Of course this could not become a universal rule, nor is there any danger that it will; but those who adopt it will find their dollars when they want them, and accumulation will follow as a necessary consequence.

Another prolific source of loss is the placing of money into new and untried enterprises, and under the control of schemers. How sane men can do such things is beyond calculation. There are enterprises, of course, which are worthy of investment; but the large class are devices to get money for other objects than the legitimate dividend proposed. How sweetly and eloquently the crafty individual will sit by your side, and sing his bewitching song of high dividends and safe returns!

Your best friend he may be, but has he shown by his fortune made in the same way that he is competent to advise, or that his recommendation is worth a straw? Not one dollar probably can he show that he has made by such a thing, yet there are men who will become so infatuated by "his talk" that they will eagerly grasp the pen and set their names to paper for thousands, and incur obligations for thousands beyond, for schemes about as likely to be profitable as a railway to the moon. Where is there a guarantee or a cent of security in the whole thing? Nothing except the *talk* of some one who wishes to make up a company, a stock, or a scheme to control your money and pass it gently from your pocket to his or one of his associates.

Such people will quietly sit down and hear a long story about an enterprise 500, 1,000 or 5,000 miles off, and take the statement second, third, or fourth hand, and greedily hand out the money to the man who could not get a personal loan of $500 on his note, or even a loan on bond and mortgage in the same place where both resided, without abundant security.

People having money in possession would always do well to hear in the first place what profits are promised, or what are probable, and if they are over seven or eight per cent., take a sudden mistrust of the thing and *fully appreciate* that some one is after your money and don't intend you shall get it back. Never mind the dividends promised or conceived. If they can be made let some one else make them, and wait till that is accomplished before you risk your money. Remember always that legal interest is about all money can earn, and be sure of the return of the principal.

If all the money that has been spent in obtaining petroleum had been invested at seven per cent. in bond and mortgage, this account would be far ahead of the real petroleum capital and profit. There is, however, a fascination about making a sudden fortune that will continue to find devotees in such hazards. But some there are who should avoid the very presence of such things and their influences, because they do not themselves understand the subject, and they are compelled to derive all their information from those whose interests are that your money should go to help theirs or their interest.

A good rule for any one who has money is to keep away from all entanglements with others. Responsibility, when the amount is comparatively trifling, may lose you your entire estate. Never sign a paper, or your name to anything that you do not fully understand, and never to a contract of any magnitude, without consulting a lawyer. The trifle you would pay him for advice may save you much in comfort and money.

No safer mode of action can be adopted by any one than keeping aloof from all intermingling of interest and responsibilities, and managing, under the best advice, your own capital; keeping always it, or as good security for money as it is, in your own hands. This will secure all the comfort that money can bring, because you get your income and avoid all legal questions and controversies; and if a man wishes to be happy, let him keep out of the law, and the way to keep out, is to see to it, that all your business is transacted legally correct, for the best money any one can spend is to pay a lawyer to keep him out of controversies, rather than pay him to get him out.

Much money is lost by speculation in things that have little or no intrinsic value. Among these, the most important is speculation in stocks. Those who have tested this subject are enabled to certify that it is the quickest and surest means of getting rid of money that is known. Some make, to be sure, but they make but to lose on the next turn of the wheel. Any one may by a single operation make, but if the thing be followed up, there is but one result. Millions have been lost by this process. There is quite a difference between speculating in stocks and buying them, when they are under value in the market for investment. This can be done always with safety. But buying stocks that do not pay a legitimate dividend, in the hope of selling to some one else as foolish as the buyer, is a strange infatuation.

In looking over the long line of our wealthy men, and the vast amount of capital sunk in this style of business, any reasonable person would suppose such operations would cease some day. But they not only continue, but increase in volume. It is like the excitement of war,— the more soldiers that fall in battle, the more will rush into its deadly carnage. It is just so in these speculations; the failure and disappearance of one large house, or operator, gives room for half a dozen smaller ones who fancy they can avoid what great experience has not avoided, and make some money where others have lost it. Such is human nature, and such it will continue, all the books, experience, and advice in the world to the contrary notwithstanding.

Money is lost in injudicious investment; that is, paying more for things than they are worth. It sometimes happens, too, that circumstances beyond the control of the most sagacious will cause depreciation in value of that which at the time was valuable. The burden of such chances can be avoided by good judgment and watchfulness, taking care to sell in proper time, if such circumstances arise. These, then, are a few, and it is believed the most common sources of the loss of money. So peculiar, however, is the action of the human mind on this subject, that although individuals see these causes in action daily around them, and book after book be written reciting them, little can be hoped for in a radical change, of these almost certain results. The reader may say to himself, all this is very well in its way, and turn from its reading to lend an irresponsible individual money, or subscribe to an extraordinarily productive gold mine in the sun, or buy stock in a petroleum well never sunk, or that never will be sunk, and only wake up to the real situation when his money has gone where millions have preceded.

CHAPTER XXI.

EARNINGS AND SAVINGS.

Object of Saving.—Duties.—Position in Life.—No meanness or penuriousness.—Ten per cent. of earnings.—Fifteen per cent. reserve.—Example—All increase.—Net profits.—Fortune should spend freely.—Spending others' money.—Wife responsible.—Fine things.—Influence.—Husband labors.—The Grundies.—Smash up. —Who responsible.—Ignorance all around.—Husband same results.—Squanders.—Wife saving.—People don't think.—No fixed principles.—Never suspect.—Sad reality.—Great Revolution.—What rule?—Spend a little less.—Principle of life.—The Savings Bank.—Real nothings.—No pleasure or position.—Surroundings and Associates.—Think how much it is.—How remedied.—Change of base.—Money improves position.—Ladder.—Cloud of hope and desire.—Platform.—Calculate independence.—Example.—Use of tables.—Great idea.—Tables of earnings and savings.

WE have now come to the whole aim and gist of money-making, considered as a means of accumulation. So far as the object of this work is concerned, the goal to be arrived at is the simple independence, or, to that point when sufficient money is accumulated and safely invested, so that the individuals or those dependent upon them shall be out of danger of falling a charge to the public, or their friends; we have the right to ask this of all, because, as has been said before, this is a *moral and political duty.* But we do not wish to be considered as asking more, though we may have gone further and shown how fortunes can be made.

Nor can we ask that more savings shall be made than

will accomplish this, and while in like manner, we may show, that by further accumulations fortunes will result. As the foundation, then, we claim that till the independence *is secured* the individual has no moral or political right to spend more than is necessary for his support, in a way commensurate with his position in life. All extravagances and useless expenditures should be avoided, and a persistent course of rigid economy pursued till the independence is accomplished.

Nor should they descend to meanness or penuriousness, but instead of gratifying every want should curtail a portion, and the principle laid down on page 229 for the professional salaried person is a sound one for every grade of life. Consider, as in that case, that ten per cent. of your earnings is not your own, but that you are your own trustee to secure your own independence and fifteen per cent. to be deposited in a Savings Institution as a reserve fund to help out in case of accident. Let the ten per cent. be invested in premiums of a ten-year endowment policy in proportion to your means, and this part of your duty in life is done, and if you do more afterward and get a fortune, well.

Taking any view of the case, either of one seeking a fortune or one seeking an independence, the operation of this cardinal rule will steady and make prosperous his whole financial life. Suppose a merchant, or trader of any kind, is in the receipt of $10,000 per annum of profit, he takes $1,000 and invests in premiums of a ten-year endowment policy, and he puts $1,500 into a Savings Bank to accumulate at six per cent. as a reserve fund. If he lives till the ten years expires, his policy will fall in, and if taken in a Cash Mutual will amount at last to $12,615.64 besides having his life insured in the mean time, and his $1,500 per annum will be $18,923.46 and the two added together will amount to $31,539.10.

Now, if he has paid his expenses and has the $7,500 invested in his business, and it has accumulated at the rate of eight per cent., he would have from this source $111,660.05, in all $143,199.15. This same rule can be applied to any conceivable income; the main feature being the life-endowment policy, by which, if death occurs, a provision is left for those dependent. This is especially imperative upon every married man on entering business. No matter how small the profits may be: the principle is the same, and the endowment policy would be small in proportion.

Net profits are entirely dependent upon expenses, or at least nearly so, for there is no occupation that does not afford a profit, that is, more income than is required to meet *necessary* expenses. To ensure savings, then, the expenses should be reduced to the minimum, which will give the maximum profit. To those who have fortunes, the more they spend, and consequently the less they save, the better for the community at large. In this way money is put in circulation, and it becomes easier for those who are striving for it to get it. But until the independence is obtained, the rule and right is directly the reverse. They have no right to spend till they have accomplished this object, for the chances are they will spend what is not their own.

Nor has any man who owes others the right to spend more than is necessary to support, in a proper manner, his relative position in life, for he, in like manner, will be found in the end to have been spending money belonging to others in case he fails. As failure is one of the chances of trade, he is not only honorably, but morally bound to save beyond his necessities till he is out of debt, then he can do as he pleases.

It then becomes a close question to decide what are necessary expenses. If the trader apes the man of fortune in his expenditures, while he is yet owing largely, the result may be most certainly conjectured. If, however, he lives moderately economically, and in proportion with his income, leaving a large portion of it to the good, success will attend in all probability. Expenditures depend entirely upon the determined will and good judgment of the person. These are, in nineteen cases out of twenty, governed entirely in families by the wife. The general rule is the man loses outside, the wife spends inside.

The old saying that the wife can throw out with a teaspoon what the husband can throw in with a shovel, is a truism. The whole question of savings rests mainly with the wife. She is responsible, and she alone, for the entire success as a general rule. The man is usually satisfied with what the wife is satisfied with. She is in very many cases responsible *directly* for the failure of the husband. She must have a fine house, fine furniture, fine clothing, carriage and horses, and fine everything, while her husband is trying to make money. She hears of his income, of his making money, and of large operations, and not knowing the course of trade, naturally supposes she is rich, and that she can lavish and spend. She says to her plastic husband, "Mrs. Grundy does so-and-so, and she has no more money than we have."

Society, dress, parties, balls, furniture and every sort of expenditure is gone into, while the husband makes shift to pay his notes from day to day, and may be straining every nerve to keep his head above water. The wife still drives and dashes in the most reckless and cruel manner, because, having started, she cannot, without losing her caste among the Grundies, fail to keep up her end in society. The husband, with no more power to stay the extravagance of home matters than to stop the current of Niagara with a quill, pays, and leaches his profits from day to day.

The end finally comes, and failure follows, and then distress often. The man hardly knows why he has failed, the wife knows still less, never for an instant supposing that she herself has plunged the dagger of disgrace into the heart of her own family. She will never, or at least has never sat down and added up the long list of follies and footed them up in thousands on thousands, spent through her own influence, the direct cause of her husband's misfortunes.

Now what is the fundamental cause of such results? An ignorance on the part of both the husband and wife of their true position. The wife is led to this course by the vain supposition that the husband *really and truly has the means* to support it, while the husband often keeps from the wife the real state of his affairs. Both are groping in the dark on the vital point of their future happiness; in truth, anticipating what they are seeking for. The husband on the other hand, by a similar course unaided by the wife, often brings about the same result.

Fast horses, clubs, suppers, dinners, and numberless extravagances squander away the earnings, while the wife is at her humble home economical and saving. She strains every nerve to save, while the heartless or heedless husband fast saps the foundation of their property, and want follows. Many would blame both husband and wife, and in a certain sense they are to blame. But they are both more to blame for their ignorance of the true principles of living than for the fact. Such people live without *thinking*. They never sit down and calculate upon the course they are pursuing, nor do they ever refer their actions or prospects to any reasonable coördinates.

They live with the idea that living is life, not that life is for a living. They have no plan of action, no fear of the future, as the child has no fear of fire till his experience has taught him that the burn is painful. They never have failed nor been in want, why should they know what it is? Those thus jeopardized may possibly read this book, but they will never suspect that they are in danger of what has been just portrayed—by no means —while to-morrow may bring the sad reality.

If every man in business, and every woman who holds the purse-strings of the home expenditure could be early in life brought by reading or experience to appreciate the terrors of want after affluence, consequent upon failure, what a revolution would be wrought in the world! The dollar that would or might prevent such a catastrophe would not be squandered in nothings till it could be done without danger—till accumulation of savings had rendered such a result next to impossible.

How are these things to be done? Every case in life is a different one; therefore, no rule can be given by which all can act. But let any one consider carefully what expenditures in the course of a week he can avoid, that he determines to make: say, once less to the theatre, one less cigar a day, one less drink, one less party a week, and so on; deny yourself something every day, and put the money into a pocket provided for the savings. Do this for a short time, and see the result. If you do it for six months your future is made, for the habit once contracted will soon run into a principle of life.

Let any one do this who will not or cannot adopt the plan of ten per cent., and fifteen per cent., referred to before, and when the week comes around put the money aside, or place it in a Savings Bank. The whole object will be accomplished ; for the moment any one has acquired the habit of saving it grows upon them. Do not undertake to be mean and niggardly, but only lay aside a part of your current expenditures in the real nothings, which neither give pleasure or position, and a new world of prosperity has opened upon your path in life.

The only obstacle to such a course lies in your surroundings or associates. The great question for each one to decide is whether you will live to please them or to please yourself, and for your own prosperity and happiness. Whether you will live to be poor and dependent or independent and beyond fear of poverty. To this end the beginner in life, by looking at the table on page seventy-eight, will see how many dollars of his independence or fortune he spends when he uselessly throws away a dollar. If he assumes that he *will* have an independence at 30 years of age, every dollar spent at 20 years of age is $2.10 at 30 ; is $4.14 at 40 ; is $8.14 at 50 ; is $16.02 at 60 ; is $31.51 at 70 ; and is $62.00 at 80.

The most satisfactory and startling manner that this subject of unnecessary yearly or daily expenditure can be brought to the mind, is to keep an account of every cent spent in the course of a year. Then, go over the list and *select such as were unnecessary or could have been avoided without interfering with your positive position in life.* Any one has but to do this and the subject will be illustrated to that mind at least. Then, to make the lesson practical and useful, stop where you are in expenditures, and change your base, to a saving of the unnecessary items, and a few years will show the magnitude of the result, and your social position will be improved, your entire character and social standing will have insensibly changed for the better.

For let the world say what it may, money *alone* improves the position of any one, and if they possess all the other qualities of the educated and, refined the goal of life in this direction is reached. Then let every one remember that the dollar in hand can be invested in such a way as to make one round in the ladder of, position, or it can be foolishly spent and leave you just where you do not desire to be, at the foot in poverty. The great trouble is that people will not *think*, will not stop to consider a course of action and analyze their condition and what they are about, but heedlessly push on in an indefinite cloud of hope and desire, expecting that Dame Fortune is either bound or not to see them through. Dame Fortune is yourself, and the sooner you find it out the sooner you will see your independence or your fortune.

We cannot leave this subject without again calling attention to the platform recommended in page 229 for the professional salaried person. By assuming that rule of action all questions of savings are included in it. If the income be large enough the ten per cent. can be directly invested in bond and mortgage at seven per cent. as a permanent fund not to be touched, to be spent The fifteen per cent. can be invested in real estate or in some productive security, and to avoid the possibility of the loss in business operations of the trust fund of ten per cent. for the benefit of the dependants, such can be placed in their name as the permanent reserve fund.

Those having small amounts of savings, the Savings Banks are the only places where such funds can be properly put, and ten per cent. of receipts thus disposed of will soon tell a handsome amount to their credit. To all such, two accounts should be opened with the Bank, one the permanent fund of ten per cent. the other as much of the fifteen per cent. as is possible to spare, in a separate account. Having then established the rule *adhere* to it, and your independence is secured, and if you live long enough your fortune too.

This then being the securest machinery to bring about a result which all desire, let no one delay in its execution. To undertake saving in any other form is simply to undertake an independent decision upon every case of expenditure that arises. This rule covers every one, and will accomplish all that is desired.

We have prepared the following tables of earnings and savings, which give all *per diem* amounts from *one cent* to *fifty dollars*, from *one year* to *fifty years*, by which any one can determine when he wishes his independence to fall in, or what he will have to save a day, to gain the amount sought. By an example their use can be understood. They are for accummulations *without* interest and with interest at 5, 6, 7, and 8 per cent. per annum, the respective amounts being improved *each six months*.

Suppose you wish to find how much you would have to save a day for ten years to accumulate 5,000. Look at the table of ten years, and run down either of the columns without interest and with interest at 5, 6, 7, or 8 per cent. You find that $1,60 cents by adding $3,130 the accumulation of $1, and $1,878 that of 60 cents, you

And how to Keep it. 263

have $5,008 without interest. So that $1,60 cents per day will accumulate in ten years, without interest, to be $5,008, and with interest the same process is had in each of the respective columns of 5, 6, 7, or 8 per cent.

These tables are interesting, and by looking at them often and studying them, the *great idea* of gain by accumulation can be grounded in the mind, and the beneficial results to the money-seeker proved. They show, too, how much per diem amounts will accumulate in any number of years.

TABLE

Showing the net amount of earnings of ONE CENT to FIFTY DOLLARS *per day* for ONE YEAR of 313 working days, without interest, and with interest at 5, 6, 7, and 8 per cent., improved each *six months*.

Savings per day.	Without interest.	With interest at 5 per cent.	With interest at 6 per cent.	With interest at 7 per cent.	With interest at 8 per cent.
1	$3 13	$3 17	$3 18	$3 18	$3 19
2	6 26	6 34	6 35	6 37	6 39
3	9 39	9 51	9 53	9 55	9 58
4	12 52	12 68	12 71	12 74	12 77
5	15 65	15 85	15 88	15 92	15 96
6	18 78	19 01	19 06	19 11	19 16
7	21 91	22 18	22 24	22 29	22 35
8	25 04	25 35	25 42	25 48	25 54
9	28 17	28 52	29 59	28 66	28 73
10	31 30	31 69	31 77	31 85	31 93
15	46 95	47 54	47 65	47 77	47 89
20	62 60	63 38	63 54	63 70	63 85
25	78 25	79 23	79 42	79 62	79 82
30	93 90	95 07	95 31	95 54	95 78
40	125 20	126 76	127 08	127 39	127 70
50	156 50	158 46	158 85	159 24	159 63
60	187 80	190 15	190 62	191 09	191 56
70	219 10	221 84	222 39	222 93	223 48
80	250 40	253 53	254 16	254 78	255 41
90	281 70	285 22	285 93	286 63	287 33
$1 00	313 00	316 91	317 69	318 48	319 26
2 00	626 00	633 82	635 39	636 95	638 52
3 00	939 00	950 74	953 08	955 43	957 78
4 00	1,252 00	1,267 65	1,270 78	1,273 91	1,277 04
5 00	1,565 00	1,584 56	1,588 47	1,992 39	1,596 30
6 00	1,878 00	1,901 47	1,906 17	1,910 86	1,915 56
7 00	2,191 00	2,218 39	2,223 86	2,229 34	2,234 82
8 00	2,504 00	2,535 30	2,541 56	2,547 82	2,554 08
9 00	2,817 00	2,852 21	2,859 26	2,866 33	2,873 34
10 00	3,130 00	3,169 12	3,176 15	3,184 77	3,192 60
15 00	4,695 00	4,753 69	4,765 42	4,777 16	4,788 90
20 00	6,260 00	6,338 25	6,350 90	6,369 55	6,385 20
25 00	7,825 00	7,922 81	7,942 37	7,961 94	7,981 50
30 00	9,390 00	9,507 37	9,530 88	9,554 32	9,577 80
35 00	10,955 00	11,091 84	11,119 32	11,146 71	11,174 10
40 00	12,520 00	12,676 50	12,707 80	12,739 10	12,770 40
45 00	14,085 00	14,261 06	14,296 28	14,331 49	14,366 70
50 00	15,650 00	15,845 63	15,884 75	15,923 88	15,963 00

TABLE

Showing the net amount of earnings of ONE CENT to FIFTY DOLLARS *per day* for FIVE YEARS of 313 working days, without interest, and with interest at 5, 6, 7, and 8 per cent., improved each *six months*.

Savings per day.	Without interest.	With interest at 5 per cent.	With interest at 6 per cent.	With interest at 7 per cent.	With interest at 8 per cent.
1	$15 65	$17 53	$17 94	$18 36	$18 79
2	31 30	35 07	35 88	36 72	37 58
3	46 95	52 60	53 82	55 08	56 37
4	62 60	70 13	71 76	73 44	75 16
5	78 25	87 67	89 70	91 80	93 95
6	93 90	105 20	107 65	110 16	112 74
7	109 55	122 73	125 59	128 52	131 53
8	125 20	140 27	143 53	146 88	150 32
9	140 85	157 80	161 47	165 24	169 11
10	156 50	175 33	179 41	183 60	187 90
15	234 75	263 00	267 11	275 39	281 84
20	313 00	350 00	358 82	367 19	375 79
25	391 25	438 33	448 52	458 99	469 74
30	469 50	526 00	538 23	550 79	563 69
40	626 00	701 33	717 64	734 39	751 58
50	782 50	876 66	897 03	917 98	939 48
60	939 00	1,052 00	1,976 46	1,101 58	1,127 37
70	1,095 50	1,227 33	1,255 87	1,285 17	1,315 27
80	1,202 00	1,402 66	1,435 28	1,468 77	1,503 16
90	1,408 50	1,578 00	1,614 69	1,652 37	1,691 06
$1 00	1,565 00	1,753 33	1,794 10	1,835 96	1,878 96
2 00	3,130 00	3,506 66	3,588 19	3,671 93	3,757 91
3 00	4,695 00	5,259 99	5,382 29	5,507 89	5,636 87
4 00	4,695 00	7,013 32	7,176 39	7,343 85	7,515 82
5 00	7,825 00	8,766 65	8,970 49	9,179 82	9,394 78
6 00	9,390 00	10,519 98	10,764 58	11,015 78	11,273 73
7 00	10,955 00	12,273 30	12,558 68	12,851 74	13,132 69
8 00	12,520 00	14,027 63	14,352 78	14,688 70	15,031 65
9 00	14,085 00	15,779 96	16,146 87	16,523 67	16,910 60
10 00	15,650 00	17,533 29	17,940 97	18,359 63	18,789 56
15 00	23,475 00	26,299 94	26,711 46	27,539 45	28,184 34
20 00	31,300 00	35,066 58	35,881 94	36,719 26	37,579 12
25 00	39,125 00	43,833 23	44,852 43	45,899 08	46,973 89
30 00	46,950 00	52,599 88	53,822 91	55,078 89	56,368 67
35 00	54,775 00	61,366 52	62,793 40	64,258 71	65,763 45
40 00	62,600 00	70,133 17	71,763 88	73,438 52	75,158 23
45 00	70,425 00	78,899 82	80,734 37	82,618 34	84,533 01
50 00	78,250 00	87,666 46	89,704 86	91,798 15	93,947 79

TABLE

Showing the net amount of earnings of ONE CENT to FIFTY DOLLARS *per day* for TEN YEARS of 313 working days, without interest, and with interest at 5, 6, 7, and 8 per cent., improved each *six months*.

Savings per day.	Without interest.	With interest at 5 per cent.	With interest at 6 per cent.	With interest at 7 per cent.	With interest at 8 per cent.
1	$31 13	$39 98	$42 05	$44 26	$46 60
2	62 26	79 95	84 10	88 52	93 21
3	93 39	119 93	126 16	132 77	139 81
4	124 52	159 91	168 21	177 03	186 41
5	156 50	199 89	210 26	222 29	233 01
6	187 80	239 86	252 31	265 56	279 62
7	219 10	279 84	294 36	309 80	326 22
8	250 40	319 82	336 52	354 06	372 82
9	281 70	369 80	378 47	398 22	419 42
10	313 00	399 77	420 52	442 58	466 03
15	469 50	599 66	630 78	666 87	699 04
20	626 00	799 95	841 04	885 15	932 05
25	782 50	999 43	1,051 30	1,111 44	1,165 07
30	939 00	1,199 32	1,261 56	1,327 73	1,398 08
40	1,252 00	1,599 10	1,682 09	1,770 31	1,864 11
50	1,565 00	1,998 87	2,102 61	2,212 89	2,330 13
60	1,878 00	2,398 64	2,523 13	2,655 46	2,796 16
70	2,191 00	2,798 42	2,943 65	3,098 04	3,262 19
80	2,504 00	3,198 19	3,364 17	3,540 62	3,728 22
90	2,817 00	3,599 97	3,784 69	3,982 19	4,194 24
$1 00	3,130 00	3,997 74	4,205 21	4,425 77	4,660 27
2 00	6,260 00	7,995 48	8,410 43	8,851 54	9,320 54
3 00	9,390 00	11,993 22	12,615 64	13,277 31	13,980 81
4 00	12,520 00	15,990 96	16,820 85	17,703 08	18,641 08
5 00	15,650 00	19,998 69	21,026 07	22,228 85	23,301 35
6 00	18,750 00	23,986 43	25,251 28	26,554 32	27,961 62
7 00	21,910 00	27,984 17	29,436 50	30,980 39	32,621 89
8 00	25,040 00	31,982 91	33,642 71	35,406 16	37,282 14
9 00	28,170 00	35,979 65	37,846 92	39,821 93	41,942 42
10 00	31,300 00	39,977 39	42,052 14	44,257 70	46,602 69
15 00	46,950 00	59,956 08	63,078 20	66,668 55	69,904 04
20 00	62,600 00	79,954 78	84,104 27	88,515 40	93,205 39
25 00	78,250 00	99,943 47	105,030 00	111,144 00	116,507 00
30 00	93,900 00	119,932 00	126,156 00	132,773 00	139,808 00
35 00	109,550 00	139,920 00	147,182 00	154,902 00	163,109 00
40 00	125,200 00	159,909 00	168,209 00	177,031 00	186,411 00
45 00	140,850 00	179,898 00	189,235 00	199,120 00	209,712 00
50 00	156,500 00	199,887 00	210,261 00	122,289 00	233,013 00

TABLE

Showing the net amount of earnings of ONE CENT to FIFTY DOLLARS *per day* for FIFTEEN YEARS of 313 working days, without interest, and with interest at 5, 6, 7, and 8 per cent, improved each *six months*.

Savings per day.	Without Interest.	With Interest at 5 per cent.	With Interest at 6 per cent.	With Interest at 7 per cent.	With Interest at 8 per cent.
1	$47	$69	$74	$81	$88
2	94	137	149	162	178
3	141	206	223	242	263
4	188	275	298	323	351
5	235	344	372	404	439
6	282	412	447	485	527
7	329	481	521	565	614
8	376	550	596	646	702
9	423	618	670	727	790
10	470	687	745	808	878
15	704	1,031	1,117	1,212	1,317
20	939	1,374	1,489	1,616	1,755
25	1,174	1,718	1,861	2,018	2,194
30	1,409	2,061	2,234	2,424	2,633
40	1,878	2,748	2,978	3,232	3,511
50	2,348	3,435	3,727	4,039	4,389
60	2,817	4,122	4,467	4,847	5,266
70	3,227	4,810	5,212	5,655	6,144
80	3,756	5,497	5,956	6,463	7,022
90	4,226	6,184	6,701	7,271	7,900
$1 00	4,695	6,871	7,446	8,079	8,777
2 00	9,390	13,742	14,891	16,160	17,555
3 00	14,085	20,612	22,337	24,237	26,332
4 00	18,785	27,483	29,782	32,316	35,109
5 00	23,475	34,354	37,228	40,395	43,886
6 00	28,170	41,225	44,673	48,474	52,664
7 00	32,865	48,095	52,119	56,550	61,441
8 00	37,560	54,966	59,564	64,633	70,218
9 00	42,255	61,837	67,060	72,716	78,996
10 00	46,950	68,708	74,456	80,789	87,773
15 00	70,425	103,162	111,683	121,184	131,659
20 00	93,900	137.415	148,911	161,600	175,546
25 00	117,375	171,769	186,139	201,974	219,432
30 00	140,850	206,123	223,367	242,368	263,319
35 00	164,325	240,477	260,594	282,748	307,205
40 00	187,800	274.830	297,822	323,158	351,092
45 00	211,275	309,185	335,050	363,553	394,978
50 00	234,750	343,539	372,278	409,947	438,865

TABLE

Showing the net amount of earnings of ONE CENT to FIFTY DOLLARS *per day* for TWENTY YEARS of 313 working days, without interest, and with interest at 5, 6, 7, and 8 per cent., improved each *six months*.

Savings per day.	Without Interest.	With Interest at 5 per cent.	With Interest at 6 per cent.	With Interest at 7 per cent.	With Interest at 8 per cent.
1	$63	$105	$118	$132	$149
2	126	211	236	265	297
3	189	316	354	397	446
4	252	422	472	529	595
5	313	527	590	662	744
6	376	633	708	794	892
7	438	738	826	926	1,041
8	501	844	944	1,059	1,190
9	563	949	1,062	1,191	1,338
10	626	1,055	1,180	1,323	1,487
15	939	1,582	1,770	1,985	2,231
20	1,252	2,110	2,360	2,646	2,974
25	1,565	2,637	2,950	3,308	3,718
30	1,878	3,165	3,540	3,970	4,461
40	2,504	4,219	4,720	5,293	5,949
50	3,130	5,274	5,900	6,616	7,436
60	3,756	6,329	7,081	7,939	8,923
70	4,382	7,384	8,260	9,262	10,410
80	5,008	8,439	9,440	10,586	11,897
90	5,634	9,494	10,620	11,909	13,384
$1 00	6,260	10,969	11,800	13,232	14,872
2 00	12,520	21,097	23,601	26,464	29,744
3 00	25,040	31,646	35,401	39,696	44,614
4 00	25,040	42,194	47,201	52,928	59,886
5 00	31,300	52,743	59,001	66,161	74,357
6 00	37,560	63,291	70,802	97,393	89,229
7 00	43,820	73,839	82,602	92,625	104,100
8 00	50,080	84,388	94,402	105,857	118,972
9 00	56,340	94,936	106,203	119,089	133,843
10 00	62,600	105,485	118,003	132,321	148,715
15 00	93,900	158,227	177,004	197,482	223,072
20 00	125,250	210,970	236,006	264,642	297,440
25 00	156,500	263,712	295,007	330,803	371,787
30 00	187,890	316,455	354,049	396,964	446,141
32 00	219,100	369,197	314,010	463,124	520,502
40 00	250,400	421,940	472,012	529,285	594,860
45 00	281,700	474,682	531,013	595,445	669,217
50 00	313,000	527,425	590,015	661,606	743,575

TABLE

Showing the net amount of earnings of ONE CENT to FIFTY DOLLARS *per day* for TWENTY FIVE YEARS of 313 working days, without interest, and with interest at 5, 6, 7, and 8 per cent., improved each *six months*.

Savings per day.	Without Interest.	With Interest at 5 per cent.	With Interest at 6 per cent.	With Interest at 7 per cent.	With Interest at 8 per cent.
1	$78	$153	$177	$205	$239
2	156	305	353	410	478
3	234	458	530	615	717
4	312	610	706	820	956
5	391	763	883	1,025	1,195
6	469	915	1,059	1,230	1,434
7	548	1,068	1,256	1,435	1,672
8	626	1,220	1,412	1,640	1,911
9	704	1,373	1,589	1,845	2,145
10	782	1,526	1,765	2,050	2,389
15	1,174	2,288	2,648	3,075	3,584
20	1,565	3,051	3,531	4,100	4,778
25	1,956	3,814	4,413	5,125	5,973
30	2,348	4,577	5,296	6,150	7,168
40	3,130	6,103	7,061	8,200	9,557
50	3,913	7,628	8,826	10,251	11,946
60	4,695	9,154	10,592	12,301	14,335
70	5,477	10,679	12,257	14,350	16,725
80	6,260	11,205	14,122	16,401	19,114
90	7,043	13,731	15,887	18,451	21,446
$1 00	7,825	15,256	17,653	20,501	23,892
2 00	15,650	30,513	35,305	41,002	47,785
3 00	23,475	45,769	52,958	61,504	71,677
4 00	31,400	61,025	70,611	82,005	95,570
5 00	39,125	76,282	88,264	102,506	119,462
6 00	46,950	91,538	105,916	123,007	143,354
7 00	54,775	106,794	125,569	143,501	167,247
8 00	62,600	122,050	141,221	164,009	191,139
9 00	70,425	137,307	158,874	184,511	214,462
10 00	78,250	152,563	176,527	205,012	238,924
15 00	117,375	228,845	264,791	307,518	358,386
20 00	156,500	305,126	353,054	410,023	477,848
25 00	195,625	381,408	441,318	512,549	597,310
30 00	234,750	457,689	529,581	615,035	716,772
35 00	273,875	533,976	612,845	717,506	836,734
40 00	313,000	610,252	706,108	820,047	945,696
45 00	352,125	686,534	794,372	922,553	1,072,308
50 00	391,250	762,815	882,635	1,025,059	1,194,620

TABLE

Showing the net amount of earnings of ONE CENT to FIFTY DOLLARS *per day* for THIRTY YEARS of 313 working days, without interest, and with interest at 5, 6, 7, and 8 per cent., improved each *six months*.

Savings per day.	Without Interest.	With Interest at 5 per cent.	With Interest at 6 per cent.	With Interest at 7 per cent.	With Interest at 8 per cent.
1	$94	$213	$255	$308	$372
2	288	425	510	615	745
3	282	638	756	923	1,117
4	376	851	1,021	1,230	1,490
5	470	1,064	1,276	1,538	1,862
6	563	1,277	1,531	1,845	2,235
7	657	1,490	1,786	2,153	2,606
8	751	1,703	2,041	2,460	2,980
9	845	1,915	2,297	2,768	3,352
10	939	2,128	2,552	2,956	3,725
15	1,409	3,192	3,828	4,613	5,587
20	1,878	4,257	5,104	6,151	7,449
25	2,348	5,321	6,329	7,689	9,311
30	2,817	6,385	7,555	9,226	11,174
40	3,756	8,513	10,207	12,302	14,898
50	4,695	10,641	12,759	15,377	18,628
60	5,634	12,770	15,311	18,453	22,347
70	6,573	14,898	17,863	21,528	26,062
80	7,512	17,026	20,414	24,604	29,796
90	8,451	19,154	22,966	27,679	33,521
$1 00	9,390	21,283	25,518	30,755	37,246
2 00	18,780	42,565	51,036	61,509	74,491
3 00	28,170	63,848	75,554	92,264	111,737
4 00	37,560	85,131	102,071	123,018	148,982
5 00	46,950	106,413	127,589	153,773	186,228
6 00	56,340	127,696	153,107	184,528	223,473
7 00	65,730	148,979	178,625	215,284	260,619
8 00	75,120	170,261	204,142	246,036	277,764
9 00	84,510	191,544	229,661	276,791	335,210
10 00	93,900	212,827	255,179	307,546	372,455
15 00	140,850	319,240	382,767	461,319	558,683
20 00	187,800	425,654	510,357	615,092	744,911
25 00	234,750	532,067	639,947	768,865	931,138
30 00	281,700	638,481	755,536	922,638	1,177,366
35 00	322,650	744,894	893,125	1,076,420	1,303,094
40 00	375,600	851,307	1,020,715	1,230,184	1,489,822
45 00	422,550	957,721	1,148,304	1,383,957	2,676,049
50 00	469,500	1,030,546	1,231,134	1,478,183	1,783,127

TABLE

Showing the net amount of earnings of ONE CENT to FIFTY DOLLARS *per day* for FORTY YEARS of 313 working days, without interest, and with interest at 5, 6, 7, and 8 per cent., improved each *six months*.

Savings per day.	Without Interest.	With Interest at 5 per cent.	With Interest at 6 per cent.	With Interest at 7 per cent.	With Interest at 8 per cent.
1	$125	$389	$503	$656	$863
2	250	777	1,006	1,312	1,728
3	375	1,166	1,509	1,969	2,588
4	500	1,555	2,012	2,625	3,451
5	704	1,944	2,515	3,281	4,313
6	751	2,333	3,018	3,937	5,176
7	876	2,721	3,521	4,594	6,039
8	1,002	3,110	4,023	5,250	6,902
9	1,127	3,498	4,526	5,906	7,764
10	1,409	3,887	5,029	6,562	8,627
15	1,878	5,831	7,544	9,843	12,940
20	2,504	7,774	10,059	13,124	17,254
25	3,130	9,718	12,573	16,405	21,567
30	3,756	11,662	15,088	19,686	25,881
40	5,008	15,549	20,117	26,248	34,508
50	6,260	19,436	25,147	32,810	43,135
60	7,512	23,323	30,176	39,373	51,762
70	8,764	27,210	35,205	45,945	60,389
80	10,016	31,098	40,235	52,497	69,016
90	11,268	34,985	45,264	59,059	77,643
$1 00	12,520	38,872	50,293	65,621	86,270
2 00	25,040	77,744	100,587	131,242	195,061
3 00	37,560	116,616	150,880	196,863	258,809
4 00	50,080	155,488	201,173	262,484	345,079
5 00	62,600	194,359	251,467	328,105	431,249
6 00	75,120	233,231	301,760	393,726	517,619
7 00	87,640	272,103	352,053	459,446	603,889
8 00	100,160	310,975	402,646	524,967	690,159
9 00	112,680	349,847	452,640	590,588	776,428
10 00	125,200	388,719	502,933	656,209	862,698
15 00	487,800	583,078	754,399	984,314	1,294,047
20 00	250,400	777,438	1,005,866	1,312,418	1,725,397
25 00	313,000	971,797	1,257,333	1,640,523	2,156,746
30 00	375,600	1,116,157	1,508,799	1,968,628	2,588,095
35 00	138,200	1,360,516	1,760,266	2,297,232	3,019,444
40 00	500,800	1,554,876	2,011,732	2,624,837	3,450,793
45 00	563,400	1,749,235	2,263,199	2,452,942	3,882,142
50 00	626,000	1,943,595	2,514,666	3,281,046	4,313,491

TABLE

Showing the net amount of earnings of ONE CENT to FIFTY DOLLARS *per day* for FIFTY YEARS of 313 working days, without interest, and with interest at 5, 6, 7, and 8 per cent., improved each *six months*.

Savings per day.	Without Interest.	With Interest at 5 per cent.	With Interest at 6 per cent.	With Interest at 7 per cent.	With Interest at 8 per cent.
1	$157	$677	$950	$1,350	$1,937
2	314	1,354	1,901	2,700	3,874
3	471	2,031	2,851	4,050	5,811
4	628	2,708	3,802	5,400	7,748
5	783	3,385	4,752	6,741	9,684
6	939	4,062	5,702	8,100	11,621
7	1,095	4,739	6,653	9,450	13,558
8	1,252	5,416	7,603	10,800	15,495
9	1,408	6,092	8,554	12,150	17,432
10	1,565	6,769	9,504	13,500	19,369
15	2,348	10,154	14,256	20,250	29,053
20	3,130	15,539	19,008	27,000	38,737
25	3,913	16,923	23,760	33,749	48,422
30	4,695	20,308	28,512	44,993	58,106
40	6,260	27,078	38,016	53,999	77,476
50	7,825	33,847	47,520	67,499	96,843
60	9,390	40,616	57,024	89,999	116,212
70	10,955	47,386	66,528	94,988	135,581
80	12,520	54,155	76,032	197,998	154,949
90	14,058	60,424	85,537	121,498	174,318
$1 00	15,650	67,694	95,041	134,998	193,687
2 00	31,300	135,388	190,081	269,995	387,373
3 00	46,950	203,082	285,122	404,993	581,060
4 00	62,600	270,775	380,162	539,990	774,756
5 00	78,250	388,469	475,203	674,988	968,433
6 00	93,900	406,163	570,984	809,985	1,162,119
7 00	109,550	473,857	665,284	944,983	1,355,806
8 00	125,200	541,551	760,325	1,079,980	1,549,493
9 00	140,850	609,245	855,365	1,214,978	1,743,179
10 00	156,500	676,939	950,406	1,349,976	1,936,866
15 00	234,750	1,015,407	1,425,606	2,024,963	2,905,299
20 00	313,000	1,353,877	1,900,812	2,699,951	3,873,732
25 00	391,250	1,692,347	2,376,015	3,374,939	4,842,165
30 00	469,500	2,030,816	2,851,218	4,049,927	5,810,598
35 00	447,750	2,369,285	3,326,412	4,724,924	6,779,031
40 00	626,000	2,707,755	3,801,624	5,399,902	7,747,564
45 00	704,250	3,046,224	4,276,827	6,074,890	8,715,897
50 00	782,500	3,384,693	4,752,030	6,749,878	9,684,330

CHAPTER XXII.

BANKING AND INSURANCE.

Banks of discount.—Making money with money.—Distinct trade.—
Banking successful.— Why.— Compared with traders.—Machinery of money-making.—Mint.—Comparison.—Must know
how.— Process of banking.—Note' done.— Lesson.—Trained
business men.— Dividends.—General principles.—Popularity
of officers.—Indiscreet Teller.—Money lost.—Treatment of
customers.—Savings banks.—How organized.—Charitable and
useful device.—Mode of doing business.--Valuable to depositors.
Influence on people.— Makes respectability.—New world.—
Gains suitors.—Compound interest tables.—Uses.—Examples.
Insurance.—Different kinds.—Money-making.--Like banking.--
Cannot afford to lose.—Winning on marine.—Property insured.
Look out.—See to your agreement.—Read it over.—Make inquiries.— Down to the ground.— Save on a loss.— Money
lost.—Look to the obligation.—Study your men.—Friends.—
Chaffer on paying.—General Principles.—Sound judgment.—
Honest intent pays well.

BANKING is of three kinds—the banks of discount and deposit, Savings Banks, and individual or private Banks. All of them have but one object, and that is to *make money with money.* This is an all-important principle for the money-maker; and to know how this is done accomplishes a great object. It is not to be presumed, here, to give such institutions or individuals any information *how* this is to be done ; for their success, generally, is a proof that they understand that. Further than that, it is an occupation, and it may be called a trade within itself, requiring long experience, extensive knowledge of values, good judgment, great firmness ; and, in fact, every business qualification in its highest perfection. By referring to banking as one of the most extensive means of making money with money, is simply to show the money-maker, after he has got his dollar, how others manage other dollars to advantage, so that he may know the danger of managing his with his trifling information—a subject that requires such superior knowledge and acquirements to do well.

There are no statistics at hand that will directly compare any other trade or business with banking, in the way of success. It is presumed, however, that it may be safely laid down that there are not five per cent. of failures in regular banking business, when there is ninety or ninety-five per cent. of failures in commercial business. Both deal in the same things, the one in the articles themselves, the other by their representation in paper. Now this fact is sufficient to awaken the mind of the merchant or trader to an investigation of the manner in which Banks handle their values ; what they do, how they do it, when they do it, and how they succeed, while I lose and fail. And now, Mr. Trader, or Merchant, if you are sufficiently awake to this fact to make the investigation, and profit by it, you have done the best day's work you ever did in your life. But the chances are, you will say, " Poh ! a Bank is one thing, and a mercantile business is another." And let me say, you say the truth, as both are conducted at the present day. The result, however, is that one is a success, while the other is a failure.

It will be interesting to the trader to look at the statistics on page 88, and read, that a bank in Boston had occasion to look back to their accounts, and the result was, that " of the *one thousand accounts* which were opened with them in starting, only six remained. They had, in forty years, either *failed* or died destitute *of property.*" The bank stood, while nine hundred and ninety-four traders, out of the thousand, had gone down.

But, it is not alone the trader who is interested in this question ; it is every one who has made his dollar, or who is in the way of making it, who is interested in knowing what machinery is used in banking, whereby money is made out of money ; and further than that, to know that it requires machinery of a peculiarly delicate nature, well-managed, to accomplish the object—at least in this special way of making money with money. Half the people who have labored for their dollar do not know that such machinery can have the least bearing upon what they have made ; that to put their dollar through this machinery, or a process like it, that it will come out one *increased in value.* The trouble being that they generally put it into a machine where it never comes out at all, and hence they never see the dollar, or its increase.

Can the machinery of a mint be made by a novice? or can it be worked by one entirely ignorant of its construction? Just as well might the man undertake to increase his dollar without the necessary knowledge of the required machinery, as to make a metallic dollar without knowing how it should be made, and a knowledge of how to make it. This trade of increasing the dollar by making the dollar work is not caught up by inspiration, or acquired in an instant ; and he who has a dollar to set at work, must know well how it is to be done, or he must find it in a machine that is known to do this kind of work well, or loss of it is the inevitable consequence. Hence the long list of failures and wide-spread poverty among our most worthy and energetic men, not to accomplish, to earn, or even to amass, but to save, because their dollar goes into the wrong-machine.

The *process* of banking is the machinery required to make money with money. Then what is this process? In the Banks of discount and deposit, a number of individuals generally put in a certain amount of money, and that is represented by stock. The stockholders assemble and elect a number of directors, and they elect a superintendent, generally called a President, and a Cashier. People deposit their money for safe keeping, and for convenience, and the original money put in by the stockholders, with the deposits, make a capital to purchase moneyed securities with—generally notes of hand, which represent property of some kind. The bank is then ready to do business, as it is called; that is, to put out their money on short dates for an increase. Up to this point, the whole matter is very simple, and any one could do it. But now comes the tug of war—whether it shall be success or failure, even in this business.

The merchant comes in with a note taken for goods sold, and says to the Cashier; "I wish you would give me the money on this." The answer is: "I will hand it to the President, and give you an answer." The President lays the paper before the Board of Directors, and if the paper is strongly endorsed, or has enough collateral to make the loan *perfectly safe*, the note is "done" as it is called, and the merchant gets the money on it. Now, Mr. Merchant, or Mr. Trader, or Mr. anybody else who has a dollar to set at work, do you see anything in this that attracts your attention? When you take a note, or part with property or money, do you do anything like this? Do you submit your transactions for approval to two sharp, experienced business men, who, not relying upon their own judgment, summon to their aid ten or twelve other first-class business men, to decide upon the *security* offered ? Remember that in the first place, they require at least two good strong names to start with, or collateral security, and then that the time of payment is very short—from thirty to ninety days.

Sometimes, even with these precautions a bank loses, but not very often. By having two names and the time of payment short, one or the other will as a rule prove good. There is no business transaction which has not some risk, the only main question being to reduce that risk as low as possible by every conceivable precaution. In this transaction of taking a note, possibly of $500, twelve to fourteen highly and long trained business men consult as to the value of the security to be taken, and every one *interested* in a money point of view in the result. An individual, therefore, who has a security to take can consult no one else who has a like interest with him. Such investments. are generally made by references to individuals who have no interest with the one who parts with his property, but whose interest, as a general rule, is to have you part with your property, that they may get pay for the property they have parted with.

Do you think a Bank would part with their money on such terms, or on such representations ? If they did every one knows what would be the result. Do you wonder then, reader, that traders fail on such a system of credits, or that Banks succeed by such care, caution, and scrutinizing discrimination ? The Banks declare and divide their earnings to the stockholders, who make new investments in like manner, while the trader makes no dividends, puts nothing away to the good, but keeps all his eggs in one basket subject to the vicissitudes of trade. Does the ordinary dealer see nothing in the adverse principles which will open his eyes to a system of business which all experience has shown but leads to disaster?

Banks of discount and deposit are useful, as a means of making money with money, to those who have comparatively large sums to set at work in this way. But there is a class of Banks called Savings Banks, where any one can in like manner set at work any sum of money, from one cent upward. But the amount of profit derived is not so great, generally, as in the Banks of discount and deposit. The Savings Banks will be treated separately hereafter, as being the most available and the best means for those unacquainted with business to set their small means to work with safety.

Although Banks present the nearest approach to perfection in the interchange of values represented by paper, there are certain general principles which will increase these earnings. These may be briefly stated to be—

First. The business qualifications of its officers.
Second. The judicious selections of its credit.
Third. The current expenses.
Fourth. General reputation.

The personal popularity of the officers of a Bank, and the manner in which customers or depositors are treated, either loses or wins money for the concern; the same general rules of polite intercourse holding in those cases as in transactions between merchants, or merchants and consumers. No shrewd business man will ever neglect this principle, whether he is in a Bank or in any other business where his profits depend upon people who have a choice, and can give their money to one or to another.

If a dealer goes into a Bank to get his own money, and an indiscreet teller makes him wait while he has an agreeable chat with his fellow-clerk, or to add up a column of figures as long as a man's arm, which he could just as well postpone, he is unfit for his place, and is a damage to the Bank, and is money lost to it. For say what you will, the dealer feels uncomfortable; and, instead of using his influence to aid that institution, he will hold back, if he does not damage it in some way. Instead of having an active friend, the Bank will have a quasi one, if not an enemy; and there is no telling when his influence, by a word, may strike to its damage or loss of money. Any other like neglect or carelessness on the part of a Bank Officer will tend to the same result.

To be polite, attentive, pleasant, and agreeable to all, while business is done on business principles, will bring dollars into the deposit-line, and keep them there. They will make friends whose influence will be exerted towards bringing new business and opening new avenues of profit. They will light up an interest in the welfare and prosperity of the institution that will stand sentinel over its interests, and sound alarms in case of danger of loss. They will infuse into its whole business a thrift and general reputation, which will roll heavily in on the deposit-line, and roll out heavily on the dividend. In case of difficulty all will pay such an institution who can.

SAVINGS BANKS.

These are institutions organized and conducted by men of knowledge and skill in financial matters, for the sole benefit of persons who wish to save and improve small sums of money, who have no knowledge where or how to place them to bring an interest, and at the same time be subject to their call. The device is eminently useful and truly charitable. The institution requires a good building to do business in, and officers to transact it. They take the deposits of money and invest in large sums at a higher rate of interest than they pay to the depositors, the difference going to pay current expenses. The interest received is generally seven per cent., from that to six per cent., and the interest paid is from five to six per cent.

The Bank holds itself ready at all times to meet any obligation on demand to the depositor. The advantages resulting to the depositor is apparent, since he cannot invest small sums safely in any other way. For the depositor generally knows nothing of business financiering, and it would be costly to get security by any other means. Then other securities are not always convertible into cash without some loss.

Too much cannot be said in favor of Savings Institutions for the protection of earnings and as incentives to economy. A sure and certain means by which in a few years, as has been seen, an independence can be obtained, and when obtained the money is within reach.

The money that the mechanic, day-laborer, house servant, or male or female operative spends in trifles which neither add to their comfort or their happiness is a powerful stream of wealth, which, if poured into a Savings Institution, soon becomes a large amount of money. The first dollar thus saved and anchored is the incentive to further additions and the taste for economy, and a desire to add will increase with each deposit.

Such an individual makes a conservative member of

society, and a good and prosperous citizen. If a man or woman has made the first deposit in a bank for savings, that moment their services are more valuable, and higher wages can be obtained from their employers. It is a guarantee—an indorsement that their course of life is governed by *saving principles*, and that they will not destroy or waste the property of their employer. No one, then, should fail to make their first deposit, and no one should fail to drill themselves to strict principles of economy. By economy is meant the leaving off of such expenses as are not necessary either for comfort or for respectability. It should also be remembered that such a course of life commands respect, and elevates the individual. Any one feels more independent, and carries the evidence of it in his whole demeanor, when free of debt, and has money at interest. If this should be disputed by any one, let them try it ; and they will find, from that moment, that they live in a new world.

A person, no matter what his walk in life, is more looked up to by his peers if he is known to be free of embarrassments, and has money at his command. The principle extends to the serving-girl, to the housemaid, and to all classes of persons. Let it be known that an industrious young woman has some money in a Bank, and has her book as the evidence, though the real contents be forever unknown, the fact gives her consequence and suitors too. No surer way for such a one to get a husband, and a good one, than to be in the possession of money of her own earnings in a Bank.

The compound interest tables are given, that any one can determine the amount of earning of any sum from ONE to ONE HUNDRED years. The earnings are given for *one dollar;* and if it be desirable to find the earnings

TABLE.—COMPOUND INTEREST.

Showing the *Amount* of $1 improved at Compound Interest for any number of years not exceeding 100.

YEARS.	1 per cent.	1½ per cent.	2 per cent.	2½ per cent.	3 per cent.	3½ per cent.	4 per cent.	4½ per cent.	5 per cent.	6 per cent.	7 per cent.	8 per cent.
1	$1 01	$1 02	$1 02	$1 03	$1 03	$1 04	$1 04	$1 05	$1 05	$1 06	$1 07	$1 08
2	1 02	1 03	1 04	1 05	1 06	1 07	1 08	1 09	1 10	1 12	1 14	1 17
3	1 03	1 05	1 06	1 08	1 09	1 11	1 12	1 14	1 16	1 19	1 23	1 26
4	1 04	1 06	1 08	1 10	1 13	1 15	1 17	1 19	1 22	1 26	1 31	1 36
5	1 05	1 08	1 10	1 13	1 16	1 19	1 22	1 25	1 28	1 34	1 40	1 47
6	1 06	1 09	1 13	1 16	1 19	1 23	1 27	1 30	1 34	1 42	1 50	1 59
7	1 07	1 11	1 15	1 19	1 23	1 27	1 32	1 36	1 41	1 50	1 61	1 71
8	1 08	1 13	1 17	1 22	1 27	1 32	1 37	1 42	1 48	1 59	1 72	1 85
9	1 09	1 14	1 20	1 25	1 30	1 36	1 42	1 49	1 55	1 69	1 84	2 00
10	1 10	1 16	1 22	1 28	1 34	1 41	1 48	1 55	1 63	1 79	1 97	2 16
11	1 12	1 18	1 24	1 31	1 38	1 46	1 54	1 62	1 71	1 90	2 10	2 33
12	1 13	1 20	1 27	1 34	1 43	1 51	1 60	1 70	1 80	2 01	2 25	2 52
13	1 14	1 21	1 29	1 38	1 47	1 56	1 67	1 77	1 89	2 13	2 41	2 72
14	1 15	1 23	1 32	1 41	1 51	1 62	1 73	1 85	1 98	2 26	2 58	2 94
15	1 16	1 25	1 35	1 45	1 56	1 68	1 80	1 94	2 08	2 40	2 76	3 17
16	1 17	1 27	1 37	1 48	1 60	1 73	1 87	2 02	2 18	2 54	2 95	3 43
17	1 18	1 29	1 40	1 52	1 65	1 79	1 95	2 11	2 29	2 69	3 16	3 70
18	1 20	1 31	1 43	1 56	1 70	1 86	2 03	2 21	2 41	2 85	3 38	4 00
19	1 21	1 33	1 46	1 60	1 75	1 92	2 11	2 31	2 53	3 03	3 62	4 32
20	1 22	1 35	1 49	1 64	1 81	1 99	2 19	2 41	2 65	3 21	3 87	4 66
21	1 23	1 37	1 52	1 68	1 86	2 06	2 28	2 52	2 79	3 40	4 14	5 03
22	1 24	1 39	1 55	1 72	1 92	2 13	2 37	2 63	2 93	3 60	4 43	5 44
23	1 26	1 41	1 58	1 76	1 97	2 21	2 46	2 75	3 07	3 82	4 74	5 87
24	1 27	1 43	1 61	1 81	2 03	2 28	2 56	2 88	3 23	4 05	5 07	6 34
25	1 28	1 45	1 64	1 85	2 09	2 36	2 67	3 01	3 39	4 29	5 43	6 85
26	1 30	1 47	1 67	1 90	2 16	2 45	2 77	3 14	3 56	4 55	5 81	7 40
27	1 31	1 49	1 71	1 95	2 22	2 53	2 88	3 28	3 73	4 82	6 21	7 99
28	1 32	1 52	1 74	2 00	2 29	2 62	3 00	3 43	3 92	5 11	6 65	8 63
29	1 33	1 54	1 78	2 05	2 36	2 71	3 12	3 58	4 12	5 42	7 11	9 32
30	1 35	1 56	1 81	2 10	2 43	2 81	3 24	3 75	4 32	5 74	7 61	10 06
31	1 36	1 59	1 85	2 15	2 50	2 91	3 37	3 91	4 54	6 09	8 15	10 87
32	1 37	1 61	1 88	2 20	2 58	3 01	3 51	4 09	4 76	6 45	8 72	11 74
33	1 39	1 63	1 92	2 26	2 65	3 11	3 65	4 27	5 00	6 84	9 33	12 68
34	1 40	1 66	1 96	2 32	2 73	3 22	3 79	4 47	5 25	7 25	9 98	13 69
35	1 42	1 68	2 00	2 37	2 81	3 33	3 95	4 67	5 52	7 69	10 68	14 79
36	1 43	1 71	2 04	2 43	2 90	3 45	4 10	4 88	5 79	8 15	11 42	15 97
37	1 45	1 73	2 08	2 49	2 99	3 57	4 27	5 10	6 08	8 64	12 22	17 25
38	1 46	1 76	2 12	2 56	3 07	3 70	4 44	5 33	6 39	9 15	13 08	18 63
39	1 47	1 79	2 16	2 62	3 17	3 83	4 62	5 57	6 70	9 70	13 99	20 12
40	1 49	1 81	2 21	2 69	3 26	3 96	4 80	5 82	7 04	10 29	14 97	21 72
41	1 50	1 84	2 25	2 75	3 36	4 10	4 99	6 08	7 39	10 90	16 02	23 46
42	1 52	1 87	2 30	2 82	3 46	4 24	5 19	6 35	7 76	11 56	17 14	25 34
43	1 53	1 90	2 34	2 89	3 56	4 39	5 40	6 64	8 15	12 25	18 34	27 37
44	1 55	1 93	2 39	2 96	3 67	4 54	5 62	6 94	8 56	12 99	19 63	29 56
45	1 56	1 95	2 44	3 04	3 78	4 70	5 84	7 25	8 99	13 76	21 00	31 92
46	1 58	1 98	2 49	3 11	3 90	4 87	6 08	7 57	9 43	14 59	22 47	34 47
47	1 60	2 01	2 54	3 19	4 01	5 04	6 32	7 92	9 91	15 47	24 05	37 23
48	1 61	2 04	2 59	3 27	4 13	5 21	6 57	8 27	10 40	16 39	25 73	40 21
49	1 63	2 07	2 64	3 35	4 26	5 40	6 83	8 64	10 92	17 38	27 53	43 43
50	1 64	2 11	2 69	3 44	4 38	5 58	7 11	9 03	11 47	18 42	29 46	46 90

And how to Keep it. 283

TABLE.—COMPOUND INTEREST.

Showing the *Amount* of $1 improved at Compound Interest for any number of years not exceeding 100.

YEARS.	1 per cent.	1½ per cent.	2 per cent.	2½ per cent.	3 per cent.	3½ per cent.	4 per cent.	4½ per cent.	5 per cent.	6 per cent.	7 per cent.	8 per cent.
51	$1 66	$2 14	$2 75	$3 52	$4 52	$5 78	$7 39	$9 44	$12 04	$19 53	$31 52	$50 65
52	1 68	2 17	2 80	3 61	4 65	5 98	7 69	9 86	12 64	20 70	33 73	54 71
53	1 69	2 20	2 86	3 70	4 79	6 19	7 99	10 31	13 28	21 94	36 09	59 08
54	1 71	2 23	2 91	3 79	4 93	6 41	8 31	10 77	13 94	23 26	38 61	63 81
55	1 73	2 27	2 97	3 89	5 08	6 63	8 65	11 26	14 64	24 65	41 32	68 91
56	1 75	2 30	3 03	3 99	5 23	6 87	8 99	11 76	15 37	26 13	44 21	74 43
57	1 76	2 34	3 09	4 09	5 39	7 11	9 35	12 29	16 14	27 70	47 30	80 38
58	1 78	2 37	3 15	4 19	5 55	7 35	9 73	12 85	16 94	29 36	50 61	86 81
59	1 80	2 41	3 22	4 29	5 72	7 61	10 12	13 42	17 79	31 12	54 16	93 76
60	1 82	2 44	3 28	4 40	5 89	7 88	10 52	14 03	18 68	32 99	57 95	101 26
61	1 83	2 48	3 35	4 51	6 07	8 15	10 94	14 66	19 61	34 97	62 00	109 36
62	1 85	2 52	3 41	4 62	6 25	8 44	11 38	15 32	20 59	37 06	66 34	118 11
63	1 87	2 55	3 48	4 74	6 44	8 73	11 83	16 01	21 62	39 29	70 99	127 55
64	1 89	2 59	3 55	4 86	6 63	9 04	12 31	16 73	22 70	41 65	75 96	137 76
65	1 91	2 63	3 62	4 98	6 83	9 36	12 80	17 48	23 84	44 14	81 27	148 78
66	1 93	2 67	3 69	5 10	7 03	9 68	13 31	18 27	25 03	46 79	86 96	160 68
67	1 95	2 71	3 77	5 23	7 25	10 02	13 84	19 09	26 28	49 60	93 05	173 54
68	1 97	2 75	3 84	5 36	7 46	10 37	14 40	19 95	27 60	52 53	99 56	187 42
69	1 99	2 79	3 92	5 49	7 69	10 74	14 97	20 85	28 98	55 73	106 53	202 41
70	2 01	2 84	4 00	5 63	7 92	11 11	15 57	21 78	30 43	59 08	113 99	218 61
71	2 03	2 88	4 08	5 77	8 16	11 50	16 19	22 76	31 95	62 62	121 97	236 09
72	2 05	2 92	4 16	5 92	8 40	11 90	16 84	23 79	33 55	66 38	130 51	254 98
73	2 07	2 96	4 24	6 07	8 65	12 32	17 52	24 86	35 22	70 36	139 64	275 38
74	2 09	3 01	4 33	6 22	8 91	12 75	18 22	25 98	36 98	74 58	149 42	297 41
75	2 11	3 05	4 42	6 37	9 18	13 20	18 95	27 15	38 83	79 06	159 88	321 20
76	2 13	3 10	4 50	6 53	9 45	13 66	19 70	28 37	40 77	83 80	171 07	346 90
77	2 15	3 15	4 59	6 69	9 74	14 14	20 49	29 65	42 81	88 83	183 04	374 65
78	2 17	3 19	4 69	6 86	10 03	14 63	21 31	30 98	44 95	94 16	195 85	404 63
79	2 19	3 24	4 78	7 03	10 33	15 15	22 16	32 37	47 20	99 81	209 56	437 00
80	2 22	3 29	4 88	7 21	10 64	15 68	23 05	33 83	49 56	105 80	224 23	471 95
81	2 24	3 34	4 97	7 39	10 96	16 22	23 97	35 35	52 04	112 14	239 93	509 71
82	2 26	3 39	5 07	7 57	11 29	16 79	24 93	36 94	54 64	118 87	256 73	550 49
83	2 28	3 44	5 17	7 76	11 63	17 38	25 93	38 61	57 37	126 00	274 70	594 53
84	2 31	3 49	5 28	7 96	11 98	17 99	26 97	40 34	60 24	133 57	293 93	642 09
85	2 33	3 54	5 38	8 16	12 34	18 62	28 04	42 16	63 25	141 58	314 50	693 46
86	2 35	3 60	5 49	8 36	12 71	19 27	29 17	44 06	66 42	150 07	336 52	748 93
87	2 33	3 65	5 60	8 57	13 09	19 94	30 33	46 04	69 74	159 08	360 07	808 85
88	2 40	3 71	5 71	8 78	13 48	20 64	31 55	48 11	73 22	168 62	385 28	873 56
89	2 42	3 76	5 83	9 00	13 88	21 36	32 81	50 27	76 89	178 74	412 25	943 44
90	2 45	3 82	5 94	9 23	14 30	22 11	34 12	52 54	80 73	189 46	441 10	1,018 92
91	2 47	3 88	6 06	9 46	14 73	22 89	35 48	54 90	84 77	200 83	471 98	1,100 43
92	2 50	3 93	6 18	9 70	15 17	26 69	36 90	57 37	89 01	212 88	505 02	1,188 46
93	2 52	3 99	6 31	9 94	15 63	24 52	38 38	59 95	93 46	225 66	540 37	1,283 54
94	2 55	4 05	6 43	10 19	16 10	25 37	39 91	62 65	98 13	239 19	578 20	1,386 22
95	2 57	4 11	6 56	10 44	16 58	26 26	41 51	65 47	103 03	253 55	618 67	1,497 12
96	2 60	4 18	6 69	10 70	17 08	27 18	43 17	68 42	108 19	268 76	661 98	1,616 89
97	2 63	4 24	6 83	10 97	17 59	28 13	44 90	71 50	113 60	284 88	708 31	1,746 24
98	2 65	4 30	6 96	11 24	18 12	29 12	46 69	74 71	119 28	301 98	757 90	1,885 94
99	2 68	4 37	7 10	11 53	18 66	30 14	48 56	78 08	125 24	320 10	810 95	2,036 82
100	2 70	4 43	7 24	11 81	19 22	31 19	50 50	81 59	131 50	339 30	867 72	2,199 76

of any other sum, multiply such sum by the amount in the proper place at any interest from *one* to *eight* per cent.: thus, wanted the compound interest of 27 dollars for 21 years at 3½ per cent. per annum. The compound interest of a dollar for that time is $2.06, multiplied by 27 dollars gives $55.62, and in like manner for any other sum.

INSURANCE.

Under this head is classed a variety of modes and kinds of Insurances. Among the most prominent, are fire, marine, inland and life insurance. They all belong to that class of business,—making money with money. They are again subdivided into cash and mutual. They are considered here more as specimens of how money can be made with money, as of interest to the money-maker, than as any special commendation of them, as the most profitable or the least profitable mode of doing so. It is more to explain their existence as a means of saving than of making.

Like banking, they are usually conducted by able business men, and in very much the same way. They are necessities to those having property at the risk of the elements, and who cannot afford to lose without embarrassments. To the money-maker they are invaluable as a means of preventing loss, and to those who have accumulated are a means of making their money work to advantage. Sometimes the profits of such business are very large; and sometimes, and more frequently than in banking, a total loss of the money invested. In all business where the profits are large, a corresponding risk is run of loss. There is a fairer chance of winning on marine than on fire insurance, all other things being equal.

But the benefit such institutions are to the moneymaker is, that, if his property is in such things as can be destroyed by the elements, he can, by the payment of a small amount of money annually, cover his loss if one occurs. Therefore, every one who is endeavoring to make money should keep such kind of property *fully* insured. An hour's neglect may lose you years of toil. Then look out when you make your agreement with a company; see that it is put into the body of the policy, and read your policy over from the first word to the last, carefully. See *what* you agree to, and *what* they agree to do. Possibly not one half the policies that are signed are read over. People suppose they are all right, and so they may be. But read, nevertheless.

If you do not know the officers to be honest and honorable men, having a high standing as such in the community, let such companies alone, they will probably not pay you if you have a loss. If, too, you know of a company chaffierng and screwing down a loss, and do not pay fairly, let it alone; these men will treat *you* in the same way in your distress. They have been paid to pay your loss in full to the extent of your policy, and should do so as cheerfully as take your money. Look more to the character of the men managing than to the capital, but look well to both. Don't trust your property in their hands without you know them, or of them, "down to the ground." You had better pay a fair company, one who will take the pains to find out what your *whole loss* is and pay it promptly, a large price at first, than have ten times that amount shaved off when your loss occurs.

No company will ever undertake this without they are

steeped in ignorance of their true interests; nor will they retain an agent for one moment who will try to *save on a loss*. It is more money out of their pockets than out of that of the insured. The manner in which losses are settled by companies draws business and profit, or repels it and makes loss. No one will ever forget the company or man who shaves him under such circumstances, nor will he forget the one who deals honestly with him.

The insured, then, may be called upon to take the promise to pay of a company for a large amount. Ask yourself would a Bank take their note for this amount, and give the money upon it. Then, to have profited duly by the lessons you have read, you must inquire of as many as twelve or fourteen successful business men if they would do so; and if they all agree, knowing the company, and would trust it, you may insure—as a safe rule, and not otherwise.

On the other hand, the company may be subject to fraud on the part of the insured. It is for their interest never to assume fraud without positive proof, or at least such proof as would convince a jury of the fact. Better pay, and look more carefully to the character of the insured next time. They will make more money in the end. Neither for their own interest should they chaffer about the payment of such a loss without they conclude to test it by law, as a compromise would injure them more than the amount saved, as one-half of those who heard of it would take it for granted that it was an unjust settlement.

The same general principles of civility and pleasant manners, and an interest in the insured, holds good in this business, as in banking business. All tells to the profit of the company and the enlargement of dividends ; and generally there is no business where sound judgment, honest intent, general reputation and policy is rewarded with more promptness than in this.

CHAPTER XXIII.

LIFE INSURANCE.

Origin of Life Insurance. — Progress. — Companies established. — Object. — Death may prevent. — Three hard problems. — Mortality table.—Life expectancy.—Duties to reader.—Four kinds of Insurance Companies. —Stock.—Mutuals.—Crowning beauty.—Mutual plan.—Twenty and ten per cent. brokerage. — Decisive. — Community recommend. — Mutual Life.— Organization. — Main feature. — Equitable principles. — Most made. — General principle. — Note and cash mutuals all profits equally divided. — Frightful exhibit. — Non-forfeiting principle.—What mutual life has done.—Good exhibit.—Whole life policies. — For whom most suitable. — Secure to wife. —Table rates.—Examples.—Grand result.—Change of ideas. —Comparison stocks and mutual.—Losses and gains.—Whole life policy illustrated.—Five and ten year payments.—Ten year payments illustrated. — Good thing. — Instalment feature. — Practical operation.—Endowment policy.—Table of rates.— What Mutual Life says.—Equitable return.—Illustration of ten year and annual endowments.—Children's endowments.—Table of rates.—Not recommended.—Surrender of policies.—Special notice.—An act.—Explanation of author.—Annuities. — Survivorship annuity.—Single life annuity.—Tables for survivorship and single life annuities.

The first public office for the insuring of lives originated with the Rev. William Anhote, D.D., of Middleton, in Lancashire, England, for the benefit of the widows of clergymen and others, and for the settling of jointures and annuities This design was undertaken and established by the "Mercers' Company," which in 1698 settled the sum of £2,888 per annum as a security for the yearly payment of £30 during the life of any widow whose husband had, in his health, subscribed £100 to the fund; and so in proportion for any greater or less amount. In 1699 another similar institution was formed, under the name of "The Society of Assurance for Widows and Orphans." In July, 1706, the first general office for this kind of security was founded by a charter from Queen Anne, and called

"The Amicable Society, or Perpetual Assurance;" and it is probable that about the same period many other projects of a like nature appeared, of which no traces are now remaining.

"The Royal Exchange Assurance Company" was established by a charter dated June 20, 1720; the original powers of which were extended by another charter, issued in the following year, to the *insurance of lives* and against casualties and accidents by fire. The "London Assurance Company" was also incorporated in 1721, in consequence of the same Act, for granting similar securities; and these appear to have been the only associations instituted for general life insurances until the year 1762, when "The Equitable Society" was formed, in consequence of the recommendation of Professor Simpson in his lectures. Mr. James Dodson also appears to have assisted in the design, by supporting the plan, and composing some of the tables. About the same period, a number of other societies were projected and formed, under the specious pretence of being institutions "for the benefit of old age," being, however, for the most part, false in principle, and mischievous in effect; but towards the conclusion of the eighteenth century, and the commencement of the present, several new and valuable companies for life insurance were founded. The following statement furnishes, perhaps, the clearest view of the advance and employment of life insurances down to the present time: In England, from 1706 to this date, upwards of 100 life insurance companies have been founded. The first life insurance company established in the United States was the "Hospital Life Insurance Company" of Boston, which commenced its operations in the year 1825. The "New York Life and Trust Company" then followed in 1829, but the life insurance department of their business was very limited. It will be seen that this subject is comparatively new in this country, few persons having availed themselves of its advantages prior to the year 1843, when the first mutual companies were established, under the names of the ."Mutual Life Insurance Company of New York," and the "New England Life Insurance Company of Boston." The next were the "State Mutual, of Worcester, Mass.," the "Mutual Benefit of Newark," and the "New York Life Insurance Company," of New York City, established in 1845. Since that date several other companies have been established in different sections of the country.— NORTON.

It will be seen from this that Life Insurance is attracting more attention each year; and, as every one knows, has now become a highly important feature in the financial world. The object is of such a nature as to commend itself to every reflecting mind. As we have insisted that it is the *moral and political duty* of all to so arrange their affairs financially, that they under *no* circumstances shall become a burden upon the public or upon friends, this department of finance seems the best way by which such a result can be obtained. For if the individual be alone, and no one dependent upon him, it will be shown that he can *accumulate* for himself, as fast as in any other way, on *small amounts*, while if he has others dependent upon him, it is the *only* way that an independence can be certainly obtained for them.

However industrious, prudent, and saving one may be under such circumstances of protection, death stands at his door to put an end at any time to such efforts, however well directed. There is then but one loop-hole of escape from such responsibility, and but one way by which any one thus situated may see his way clear, and conquer even the efforts of death to prevent. The life insurance meets this case; and while it does this effectually, if it at the same time accomplishes another end, of making money make money to the best advantage, it is still better; but if still again it shows how, and *does* keep it, a treble result is obtained; and three harder problems are not to be found in the range of financial skill. If, then, their solution can be accomplished by the most simple and uneducated in finance, here may be said to be the Eldorado of the protector's hope, if not of the unskilled money-maker and saver.

Let every one, then, who has such obligations upon him, consider well their binding force, politically and socially, if he has no promptings of affection or love to the same end. As a means of quickening these considerations, let him look over a mortality table, which we furnish, with his expectancy of life, and it will in all probability arouse him to sudden and energetic action in the right direction, before his opportunities to do so are ended, with no chance to retrace or amend.

TABLE

Showing the probable number of persons living at the end of each year out of every 1,000 born at the same time, and the life expectancy; as calculated from the Carlisle Table of Mortality.

Age.	No. Living.	Expec.	Age.	No. Living.	Expec.	Age.	No. Living.	Expec.	Age.	No. Living.	Expec.
1	846	44⅔	27	579	36½	53	421	19	79	108	5⅘
2	778	47½	28	575	35⅔	54	414	18¼	80	95	5½
3	727	50	29	570	35	55	407	17½	81	84	5¼
4	700	50¾	30	564	34⅓	56	400	17	82	72	5
5	680	51¼	31	558	33⅔	57	392	16¼	83	62	4⅔
6	668	51⅛	32	553	33	58	384	15½	84	53	4⅜
7	659	51	33	547	32⅓	59	375	15	85	44	4⅛
8	654	50¼	34	542	31⅔	60	364	14⅓	86	37	3⅞
9	649	49½	35	536	31	61	352	14	87	30	3¾
10	646	49	36	531	30⅓	62	340	13⅓	88	23	3⅝
11	643	48	37	525	29⅔	63	327	13	89	16	3½
12	640	47¼	38	519	29	64	314	12¼	90	14	3¼
13	637	46½	39	514	28¼	65	302	11¾	91	10	3¼
14	633	45¾	40	507	27½	66	289	11¼	92	7	3⅜
15	630	45	41	501	27	67	277	10¾	93	5	3½
16	626	44¼	42	494	26⅓	68	265	10¼	94	4	3½
17	622	43½	43	487	25¾	69	252	9¾	95	3	3½
18	618	43	44	480	25⅛	70	240	9⅛	96	2	3½
19	613	42⅛	45	473	24½	71	228	8⅔	97	2	3¼
20	609	41½	46	466	24	72	214	8⅛	98	1	3
21	605	40¾	47	459	23⅙	73	200	7¾	99	1	2¾
22	600	40	48	452	22½	74	184	7⅓	100	1	2¼
23	596	39⅓	49	446	22	75	167	7	101	1	1¾
24	592	38½	50	440	21⅛	76	151	6⅔	102	0	
25	588	38	51	434	20⅜	77	136	6⅜	103	0	
26	584	37⅛	52	428	19⅔	78	121	6	104	0	

The basis of life insurance is laid in what are denominated Mortality Tables. They are prepared by taking a large number of cases, and from experience ascertaining the average extent in duration of life, from any given age. The results vary in different parts of the world. The table now in use as a basis, with slight variations in practice in this country, is taken from observations for nine years, ending in 1787, at Carlisle, in England. The length of time any one has by their chances to live is called their *life expectancy*. A close inspection of this table will show what the life insurance is intended to guard against.

So far as the objects of this work are involved in this very important principle of life insurance, we have but two duties to perform to the reader.

First—To show the best means of using it.

Second—To point out the safest and most lucrative plan to use it.

This article, and for this object, was first written about seven years ago, and the conclusions arrived at then have materially changed in its favor within that time. All, however, we hold ourselves responsible for now, is simply to furnish *facts*, and give an individual opinion upon them, which it is believed will be borne out by subsequent results.

Insurance companies are principally founded upon *four* different bases: the cash stock and cash premiums, in which the insured have no interest in the profits, the other *three* being mutual, in which the insured have an interest in the profits. Of these latter some have a cash capital, and the premiums are paid in cash and in notes. Others have no cash capital, and the premiums are paid in like manner; while others have no cash capital, and the premiums are all paid in cash. All have the same object; and it is for the insured to say, after a careful investigation of the foundations upon which they are raised, and the benefits flowing to the insured, which one of the four classes he will select. A life policy is something of an undertaking, and especially if the insured has no aid from any source to ease his payments. For as he grows older, as a general thing his ability to pay becomes less, and from this cause may endanger his profits of previous payments.

The mutual plan obviates this controlling objection to life insurance, and by division of profits lightens the payments from year to year, and in the most successful mutual cash company now doing business in the United States, they cease altogether in *sixteen years*. This is the *crowning beauty* of the mutual cash plan, and, as a consequence, the business is not only increasing but assuming gigantic proportions. Results in business operations are the true tests of merit of the kind of business done. Individual opinions may be of some value as to the best of the three modes of mutual insurance, but this is proof positive.

One thing is certain, that no mutual company can do a successful business on notes without the notes are paid; and if the insured gets no benefit the cash plan is the safest, for then he knows what he can do, and acts accordingly, while in the plan of giving notes an undertaking is gone into which may or may not be within his control to carry out. There is one fact connected with the two modes of insurance which the insured should know. In the mutual note and cash, the brokerage paid for procuring insurance is *twenty per cent.* on cash portion, while in the cash mutual it is but *ten*. This to a shrewd business-man is a *significant fact*, and so far as we would be concerned, if we were about to insure, would be *decisive*.

Having looked at this point as part of the expenses of the mutual plan, there are others that bear upon it in like manner. The larger the business done the less will be the expense to be borne by each one insured, and the larger will be the dividend of profits arising. The truth of the whole matter lies just here: the most successful company, or that which has received the largest amount of public patronage, and especially so when the brokerage for procuring insurance is one-half less than others, is the highest recommendation such style of company can have, for it is not an individual opinion, but the opinion of the *community*.

Then, in a word, to those about to insure, look for *that* company, and insure in it. Your money is safe, and your beneficiaries will be paid, calculating on human probabilities. Upon the same general principle that you select the heaviest bank to deposit your money in, although there may be others equally good, of smaller means.

The most successful mutual cash company in the United States, or in the world, is the Mutual Life Insurance Company of New York. Those who insure in that company become partners, and by the charter have *no liabilities of loss*, but participate in the profits. They have made very decided improvements in the style of their business, for the benefit of the insured, since its first organization, and the result of these changes has increased its business within the last year nearly one-half of its whole business outstanding at that time.

The main feature which has given the greatest impetus to their popularity among seekers after life insurance, is the equitable division of profits among the insured. In 1862 they adopted the contribution plan originated by their actuary, Mr. Sheppard Homans, by which every policy-holder receives his dividend of profits just in proportion to the interest he has in the funds of the company. This feature originated with them, and they are now receiving as a company the benefit of such a just arrangement. Other companies have adopted, and are following, the example of the Mutual Life.

To explain this more fully, one man insured in 1850, and one in 1860, for the same amount. The one insured in 1850 has paid more money into and has more to his credit than the one who insured in 1860. The dividend of profits is now made in proportion to the amount to each one's credit, by which operation each gets his just share of profit.

This principle is the one so closely pressed in this work, and the illustration of it in the success of the Mutual Life is a strong indorsement of the opinion. To do business for the *interest* of those you do business for, is a sure road to success. It inspires confidence and makes innumerable friends, beside those benefited directly. Every dollar an individual loses by a life insurance company is *two* dollars taken out of its earnings in the future, though one may be added temporarily. We mean *loss beyond the just charge for the risk for the time the insured pays, and if it be in a mutual, a just and accurate proportion of the expenses for the time insured.* The position of a life insurance company to make money out of those they pretend to be protecting for a charitable end, is a false one. The true principle should be that *whatever the insured pays to a company as premium on any risk, should stand to his credit till death occurs, or the just proportion refunded.* Because the company would *make the most money by it*, besides being the protector of the unfortunate. Instead of taking from those who could pay no longer what they had intrusted to the care of the company, the company would be sought for as a bank of savings, to return or at least keep for their benefit their hard earnings. A savings bank will not close its books and refuse to pay a depositor what he has earned because he can make no more money, nor should a life insurance company do the equivalent.

In the mutuals, note and cash system, those insuring at different times for the same amount get the same amount of dividend. So that if the company receives a large accession to its business, the new-comers take what really belongs to the older insurers; a system of injustice that soon becomes burdensome even to those who now insure, and as the business increases becomes more and more so.

Another feature in the Mutual Life Insurance Company of New York, is the non-forfeiting of policies when the individual becomes unable to pay. In former years, and before the adoption of this plan, thousands were deterred from insuring by the large excess of policies forfeited over those actually paid. Thus, in 1859, this company forfeited 302 policies; cancelled, 136; surrendered, 266; expired, 80; paid from death, 98. A frightful exhibit to one who had the idea of insuring his life.

These things are now ameliorated, and any policyholder, who has paid money into the company on a policy, can get an equitable return or paid-up policy for the money which he has paid. Of course he cannot get all, for his life has been insured in the meantime, and if he had died the company would have been bound to pay the whole amount of the policy. Other companies of like construction have adopted and are following the excellent and popular example of this company in these respects. To get this advantage *now*, however, the policyholder must apply before his premium becomes due.

The success of this company has been so amazing, that although they have paid claims by death of $6,464,713, in less than twenty-five years, they have never yet for any purpose touched a dollar of cash premiums paid in, but have been able to meet all demands from the profits of business without touching moneys paid as premiums. They have paid in the past twenty-three years dividends to their policy-holders, $10,176,388 in cash, or equivalent additions to their policies of $22,000,000, and now hold cash assets of $20,000,000. This is an exhibit which removes all human doubt as to ultimate security of the policy-holder, for if every dollar of its assets were swept away now invested in bonds and mortgages, real estate, in buildings, State and United States bonds, and cash on hand, the regular premiums payable in cash would not be consumed, in all probability, in payment of policies falling due.

This state of things has been brought about by the *equity* of the plan of doing the business, and the general *economy* of its management. The prudent investment of its funds, cash system in its transactions, scrutiny of the risks taken, and low expenses, have enabled the company to make dividends to life policy-holders, so that their dividends exceed their annual premiums after a run of the policy for *sixteen years*. The dividends are either payable in cash, at the option of the insured, or can be applied to extinguish premiums or increase insurance.

With a full conviction that this company offers the largest inducements to life insurance seekers, we have taken the liberty to use their tables in this work, to show to those whose wish it is to make provision in this way for themselves or those dependent upon them, the mode of operation. There are undoubtedly other companies equally responsible with this, but none probably who will pretend to question the supposed facts herein stated.

WHOLE LIFE POLICIES.

These can be paid for in four ways; in *annual* premiums in first *ten* annual payments, or in first *five* annual payments, or in one payment. Below are the tables of the Mutual Life, and the rates are about the same in all mutual companies.

WHOLE LIFE TABLE.

Premiums for an insurance of $1,000 (other amounts to extend to $20,000, in same proportion), in the MUTUAL LIFE INSURANCE COMPANY OF NEW YORK.

Age.	Annual Payments for Five Years.	Annual Payments for Ten Years.	Annual Payments for Life.	Age.	Annual Payments for Five Years.	Annual Payments for Ten Years.	Annual Payments for Life.	Age.	Annual Payments for Five Years.	Annual Payments for Ten Years.	Annual Payments for Life.
14–25	$71 89	$41 95	$19 89	39	$95 38	$56 21	$30 66	53	$128 61	$77 81	$52 71
26	73 34	42 82	20 47	40	97 37	57 44	31 73	54	131 44	79 78	55 07
27	74 82	43 71	21 07	41	99 41	58 71	32 86	55	134 34	81 83	57 58
28	76 34	44 62	21 70	42	101 51	60 02	34 05	56	137 32	83 98	60 25
29	77 88	45 55	22 35	43	103 66	61 38	35 30	57	140 38	86 22	63 10
30	79 46	46 51	23 02	44	105 87	62 78	36 63	58	143 52	88 57	66 14
31	81 07	47 48	23 73	45	108 15	64 23	38 04	59	146 76	91 04	69 38
32	82 72	48 48	24 46	46	110 49	65 74	39 53	60	150 09	93 63	72 84
33	84 41	49 50	25 23	47	112 91	67 31	41 11	61	153 51	96 35	76 53
34	86 13	50 55	26 03	48	115 38	68 92	42 78	62	157 04	99 21	80 46
35	87 89	51 62	26 87	49	117 92	70 59	44 55	63	160 67	102 21	84 65
36	89 70	52 72	27 75	50	120 51	72 31	46 42	64	....	105 37	89 12
37	91 55	53 86	28 67	51	123 15	74 08	48 39	65	....	108 68	93 86
38	93 44	55 02	29 64	52	125 85	75 91	50 49				

These policies are more especially suitable for all salaried persons, or those having a small stated income. Though no person in trade, or in any occupation about which there is risk of failure, should fail to lay aside enough to pay for a life policy which would give them some reserve fund in case of accident ; *and be careful not to insure in any company that does not secure a non-forfeit-*

able benefit for what you do pay. Look at the vicissitudes of commercial life and see what proportion fall by the wayside into actual poverty that could, while their thousands were passing like snow-flakes, have secured to themselves and their families, a home, without missing the trifle in money that it would have cost.

No one is free from such chances of calamity, and the *life policy to the wife, under certain restrictions named hereafter, cannot be reached by the creditor.* At the high tide of prosperity which generally takes place in a man's life about thirty-five years of age, a life policy of ten thousand dollars will cost in the Mutual Life in ten annual payments, cash dividends applied, about $3,200—an amount which is often lost by injudicious credits, or in some odd speculation. If men could see the down-hill side of life as it will be, very few would be without this comfort to purchase a snug little home to shelter those they cherish and have always the good-will to protect.

The plan of paying in five or ten years is a beautiful feature in life insurance, as any one can make good the payments in an ordinary business, and secure, without knowing or feeling, that this anchor to the windward has been laid. While fortune smiles and success runs high, few ever cast a glance into the chances of the future. It would be better if they did, and study statistics.

We give examples of a few policies now running to show the increase, and dividends paid.

EXAMPLES of Life Policies, of $1,000 each, in the MUTUAL LIFE INSURANCE COMPANY OF NEW YORK.

Age at Issue.	Year when Issued.	Present Age.	Annual Premium.	Total Paid in Years 1863–6.	Cash Dividend, 1866.	Per cent on Premiums Paid.	Additions for Dividend of 1866.	Total Additions for Whole Time.
30	1863	33	$23 02	$69 06	$24 73	36	$71 47	$71 47
	1858	38	23 02	69 06	38 97	56	101 56	269 19
	1853	43	23 02	69 06	54 63	79	127 62	469 17
	1848	48	23 60	70 80	75 65	107	157 77	648 61
	1843	53	23 60	70 80	92 03	130	171 37	767 88
35	1863	38	26 87	80 61	31 31	39	81 60	81 60
	1858	43	26 87	80 61	47 35	59	110 62	307 56
	1853	48	26 87	80 61	66 90	83	139 15	550 67
	1848	53	27 50	82 50	87 14	106	162 26	667 21
	1843	58	27 50	82 50	114 84	139	191 83	918 13
40	1863	43	31 73	95 19	36 60	38	85 51	85 51
	1858	48	31 73	95 19	57 85	61	120 65	330 79
	1853	53	31 73	95 19	76 97	81	143 32	521 60
	1848	58	32 00	96 00	99 40	103	166 06	672 21
	1843	63	32 00	96 00	129 50	135	195 73	808 87
45	1863	48	38 04	114 12	44 12	39	01	92 01
	1858	53	38 04	114 12	65 06	57	121 16	330 70
	1853	58	38 04	114 12	89 64	79	149 76	536 08
	1848	63	37 30	111 90	117 63	105	177 90	673 60
	1843	68	37 30	111 90	153 07	137	211 71	830 72

The above table exhibits the dividend of 1866 upon policies in force.

The policy for $1,000 issued in the year 1843, at age 30, having a dividend of 130 per cent., not only has the entire future premium cancelled, but is practically a paid-up policy for $1,767.88. This amount will gradually increase every year during the life of the person assured.

No more cash premiums are required on any of the above policies issued previous to the year 1853.

The average annual dividend (of 1866) on all policies issued in the first ten years of the company's history (1843–52 inclusive), is 103 per cent. (in cash value) on the annual premiums.

As the groundwork of life insurance is laid in the absolute money paid, it is interesting to the insured to know how to determine the best companies to insure in order to get the largest amount for their money. Not the company that promises the most, but the one that by calculation from what it has accomplished in a series of years, is still increasing. In the old style of insurance, it was supposed if they paid a dividend on their cash capital and had a surplus in premiums the concerns were doing well.

The mutual plan, however, has changed these ideas, and a new state of things has arisen. The comparison between the cash stock cash premium companies, wherein the insured have no interest in the profits, and in case of death only receive the amount of their policy, no matter how long it has run, and the mutual plans, leads to wonderful differences, especially on long dates. On long runs of such policies the losses to the insured become terrific in the cash stock companies, and are superior only on the first year to the best cash mutuals.

In order to make the comparison understandingly, we will take the extreme case where one in one thousand lives to the age of 101. There is one such, according to the Carlisle table of mortality. We will suppose that he insures a whole life for $13,525, at the age of 30 years, and that he pays into the cash stock company his yearly premium till he is 101 years old: that is, for 71 years. The yearly premium is $230.20, or, in other words, a trifle more than 73 cents per day for 313 days. This, by the table of earnings, will give for 71 years, at 5 per cent., $146,193.66. From this it will be seen that if the annual payment had been deposited in a savings bank, at 5 per cent. compound interest, instead of having been paid to the cash stock company, this sum would have been to the credit of the insured, whereas all he would get from the insurance company would be the amount of his policy, $13,525. Hence, by insuring instead of investing in that way, his estate would have made a *dead loss* of $132,668.66.

Suppose, instead of insuring in the stock company for $13,525, he had insured for $10,000 in a cash mutual, premium $230.20, that equalled in profits the accumulations in the savings bank of 5 per cent., the estate of the insurer would have had $146,193.66; consequently, he would have lost $132,668.66 in the stock company on a policy of $13,525, as against an investment in a savings bank, and gained in a cash mutual company doing as well as the bank, in profits, $146,193.66, on a policy of $10,000.

Suppose, however, we consider the subject with reference to a six per cent. investment in a savings bank and a life insurance in a cash stock and cash premium company on this same life. The savings bank will have to the credit of the assured the sum of $242,472.15, while the cash stock company would have $13,525 to the credit of the assured. If the cash mutual life, on a policy of $10,000, would do for the assured as well as the savings bank, he would have the same amount, $242,472.15. The assured would lose $228,947.15 in the cash stock on a policy of $13,525, and receive $242,472.15 in the cash mutual on a policy of $10,000. It is doubtful, however, whether the cash mutual will ever be able to do as well for the assured as six per cent. on the annual rates, though the Mutual Life now does as well as six per cent. on the money paid in.

The mode of getting at this result from the tables

in this book is, first to ascertain the daily payment for 313 days, being 73 cents. This, by table of earnings, in 50 years will give $68,559.24; compounded at 6 per cent. for 21 years gives $233,101.41; and 73 cents for the same 21 years will give in earnings $9,370.74, and added together gives $242,472.15.

The yearly premium in the stock companies is less on the same amount of policy on the start than in the cash mutual, being in the stock company $170.20 on $10.000, at 30 years of age, while it is $230.20 in the mutual. The total amount of cash paid by the insured in the case cited would be, in the stock company, $12,084.20, while in the mutual, on the basis of dividend of 1866, it would be $3,069.43, without noticing interest. The first yearly premiums differ $60, the second are about the same, while in the mutual they decrease rapidly, and in the other they remain the same always.

We will now give an example of the operation of a whole life policy in the Mutual Life of New York, on next page, on the basis of dividend of February 1, 1866.

From this we find that in ten years there is an addition in *value* to the policy of $3,247.99; in fifteen years, of $5,631.29; in twenty-five, of $12,152.50. That there was in the first ten years, of *actual cash paid*, of $1,691.17; for fifteen years, of $2,284.83; for twenty-five years, of $3,050.43. If the whole premiums had been paid without dividends to help, in the first ten years, there would have been paid in cash, $2,687.00; for the first fifteen years, $4,030.50; for the first twenty-five years, $6,717.75.

By examination it will be seen that the insured at the end of the first year has added $254.24 to the value of his policy, and had his life insured for $10,000 for $14.46,

WHOLE LIFE POLICY for $10,000, issued at age of 35, Annual Premium, $268.70.

Date.	Dividend on Policy proper.	Net premium required, Deducting Dividends.	Dividedn from Additions.	Total Annual Dividend.	Corresponding Addition to Policy.	Total Amount of Additions.	Total Amount of Policy and Additions.
End of 1st Year.	$93 53	$175 17	......	$93 53	$254 24	$254 24	$10,254 24
2d	97 68	171 02	$3 36	101 04	268 96	523 20	10,523 20
3d	101 48	167 22	7 06	108 54	282 87	806 07	10,806 07
4th	105 40	163 30	11 10	116 50	297 17	1,103 24	11,103 24
5th	109 46	159 24	15 53	124 99	311 99	1,415 23	11,415 23
6th	113 87	154 83	20 39	134 26	327 87	1,743 10	11,743 10
7th	118 97	149 73	25 75	144 72	345 69	2,088 79	12,088 79
8th	124 68	144 02	31 89	156 57	365 75	2,454 54	12,454 54
9th	130 76	137 94	38 14	168 90	385 87	2,840 41	12,840 41
10th	136 89	131 81	45 63	182 52	407 58	3,247 99	13,247 99
11th	142 80	125 90	53 60	196 40	428 73	3,676 72	13,676 72
12th	148 78	119 92	62 27	211 05	450 33	4,127 05	14,127 05
13th	154 56	114 14	71 66	226 22	471 79	4,598 84	14,598 84
14th	166 81	101 89	81 69	248 50	506 55	5,105 39	15,105 39
15th	171 44	97 26	92 50	263 94	525 90	5,631 29	15,631 29
16th	175 01	93 69	103 62	278 63*	542 71	6,174 00	16,174 00
17th	178 16	90 54	115 10	293 26	558 45	6,732 45	16,732 45
18th	182 05	86 65	127 44	309 49	576 30	7,308 75	17,308 75
19th	187 06	81 64	141 01	328 07	597 47	7,906 22	17,906 22
20th	193 71	74 99	156 12	349 83	623 24	8,529 46	18,529 46
21st	201 50	67 20	172 93	374 43	652 73	9,182 19	19,182 19
22d	210 07	58 63	191 44	401 51	685 09	9,867 28	19,867 28
23d	219 59	49 11	211 92	431 51	720 88	10,588 16	20,588 16
24th	230 21	38 49	234 81	465 02	760 87	11,349 03	21,349 03
25th	241 30	27 40	259 89	501 19	803 47	12,152 50	22,152 50

* It will be seen that when the dividends are allowed to remain with the company, the policy and additions become paid up in full in sixteen years; or, in other words, the annual dividends exceed the annual premiums.

or a little over five per cent. on his premium. At the end of the second year he has paid in all, *in cash*, $443.87, and has added to the value of his policy $523.20—costing nothing to insure, and has made $79.33, being a trifle short of eighteen per cent. on the amount of cash paid in or invested. At the end of the third year he has paid in all, in cash, $614.89, and has added to the value of his policy $806.07, costing nothing to insure, and has made $191.18, being a trifle over thirty-one per cent. upon the cash invested. At the end of the fourth year ne has paid in all, in cash, $782.11, and has increased the value of his policy $1,103.24, costing nothing to insure, and has made $321.13, being about forty-three per cent. upon the investment. At the end of the fifth year he has paid $945.41, and increased the value of his policy $1,415.23, and has made $469.82; a trifle short of fifty per cent. upon the investment, and so on.

It must be remembered that although the additions to the policy are not *accumulated interest*, they are nevertheless *dollars*, which will be paid to the policy-holder in case of death. Hence it matters not to him what it is or how it is calculated; the money will be found when due. It must be borne in mind, too, that if death occurs in either of these years, the heir of the policy-holder not only gets what we have called profits, but he gets also the amount of policy, $10,000.

Considering the subject of life policy in any point of view, and especially in that of a cash mutual, where the first premium is the heaviest payment, and that they decrease rapidly as the age increases, and finally the payments cease altogether, and the inability, from inexperience, of those having money to manage it, the conclusion must inevitably result in the minds of those having experience in investments, that it is the best that the largest class of people can make, independent of the insurance itself; but when this is taken into account also, it is surely strange that any one who has dependants, and has not ample means, should fail to avail himself of the advantage. Nothing but an ignorance of the subject would prevent.

The quicker, however, any one can secure the benefits of a *paid-up policy, the better*. Hence, life policies can be paid for in *five* or *ten* annual payments, and the rates have been given heretofore. Change of circumstances may render payments, however small, difficult or impossible, and the insured would not get the full value, as he would if he continued the payments to the end. The Mutual Life of New York set forth the following for all such policies:

> 1. The company will purchase ordinary life policies after the second year's premium has been paid, and give therefor the equitable cash value or an equivalent paid-up policy. The cash value varies with the age of the policy from thirty to ninety per cent. of the premiums paid, averaging about sixty-six per cent. The equivalent paid-up policy ALWAYS exceeds the total amount of premiums paid.
>
> 2. Life policies issued on the ten-payment plan, and all endowment policies, have a like surrender-value from the moment the first premium is paid, even if it be only a quarterly premium.

We give an example on next page of the operation of a whole life policy, premium paid in *ten* yearly payments in this company, on the basis of dividend of 1866.

This style of life policy is especially recommended, for many reasons, and if these reasons are good for it, they are still better for the payments in *five* years. It will be noticed that the additions in the whole life annual payments in twenty-five years, are $12,152.50, while in this they are $14,741.46, and in the five yearly payments would be still more. For the principle in all cases holds good, that the quicker you pay the more you get in value on the policy.

A new feature has lately been introduced by the Mutual Life, on life policies, and we can do no better than quote, on next page, what they say on that subject. It is without doubt a most beautiful idea, and will commend itself to those whose objects it will forward, if not consummate, in the best way.

TEN YEAR Whole Life Policy for $10,000, issued at age of 35. Annual Premium, $516.21.

Date.	Dividend from Policy.	Annual Premium required, Deducting Dividends.	Dividend from Additions.	Total Annual Dividend.	Corresponding Addition to Policy.	Total Additions.	Total Amount of Policy and Additions.
End of 1st Year.	$119 26	$396 94	......	$119 26	$324 18	$324 18	$10,324 18
2d	128 57	387 63	$4 28	132 85	353 64	677 82	10,677 82
3d	138 19	378 01	9 14	147 33	383 96	1,061 78	11,061 78
4th	148 28	367 92	14 63	162 91	415 56	1,477 34	11,477 34
5th	159 05	357 15	20 79	179 84	448 91	1,926 25	11,926 25
6th	170 89	345 31	27 75	198 64	485 10	2,411 35	12,411 35
7th	183 76	332 44	35 62	219 38	524 03	2,935 38	12,935 38
8th	197 81	318 39	44 82	242 63	566 80	3,502 18	13,502 18
9th	212 78	303 42	54 41	267 19	610 42	4,112 60	14,112 60
10th	228 35*	Nothing.	66 07	294 42	657 47	4,770 07	14,770 07
11th	159 64	Nothing.	78 72	238 36	520 33	5,290 40	15,290 40
12th	163 45	Nothing.	89 60	253 05	539 94	5,830 34	15,830 34
13th	167 14	Nothing.	101 23	268 37	559 70	6,390 04	16,390 04
14th	170 56	Nothing.	113 51	284 07	579 06	6,969 10	16,969 10
15th	173 59	Nothing.	126 27	299 86	597 47	7,566 57	17,566 57
16th	175 91	Nothing.	139 23	315 14	613 82	8,180 39	18,180 39
17th	177 89	Nothing.	152 51	330 40	629 18	8,809 57	18,809 57
18th	180 33	Nothing	166 75	347 08	646 29	9,455 86	19,455 86
19th	183 68	Nothing.	182 44	366 12	666 77	10,122 63	20,122 63
20th	187 79	Nothing.	199 88	387 67	690 66	10,813 29	20,813 29
21st	192 80	Nothing.	219 23	412 03	718 28	11,531 55	21,531 57
22d	198 32	Nothing.	240 43	438 75	748 63	12,280 20	22,280 20
23d	204 40	Nothing.	263 74	468 14	782 08	13,062 28	23,062 28
24th	211 25	Nothing.	289 68	500 93	819 63	13,881 91	23,881 91
25th	218 28	Nothing.	317 89	536 17	859 55	14,741 46	24,741 46

* The ten years having expired, the premiums are paid up in full, and the annual dividends may be used either to increase the amount insured, or as an annual cash income.

THE INSTALMENT FEATURE.

To meet the choice of such present or future members as may prefer to have the amount insured paid in instalments to their widows or heirs, rather than in one sum, this company is prepared to issue policies covenanting that in lieu of the payment of the policy and additions thereto in one sum, an equitable amount, to be determined by the company, may be paid annually or semi-annually for any specified number of years (say from five to twenty-five years).

This form of annuity will remove the anxiety which may exist in the minds of some policy-holders, lest the future provision they have made for their families should be ineffectual or transitory in its duration, either through unsafe investments, unwise expenditure, or other uncertainties incidental to contingent trusts.

It is not only free from the ordinary dangers of investment, but its punctual and full payment is secured by the LARGE AND SOLID CASH RESOURCES and good faith of this institution, which thus, to a certain extent, becomes the GUARDIAN or TRUSTEE of the survivors. Hence the provision may be considered, humanly speaking, beyond any adverse contingency.

All such deferred payments or annuities will share equitably in the profits or dividends of the company. They will also, when desired, be made inalienable by the beneficiaries.

TABLE

Showing the Practical Operation of the Instalment System. Example, $10,000 in Ten Annual Instalments. Other Amounts in same proportion.

Beginning of Year.	Amount remaining with Company.	Amount of Instalment paid.	Interest on balance remaining with Company.		Total amount of each Instalment.	
			6 per cent.	7 per cent.	6 per cent.	7 per cent.
1	$10,000	$1,000	...	...	$1,000	$1,000
2	9,000	1,000	$540	$630	1,540	1,630
3	8,000	1,000	480	560	1,480	1,560
4	7,000	1,000	420	490	1,420	1,490
5	6,000	1,000	360	420	1,360	1,420
6	5,000	1,000	300	350	1,300	1,350
7	4,000	1,000	240	280	1,240	1,280
8	3,000	1,000	180	210	1,180	1,210
9	2,000	1,000	120	140	1,120	1,140
10	1,000	1,000	60	70	1,060	1,070

ENDOWMENT POLICIES.

The next in order, but by no means the less important mode of effecting life insurance, is the ENDOWMENT policy. By this one can have his life insured and have the amount of policy paid to himself at any age after *ten years* intervene. There is not a merchant, trader, or any one subject to the misfortunes of business, that should not have an *endowment policy*. It is the *best pos-*

ENDOWMENTS.

Premiums Payable ANNUALLY, and in TEN Annual Payments, on Assurance of $1,000.

Age.	At Death or 40.		At Death or 45.		At Death or 50.		At Death or 55.		At Death or 60.		At Death or 65.	
	In Ten Annual Payments.	In Annual Payments.	In Ten Annual Payments.	In Annual Payments.	In Ten Annual Payments.	In Annual Payments.	In Ten Annual Payments.	In Annual Payments.	In Ten Annual Payments.	In Annual Payments.	In Ten Annual Payments.	In Annual Payments.
20	$72 82	$42 28	$65 09	$32 83	$59 30	$26 98	$55 30	$23 20	$52 48	$20 73	$50 68	$19 14
21	74 75	45 04	66 58	34 58	60 56	28 19	56 24	24 10	53 26	21 45	51 39	19 75
22	76 80	48 12	68 16	36 48	61 80	29 49	57 22	25 06	54 08	22 20	52 07	20 38
23	78 95	50 56	69 82	38 55	63 09	30 89	58 26	26 08	54 93	23 00	52 81	21 05
24	81 23	55 44	71 57	40 83	64 46	32 39	59 34	27 17	55 83	23 84	53 58	21 74
25	83 63	59 85	73 42	43 34	65 89	34 01	60 49	28 32	56 77	24 73	54 39	22 47
26	......	64 89	75 36	46 11	67 41	35 78	61 69	29 56	57 75	25 67	55 24	23 23
27	......	70 82	77 41	49 20	69 00	37 69	62 95	30 88	58 78	26 66	56 13	24 04
28	......	77 52	79 58	52 65	70 67	39 79	64 27	32 31	59 87	27 72	57 06	24 89
29	......	85 58	81 86	56 55	72 44	42 08	65 67	33 84	61 00	28 84	58 03	25 78
30	......	95 26	84 28	60 96	74 31	44 61	67 13	35 49	62 20	30 04	59 05	26 72
31	......	......	......	66 01	76 27	47 40	68 68	37 28	63 45	31 32	60 12	27 72
32	......	......	......	71 85	78 34	50 51	70 30	39 23	64 77	32 68	61 24	28 77
33	......	......	......	78 67	80 53	53 98	72 01	41 35	66 15	34 15	62 41	29 89
34	......	......	......	86 73	82 85	57 89	73 82	43 68	67 61	35 73	63 64	31 08
35	......	......	......	96 41	85 30	62 32	75 72	46 24	69 13	37 43	64 94	32 35
36	......	......	......	......	......	67 39	77 73	49 06	70 75	39 28	66 29	33 70
37	......	......	......	......	......	73 25	79 85	52 21	72 44	41 28	67 72	35 15
38	......	......	......	......	......	80 08	82 10	55 72	74 23	43 47	69 21	36 70
39	......	......	......	......	......	88 16	84 47	59 67	76 11	45 86	70 79	38 37
40	......	......	......	......	......	97 87	86 98	64 15	78 10	48 49	72 44	40 17
41	......	......	......	......	......	......	......	69 27	80 21	51 39	74 19	42 12
42	......	......	......	......	......	......	......	75 18	82 44	54 62	76 03	44 24
43	......	......	......	......	......	......	......	82 07	84 80	58 22	77 98	46 55
44	......	......	......	......	......	......	......	90 22	87 32	62 27	80 05	49 08
45	......	......	......	......	......	......	......	100 00	90 00	66 86	82 24	51 85
46	......	......	......	......	......	......	......	......	72 10	84 57	54 91
47	......	......	......	......	......	......	......	......	78 13	87 05	58 30
48	......	......	......	......	......	......	......	......	85 15	89 70	62 08
49	......	......	......	......	......	......	......	......	93 43	92 52	66 30
50	......	......	......	......	......	......	......	......	103 32	95 54	71 06
51	......	......	......	......	......	......	......	......	......	......	76 46
52	......	......	......	......	......	......	......	......	......	......	82 65
53	......	......	......	......	......	......	......	......	......	......	89 83
54	......	......	......	......	......	......	......	......	......	......	98 26
55	......	......	......	......	......	......	......	......	......	......	108 31

sible way of investing and saving profits. Taken out in the name of the wife, no creditor can touch it, under certain restrictions named hereafter; and while it is a safe, swift, and sure way to accumulate, its benefits may come at a time when money will be sweet. As has been said before, take ten per cent. of your profits and invest them in an endowment policy, and you will never see the day you will regret it; and you will undoubtedly see the time that you will be truly thankful, whether you are unfortunate or not, that some one has told you of such a plan of accumulating and saving.

The preceding table gives the rates of the Mutual Life Insurance of New York.

We give what the Company says of this species of Life Insurance :—

ENDOWMENTS.

We solicit from the reader a careful consideration of this system. An endowment policy is a double contract, by which the company agrees to pay a certain sum to the person insured at a specified age, with the promise that if he dies before attaining that age, the sum named in the policy shall be paid at once. The plan combines the advantages of a life insurance, a savings bank, and safe investment. It is simply an annual deposit of funds, to be repaid to the depositor with a fair rate of interest at a specified time. It is believed to be BETTER than a deposit in a savings bank, because NO CREDITOR CAN REACH A WIFE'S POLICY, and also because if the assured should die after having made only one payment of premium, his heirs would be entitled to the full sum insured. The system commends itself to wealthy men, and also to persons living upon a stated income, the result of personal labor.

This is a peculiar feature with this company, as no other companies can present the security we offer, or the profits which we are enabled to divide, so as to make the investment a good one to the applicant; and the rates for such policies are from 10 to 30 per cent. lower than those charged by other and smaller institutions.

The following endowment policies have been paid to the owners, and it will be seen that they received a SURPLUS above all they had paid to the company, with compound interest at six per cent., and no charge whatever for expenses or cost of insurance meanwhile.

ENDOWMENT ASSURANCES.

All the Policies of this Class which have matured thus far, are included in the following list.

Number of Policy.	Date of Issue.	Amount of Policy.	Annual Premium.	Description.	When Paid.	Amount paid by the Company.
17826	1857	$5,000	$576 80	Death or 60	1865	$6,634 01
18905	"	2,000	253 74	" 55	"	2,662 80
19949	1858	5,000	622 87	" 50	"	6,602 59
18538	1857	2,000	223 88	" 55	1866	2,705 07
18991	"	2,500	274 33	" 50	"	3,354 38
18992	"	2,500	274 33	" 50	"	3,467 81
18153	"	5,000	541 30	" 45	"	6,711 97

Let any merchant or trader but read the statistics given heretofore of successes and failures in business and consider whether it is not wise for himself, and especially if he has dependants upon him, to set aside a portion of his profits in this way, to guard against a day of misfortune. Is it wise to risk *all* in business, when you know yourself that things may occur beyond your control that will sweep away *all* your earnings? Men cannot control events. There may be accidents or changes that will come upon the most prudent and far-seeing. Then anchor a little while you can; for even in this enterprise, if you become unable to pay your premiums for the whole time, you will not lose what you have paid, for the company, by an equitable scale, will pay you an equitable amount. We quote what they say on this subject:

ENDOWMENTS.—ON THE TEN YEAR PLAN.

PAYMENTS CEASE ENTIRELY AT THE END OF TEN YEARS; with the privilege of surrendering before the expiration of the ten years, and taking a policy for the proportionate amount. If the holder of a policy for $10,000 on this plan should desire to discontinue the payments of premiums before the end of the ten years, the company will give, on the surrender of the original policy, a similar endowment assurance policy paid up in full, which,

If at the end of two years, shall exceed $2,000
" " " three " " 3,000
" " " four " " 4,000
" " " five " " 5,000
" " " six " " 6,000
" " " seven " " 7,000
" " " eight " " 8,000
" " " nine " " 9,000

This plan of paying for a policy by a definite number of annual instalments must commend itself to every thoughtful man, as it obviates one of the greatest objections to life insurance, namely, the uncertainty of being able to continue the customary payments of premiums during the later years of life.

We give the practical working of a *Ten Year* payment endowment policy, and one in which the premiums are

"TEN YEAR" Endowment Assurance Policy for $10,000, issued at age of 35, payable at Death or at 60 years of age. Annual Premium, $691.30.

Date.	Dividend on Policy proper.	Net Premium required, deducting Dividends.	Dividend from Additions.	Total Annual Dividend.	Corresponding Addition to Policy.	Total Amount of Additions.	Total Amount of Policy and Additions.
End of 1st Year.	$185 32	$505 98	......	$185 32	$399 66	$399 66	$10,399 66
2d	198 99	492 31	$6 25	205 24	430 91	830 57	10,830 57
3d	212 92	478 38	13 30	226 22	462 20	1,292 77	11,292 77
4th	227 34	463 96	21 18	248 52	493 90	1,786 67	11,786 67
5th	243 38	447 92	29 96	273 34	528 16	2,314 83	12,314 83
6th	258 39	432 91	39 82	298 21	560 00	2,874 83	12,874 83
7th	275 31	415 99	51 09	326 40	595 46	3,470 29	13,470 29
8th	293 05	398 25	63 02	356 07	630 74	4,101 03	14,101 03
9th	311 91	379 39*	76 81	388 72	663 37	4,769 40	14,769 40
10th	330 67	Nothing.	91 77	422 44	704 74	5,474 14	15,474 14
11th	197 92	Nothing.	108 34	306 26	495 52	5,969 66	15,969 66
15th	219 78	Nothing.	165 71	385 49	549 51	8,088 62	18,088 62
16th	224 95	Nothing.	181 99	406 94	561 44	8,650 06	18,650 06
20th	249 49	Nothing.	259 67	509 16	613 27	11,020 78	21,020 78
21st	257 10	Nothing.	283 34	540 44	628 27	11,649 05	21,649 05
24th	280 86	Nothing.	362 88	643 74	669 48	13,617 92	23,617 92
25th	288 45	Nothing.	391 97	680 42	680 42	14,298 34	24,298 34

* The ten years having expired, the premiums are paid up in full, and the annual dividends may be used either to increase the amount insured, or as an annual cash income.

paid during its time in the Mutual Life Insurance Company of New York, upon the basis of dividend of 1866.

ENDOWMENT Assurance Policy for $10,000, issued at age of 35 years, payable at Death or at 60 years of age. Annual Premium, $374.30.

Date.	Dividend on Policy proper.	Net Premium required, deducting Dividends.	Dividend from Additions.	Total Annual Dividend.	Corresponding Addition to Policy.	Total Amount of Additions.	Total Amount of Policy and Additions.
End of 1st Year.	$102 07	$272 23	......	$102 07	$220 12	$220 12	$10,220 12
2d	108 93	265 37	$3 44	112 37	235 93	456 05	10,456 05
3d	115 70	258 60	7 30	123 00	251 31	707 36	10,707 36
4th	122 63	251 67	11 59	134 22	266 75	974 11	10,974 11
5th	129 83	244 47	16 34	146 17	282 44	1,256 55	11,256 55
6th	137 86	236 44	21 61	159 47	299 47	1,556 02	11,556 02
7th	146 18	228 12	27 65	173 83	317 12	1,873 14	11,873 14
8th	155 30	219 00	34 02	189 32	335 37	2,208 51	12,208 51
9th	165 32	208 98	41 37	206 69	355 39	2,563 90	12,563 90
10th	174 90	199 40	49 33	224 23	374 07	2,937 97	12,937 97
15th	224 78	149 52	101 57	326 35	465 22	5,087 02	15,087 02
16th	234 20	140 10	114 46	348 66	481 02	5,568 04	15,568 04
20th	279 02	95 28	177 35	456 37	549 69	7,657 97	17,657 97
21st	292 85	81 45	196 88	489 73	569 33	8,227 30	18,227 30
25th	350 00	24 30	289 89	639 89	639 89	10,688 11	20,688 11

We give also an endowment table for children, by which it is claimed a fund can be provided for their collegiate education, or for the purposes of support. In very many cases this might not only be useful, but necessary.

We cannot see the benefit of such endowments as compared with a deposit in savings banks, and certainly not as compared with life endowment policies. We cannot see the benefit of *any* plan of life insurance or endowments where the earnings may be lost at a time when they are the most needed. It would be far better where no life policy exists, to deposit in savings bank, where the earnings would be at command when money is sweet to alleviate distress, and cover the achings of poverty.

CHILDREN'S ENDOWMENT TABLE.

Annual Premiums charged to secure Endowments of $1,000.

Present Age.	Payable at the age of 18.		Payable at the age of 21.		Payable at the age of 25	
	No premiums returned in case of previous Death.	All Premiums returned in case of previous Death.	No Premiums returned in case of previous Death.	All Premiums returned in case of previous Death.	No Premiums returned in case of previous Death.	All Premiums returned in case of previous Death.
1	$40 38	$46 78	$31 80	$37 16	$23 85	$28 21
2	44 77	50 30	34 90	39 64	25 93	29 89
3	49 52	54 44	38 18	42 52	28 09	31 81
4	54 75	59 32	41 71	45 86	30 36	33 99
5	60 68	65 06	45 60	49 67	32 82	36 44
6	67 50	71 85	49 97	54 07	35 50	39 18
7	75 52	79 94	54 93	59 13	38 47	42 27
8	85 13	89 69	60 65	65 01	41 79	45 74
9	96 87	101 66	67 33	71 90	45 54	49 66
10	111 58	116 66	75 24	80 07	49 80	54 13
11	130 53	135 96	84 78	89 88	54 70	59 24
12	155 88	161 71	96 49	101 89	60 39	65 15
13	191 45	197 78	111 18	116 91	67 06	72 06
14	244 93	251 89	130 13	136 22	74 99	80 22
15	......	......	155 49	161 97	84 55	90 03
16	......	......	191 10	198 02	96 30	102 01
17	......	......	244 64	252 09	111 03	117 00
18	......	......	......	......	130 03	136 29

We subjoin the following information for such as might be induced to consider the subject of life insurance favorably, as being interesting to them. We take it from the yearly report of the Mutual Life.

SURRENDER OF POLICIES.

Should the original motive for effecting an assurance in this company cease before the termination of life, the party may surrender his policy, provided it has run two years, for an equitable consideration, which may be paid to him in cash by the company on its surrender. Or, if it is found inconvenient to continue the payment of the annual premium, the company will grant a new policy, which, without further payment, will assure to the representatives of the party, at his death, a reversionary sum equivalent to the present value of the policy on surrender.

SPECIAL NOTICE.

The following rules and usages of the company established by the board, and governing it in its transactions with its agents and the insured, are published for the guidance and information of policy-holders.

The agreement is mutual, as expressly stipulated in the application and the policy, that unless the premium is paid on or before the day it becomes due, the policy is forfeited and void.

All premiums are due and payable at the office of the company, in the city of New York, but for the convenience of policy-holders residing at a distance, they may be paid to an agent, but only on the production of a receipt signed by the President or Secretary, who are alone authorized to sign receipts on the part of the company. When receipts are delivered to a policy-holder by an agent, such agent should countersign the same as an evidence of payment to him.

Agents are not authorized to receive any premium, on the part of the company, unless they shall have been furnished with a receipt therefor, signed by the President or Secretary, as no payment made to an agent, without such receipt being given in return by him, is considered valid by the company.

Should any policy-holder tender payment of a premium to an agent, for which no receipt has been furnished, the following conditional receipt may be given by the agent, and no other:

"CONDITIONAL RECEIPT.

Received, , 186 , from , $, stated to be the amount of a premium due this day on Policy No. , issued by the Mutual Life Insurance Company of New York, upon the life of , for the sum of $, and in favor of . Said alleged premium is to be held by the undersigned until application can be made to the company to accept the same and forward their receipt. If such receipt be forwarded, this conditional receipt is to be exchanged therefor; if the company's receipt be not forwarded, the money is to be returned, and this conditional receipt cancelled.

(Signed) J. D., Agent."

Agents are not authorized to make, alter, or discharge contracts, waive forfeitures, name an extra rate for special risks, or bind the company in any way, their duties being simply the reception and transmission of applications for policies and premiums under the rules and instructions laid down in their letters of appointment.

The company may, but solely as an act of grace or courtesy, and when the interests of the company will not be impaired in any way thereby, restore a forfeited policy. When a restoration is applied for, the application must invariably be accompanied by a certificate as to the health of the person whose life was insured, and at his expense, from a physician acceptable to the company. The agent forwarding such application will be then notified of the decision made in the case.

In all cases of restorations of forfeited policies, and in all cases where the premium is received after the day on which it became due, although the policy may not have been formally cancelled on the company's books, the renewal or revival of the policy, in whatever form made, will be, in accordance with the decision of the Commissioners of Internal Revenue, subject to stamp tax the same as if a new policy had been issued.

Agents of the company are not, under any circumstances, authorized to indorse the receipt of premiums on the policy.

Should the policy-holder so desire, the agent will send the policy and all' previous receipts to this company, and the premiums will then be entered upon it by the President or Secretary, and the policy returned.

It is entirely optional with the policy-holder to communicate directly with the company or through an agent. If he should elect the latter method, such agent in all communications and payments acts as his representative.

AN ACT FOR THE BENEFIT OF MARRIED WOMEN IN INSURING THE LIVES OF THEIR HUSBANDS. PASSED MARCH, 1858.

The People of the State of New York, represented in Senate and Assembly, do enact as follows:

§ 1. It shall be lawful for any married woman, by herself, and in her name, or in the name of any third person, with his assent, as her trustee, to cause to be insured, for her sole use, the life of her husband, for any definite period, or for the term of his natural life ; and in case of her surviving her husband, the sum or net amount of the insurance becoming due and payable by the terms of the insurance, shall be payable to her, to and for her own use, free from the claims of the representatives of the husband, or of any of his creditors; but such exemption shall not apply where the amount of premium annually paid out of the funds or property of the husband shall exceed three hundred dollars.

§ 2. In case of the death of the wife before the decease of her husband, the amount of the insurance may be made payable after death to her children, for their use, and to their guardian, if under age.

The author of this work has some explanation to make to his readers why he has spoken of the Mutual Life of New York instead of other companies who may be as good and insure on as favorable or more favorable terms than they. He would say that he has not, directly or indirectly, any interest in any life company in the world, because he is fortunate enough, at present, not to need their aid in the way of insurance. He happens to know the officers of the company, and believes they are all entirely trustworthy, and also knows that it has been the most successful mutual company in the world. He therefore has felt himself bound, in a conscientious discharge of duty to his readers, to say what he has without disparagement to any one else.

ANNUITIES.

We give tables of rates of what are called survivorship annuities, and annuities on a single life. It will be seen that the survivorship annuities are intended to benefit *one person only*. For this single object it will be seen to be the *cheapest, most effective, and indeed the* ONLY *method of securing a definite, certain, and* PERMANENT SUPPORT *to a surviving* WIFE *or* NOMINEE. We give what the Mutual Life says of these policies.

> By this plan a husband may secure to his widow the payment (in annual, or, if preferred, in semi-annual or quarterly instalments *without extra charge)* of an annuity sufficient to maintain her in comfort and independence during the remainder of her life. This provision is not only free from the ordinary dangers of investment and of dependence upon designing or inexperienced persons; but its punctual and full payment is secured upon the promises, large resources, and good faith of this institution, which thus, to a certain extent, becomes the *guardian* or *trustee* of the survivor: and hence the provision may be considered, humanly speaking, *beyond any adverse contingency.*
> In the same manner, a parent, sister, or child may, by such a provision, be made independent both of friends and of charity, when their natural protector shall have been removed by death.
> Although a survivorship annuity is intended for the benefit of one

person exclusively, yet a family may be provided for, and more economically than by any other method, by taking a policy for each person separately, with the additional advantage of being able to *modify the annuity to suit each individual case.*

In addition, rates of premium are given in the tables on the following pages, by which, in case the *nominee* or person for whom the benefit was intended *should die first, all payments* made to the Company *will be* RETURNED *to the insurer.* This feature is especially recommended.

The premiums on these policies may be paid annually, semi-annually, or quarterly, or by a single payment.

Annuities for a single life are not likely to be very popular in this country, where investments in large sums can be made in real estate, bonds and mortgages, State and United States bonds, and bank stocks, at seven per cent., while the annuities are calculated in the best companies on a basis of only four per cent. The companies could undoubtedly do better than this if there was a certainty of money remaining at present interest for a long series of years. It would not be prudent, however, to make such calculations, as money over the water, on the average, does not command as much as this. Persons, however, might find annuities in this country on that basis of interest advantageous, and especially so if they were of strong constitutions, and belonged to a lineage of great longevity.

Any one can understand the survivorship annuity tables on inspection, as they explain themselves. For the annuity tables on a single life, we will give an example. Suppose you wish to find the rate on a single life at 40 years, on a basis of interest of 6 per cent. Opposite 40 years, and under the line of six per cent., you will find you must pay $12.002 for one dollar of yearly income.

And how to Keep it. 319

ANNUAL PREMIUMS necessary to secure a Survivorship Annuity of $100. When the Nominee is older than the Life Insured, without return of Premiums Paid, in case the Nominee dies first.

Age	Nominee 1 year older.	Nominee 2 years older.	Nominee 3 years older.	Nominee 4 years older.	Nominee 5 years older.	Nominee 6 years older.	Nominee 7 years older.	Nominee 8 years older.	Nominee 9 years older.	Nominee 10 years older.	Nominee 15 years older.	Nominee 20 years older.	Nominee 25 years older.	Nominee 30 years older.
	$	$	$	$	$	$	$	$	$	$	$	$	$	$
20	20 35	20 00	19 66	19 31	18 97	18 62	18 28	17 94	17 60	17 26	15 58	13 94	12 35	10 79
21	20 45	20 09	19 73	19 37	19 01	18 66	18 30	17 94	17 59	17 24	15 50	13 82	12 19	10 60
22	20 56	20 19	19 81	19 44	19 06	18 69	18 32	17 95	17 59	17 22	15 43	13 69	12 02	10 41
23	20 68	20 29	19 90	19 51	19 12	18 73	18 35	17 96	17 58	17 20	15 35	13 57	11 86	10 21
24	20 80	20 40	19 99	19 58	19 18	18 78	18 38	17 98	17 59	17 19	15 27	13 44	11 69	10 02
25	20 94	20 51	20 09	19 67	19 25	18 83	18 41	18 00	17 59	17 18	15 20	13 31	11 52	9 82
26	21 08	20 64	20 20	19 76	19 32	18 89	18 46	18 03	17 60	17 18	15 13	13 19	11 35	9 63
27	21 24	20 78	20 32	19 86	19 40	18 95	18 50	18 06	17 62	17 18	15 06	13 06	11 19	9 43
28	21 40	20 92	20 45	19 97	19 50	19 03	18 56	18 10	17 64	17 18	14 99	12 93	11 02	9 24
29	21 58	21 08	20 58	20 09	19 60	19 10	18 62	18 14	17 66	17 19	14 92	12 81	10 85	9 05
30	21 78	21 25	20 73	20 22	19 70	19 19	18 69	18 19	17 70	17 21	14 86	12 69	10 69	8 86
31	21 98	21 44	20 90	20 36	19 82	19 29	18 77	18 25	17 74	17 23	14 80	12 57	10 52	8 66
32	22 21	21 64	21 07	20 51	19 95	19 40	18 86	18 32	17 78	17 26	14 75	12 45	10 36	8 48
33	22 44	21 85	21 26	20 68	20 10	19 52	18 95	18 39	17 84	17 29	14 70	12 33	10 20	8 29
34	22 70	22 08	21 47	20 86	20 25	19 65	19 06	18 48	17 91	17 34	14 65	12 22	10 05	8 10
35	22 98	22 33	21 69	21 05	20 42	19 80	19 18	18 58	17 98	17 39	14 62	12 12	9 89	7 92
36	23 27	22 60	21 93	21 27	20 61	19 96	19 32	18 69	18 07	17 46	14 59	12 02	9 74	7 74
37	23 59	22 89	22 19	21 49	20 81	20 13	19 47	18 81	18 17	17 54	14 56	11 92	9 60	7 57
38	23 93	23 20	22 47	21 74	21 03	20 33	19 63	18 95	18 28	17 63	14 55	11 83	9 45	7 39
39	24 30	23 53	22 77	22 01	21 27	20 53	19 81	19 10	18 41	17 73	14 55	11 75	9 32	7 23
40	24 69	23 89	23 09	22 30	21 53	20 76	20 01	19 27	18 55	17 85	14 55	11 67	9 18	7 06
41	25 11	24 27	23 44	22 62	21 81	21 01	20 23	19 46	18 71	17 98	14 57	11 60	9 05	6 89
42	25 57	24 69	23 82	22 96	22 11	21 28	20 47	19 67	18 89	18 13	14 60	11 54	8 94	6 73
43	26 05	25 13	24 22	23 32	22 44	21 58	20 73	19 90	19 09	18 30	14 64	11 49	8 82	6 58
44	26 58	25 61	24 66	23 72	22 80	21 90	21 02	20 15	19 31	18 49	14 69	11 45	8 72	6 42
45	27 13	26 12	25 13	24 15	23 19	22 25	21 33	20 43	19 55	18 70	14 77	11 42	8 62	6 27
46	27 73	26 68	25 64	24 62	23 61	22 63	21 67	20 73	19 82	18 93	14 86	11 40	8 54	....
47	28 38	27 27	26 18	25 11	24 07	23 04	22 04	21 06	20 11	19 19	14 96	11 40	8 44	....
48	29 06	27 90	26 76	25 65	24 55	23 48	22 44	21 42	20 43	19 47	15 08	11 40	8 36	....
49	29 78	28 57	27 38	26 21	25 07	23 95	22 86	21 80	20 77	19 77	15 22	11 42	8 28	....
50	30 55	29 28	28 03	26 81	25 62	24 45	23 32	22 21	21 15	20 09	15 37	11 44	8 20	....
51	31 36	30 03	28 72	27 44	26 20	24 98	23 79	22 64	21 52	20 44	15 53	11 46	....	....
52	32 20	30 81	29 44	28 11	26 80	25 53	24 29	23 09	21 92	20 79	15 70	11 49	....	....
53	33 09	31 63	30 20	28 80	27 44	26 11	24 82	23 56	22 35	21 17	15 87	11 52	....	....
54	34 02	32 49	30 99	29 52	28 10	26 71	25 36	24 05	22 79	21 56	16 06	11 53	....	....
55	34 98	33 38	31 81	30 28	28 78	27 33	25 93	24 56	23 24	21 96	16 24	11 53	....	....
56	35 99	34 30	32 66	31 06	29 50	27 98	26 51	25 09	23 71	22 38	16 43	11 52	....	....
57	37 03	35 26	33 54	31 86	30 23	28 65	27 11	25 62	24 19	22 80	16 61	11 49	....	....
58	38 10	36 25	34 45	32 69	30 98	29 33	27 73	26 18	24 68	23 23	16 78	11 43	....	....
59	39 21	37 27	35 38	33 54	31 76	30 03	28 36	26 74	25 18	23 67	16 93	11 35	....	....
60	40 35	38 32	36 34	34 42	32 55	30 74	29 00	27 31	25 68	24 11	17 07	11 22	....	....

ANNUAL PREMIUMS necessary to secure a Survivorship Annuity of $100. Where the Nominee, or Person for whom the Annuity is intended, is younger than the Life Insured, without return of Premiums Paid, in case the Nominee dies first.

Age.	Equal Ages.	Nominee 1 year younger.	Nominee 2 years younger.	Nominee 3 years younger.	Nominee 4 years younger.	Nominee 5 years younger.	Nominee 6 years younger.	Nominee 7 years younger.	Nominee 8 years younger.	Nominee 9 years younger.	Nominee 10 years younger.	Nominee 15 years younger.	Nominee 20 years younger.	Nominee 25 years younger.
	$	$	$	$	$	$	$	$	$	$	$	$	$	$
20	20 69	21 03	21 37	21 71	22 05	22 38	22 71	23 04	23 36	23 68	24 00	....	....	....
21	20 81	21 17	21 52	21 88	22 23	22 57	22 92	23 26	23 60	23 93	24 26	....	....	....
22	20 93	21 30	21 68	22 05	22 41	22 78	23 14	23 50	23 85	24 20	24 54	....	....	....
23	21 07	21 45	21 84	22 23	22 61	22 99	23 37	23 74	24 11	24 48	24 84	....	....	....
24	21 21	21 61	22 02	22 42	22 82	23 22	23 61	24 00	24 39	24 77	25 15	....	....	....
25	21 36	21 78	22 20	22 63	23 04	23 46	23 87	24 28	24 69	25 09	25 48	27 35	....	....
26	21 52	21 96	22 41	22 85	23 28	23 72	24 15	24 58	25 00	25 42	25 83	27 79	....	....
27	21 70	22 16	22 62	23 08	23 54	23 99	24 44	24 89	25 33	25 77	26 20	28 26	....	....
28	21 89	22 37	22 85	23 33	23 80	24 28	24 75	25 22	25 68	26 14	26 60	28 75	....	....
29	22 09	22 59	23 09	23 59	24 09	24 59	25 08	25 57	26 06	26 54	27 02	29 28	....	....
30	22 30	22 82	23 35	23 87	24 40	24 92	25 43	25 95	26 46	26 96	27 46	29 83	31 97	....
31	22 53	23 08	23 63	24 17	24 72	25 27	25 81	26 35	26 88	27 41	27 93	30 42	32 67	....
32	22 78	23 35	23 92	24 50	25 07	25 64	26 21	26 77	27 33	27 88	28 43	31 05	33 41	....
33	23 04	23 64	24 24	24 84	25 44	26 04	26 63	27 22	27 81	28 39	28 96	31 71	34 19	....
34	23 32	23 95	24 58	25 20	25 83	26 46	27 08	27 70	28 31	28 92	29 53	32 41	35 02	....
35	23 63	24 28	24 94	25 59	26 25	26 91	27 56	28 21	28 85	29 49	30 12	33 16	35 90	38 32
36	23 95	24 64	25 33	26 01	26 70	27 39	28 07	28 75	29 43	30 10	30 76	33 95	36 84	39 39
37	24 30	25 02	25 74	26 46	27 18	27 90	28 62	29 33	30 04	30 74	31 44	34 79	37 84	40 52
38	24 68	25 43	26 18	26 93	27 69	28 44	29 20	29 95	30 69	31 43	32 16	35 69	38 89	41 72
39	25 08	25 86	26 65	27 44	28 23	29 02	29 81	30 60	31 38	32 16	32 93	36 64	40 02	43 00
40	25 51	26 33	27 15	27 98	28 81	29 64	30 47	31 30	32 12	32 94	33 75	37 65	41 21	44 36
41	25 97	26 82	27 69	28 56	29 43	30 30	31 17	32 04	32 90	33 76	34 61	38 72	42 48	45 80
42	26 46	27 36	28 26	29 17	30 09	31 00	31 92	32 83	33 74	34 64	35 54	39 87	43 83	47 34
43	26 99	27 93	28 88	29 83	30 79	31 75	32 71	33 67	34 63	35 58	36 52	41 09	45 27	48 98
44	27 55	28 54	29 53	30 54	31 54	32 55	33 56	34 57	35 58	36 58	37 58	42 39	46 81	50 73
45	28 16	29 19	30 24	31 29	32 35	33 41	34 47	35 53	36 59	37 64	38 69	43 77	48 44	52 59
46	28 81	29 89	30 99	32 09	33 20	34 32	35 43	36 55	37 67	38 78	39 88	45 24	50 18	54 57
47	29 50	30 63	31 78	32 94	34 11	35 28	36 46	37 64	38 81	39 98	41 15	46 81	52 04	56 69
48	30 23	31 43	32 63	33 85	35 08	36 31	37 55	38 79	40 03	41 26	42 49	48 47	54 00	58 94
49	31 02	32 27	33 53	34 81	36 10	37 40	38 70	40 01	41 32	42 62	43 92	50 24	56 10	61 33
50	31 84	33 16	34 48	35 83	37 28	38 55	39 92	41 30	42 68	44 05	45 42	52 11	58 32	63 88
51	32 71	34 09	35 48	36 90	38 32	39 76	41 21	42 66	44 11	45 56	47 00	54 08	60 67	66 58
52	33 62	35 07	36 54	38 02	39 52	41 03	42 56	44 09	45 62	47 15	48 68	56 17	63 16	69 44
53	34 58	36 10	37 64	39 20	40 77	42 37	43 97	45 58	47 20	48 82	50 44	58 37	65 80	72 47
54	35 58	37 17	38 79	40 43	42 09	43 77	45 46	47 16	48 87	50 58	52 28	60 69	68 58	75 68
55	36 62	38 29	39 99	41 72	43 46	45 23	47 01	48 81	50 61	52 42	54 22	63 13	71 51	79 09
56	37 71	39 46	41 25	43 06	44 90	46 76	48 64	50 53	52 43	54 34	56 25	65 69	74 61	82 69
57	38 83	40 67	42 55	44 46	46 39	48 35	50 33	52 33	54 34	56 36	58 38	68 39	77 88	86 49
58	39 99	41 93	43 90	45 91	47 95	50 01	52 10	54 21	56 33	58 46	60 60	71 22	81 33	90 52
59	41 20	43 23	45 30	47 41	49 56	51 74	53 94	56 16	58 41	60 66	62 92	74 19	84 95	94 77
60	42 44	44 57	46 75	48 97	51 23	53 53	55 85	58 20	60 56	62 95	65 34	77 30	88 77	99 27

And how to Keep it. 321

VALUE OF ANNUITIES ON A SINGLE LIFE.

Calculated on a basis of 4, 5, 6, 7, 8, 9, and 10 per cent. (Carlisle Table of Mortality.)

Age.	4 per cent.	5 per cent.	6 per cent.	7 per cent.	8 per cent.	9 per cent.	10 per ct
1	$16,554	$13,995	$12,078	$10,605	$9,439	$8,502	$7,732
2	17,726	14,983	12,925	11,342	10,088	9,080	8,251
3	18,715	15,824	13,652	11,978	10,651	9,584	8,705
4	19,231	16,271	14,042	12,322	10,957	9,858	8,954
5	19,592	16,590	14,325	12,574	11,184	10,064	9,141
6	19,745	16,735	14,460	12,698	11,298	10,168	9,237
7	19,790	16,790	14,518	12.756	11,354	10,221	9,287
8	19,764	16,786	14,526	12,770	11,371	10.240	9.306
9	19,691	16,742	14,500	12,754	11,362	10,236	9,304
10	19,583	16,665	14,448	12,717	11,334	10,214	9,286
11	19,458	16,581	14,384	12,669	11,296	10,183	9,261
12	19,334	16,494	14,321	12,621	11.259	10,153	9,238
13	19,209	16,406	14,257	12,572	11,221	10.123	9,213
14	19,081	16,316	14,191	12,522	11,182	10,091	9,187
15	18,995	16,227	14,126	12,473	11,144	10,061	9.161
16	18,836	16,144	14,067	12,429	11,111	10,034	9,140
17	18,721	16,066	14,012	12,389	11,081	10,011	9,122
18	18,606	15,987	13,956	12,348	11,051	9,988	9,104
19	18,486	15.904	13,897	12,305	11,019	9,963	9,085
20	18,361	15.817	13,835	12,259	10.985	9,937	9,064
21	18,231	15.726	13,769	12,210	10,948	9,909	9,041
22	18,093	15,628	13,697	12,156	10,906	9,876	9,015
23	17,950	15,525	13,621	12.098	10,861	9,841	8,987
24	17,800	15,417	13,541	12,037	10,813	9,802	8,955
25	17,644	15.303	13,456	11,972	10,762	9,761	8,921
26	17,485	15,187	13,368	11,904	10,709	9,718	8,886
27	17,320	15,065	13,275	11,832	10,652	9,671	8,847
28	17,154	14,942	13,182	11,759	10.594	9,624	8,808
29	16,996	14,827	13,096	11,693	10,542	9,582	8,773
30	16,852	14,723	13,020	11,636	10,498	9,548	8,747
31	16,705	14.617	12,942	11,578	10,454	9,514	8,719
32	16.552	14,506	12,860	11,516	10,407	9,476	8.690
33	16,390	14,387	12,771	11,448	10.355	9,435	8,657
34	16,219	14,260	12,675	11,374	10,297	9,389	8.619
35	16,041	14,127	12,573	11,295	10,235	9,339	8.578
36	15,855	13,987	12,465	11,211	10,168	9.285	8,534
37	15 665	13,843	12,354	11,124	10,098	9.228	8.488
38	15.471	13,695	12,239	11,033	10.026	9,169	8,439
39	15,271	13.542	12,120	10,939	9,950	9,107	8,388
40	15,073	13,390	12,002	10,845	9,875	9,046	8,337
41	14,883	13,245	11,890	10,757	9,805	8,991	8,292
42	14.694	13,101	11,779	10,671	9.737	8,937	8,249
43	14,505	12.957	11,668	10,585	9,669	8,883	8,206
44	14,308	12 806	11,551	10.494	9.597	8,826	8,160
45	14.104	12.648	11,428	10.397	9,520	8.764	8,111
46	13,889	12,480	11.296	10,292	9.436	8,607	8,056
47	13,662	12,301	11,154	10,178	9.344	8,622	7.995
48	13,419	12,107	10,998	10.052	9,241	8,537	7,925
49	13.153	11,892	10,823	9,908	9.121	8,437	7,840
50	12,869	11,660	10,631	9,749	8,987	8,324	7,744
51	12,565	11,410	10,422	9,573	8,838	8,197	7,634

Value of Annuities on a Single Life.

Calculated on a basis of 4, 5, 6, 7, 8, 9, and 10 per cent. (Carlisle Table of Mortality.)

Age.	4 per cent.	5 per cent.	6 per cent.	7 per cent.	8 per cent.	9 per cent.	10 per ct.
52	$12,257	$11,154	$10,208	$9,392	$8,684	$8,064	$7.519
53	11,945	10,892	9,988	9,205	8,523	7,926	7.399
54	11,626	10,624	9,761	9,011	8,356	7.781	7 272
55	11,299	10,347	9,524	8.807	8,179	7.627	7,137
56	10,966	10,063	9,280	8.595	7,995	7,465	6,994
57	10,625	9,771	9,027	8,375	7,802	7,294	6,843
58	10.286	9,478	8,772	8.153	7,606	7.120	6,687
59	9.963	9.199	8,529	7,940	7,418	6.954	6 539
60	9,663	8,940	8,304	7.743	9,245	6,800	6,402
61	9,398	8,712	8,108	7.572	7,095	6,669	6 285
62	9,136	8,487	7,913	7.403	6,947	6,539	6,171
63	8,871	8,258	7,714	7.229	6,795	6,404	6 052
64	8,593	8,016	7,502	7.042	6.630	6.258	5.922
65	8,307	7,765	7,281	6,847	6,457	6,104	5,784
66	8,009	7,503	7,049	6,641	6,272	5,938	5 635
67	7.699	7,227	6,803	6,421	6 075	5,760	5,474
68	7,379	6,941	6,546	6,189	5,866	5,570	5,301
69	7.048	6,643	6,277	5,945	5,643	5,368	5,115
70	6,709	6,336	5,988	5,690	5,410	5.153	4,918
71	6,357	6,015	5,704	5 420	5.160	4.923	4.704
72	6,025	5,711	5,424	5,162	4,922	4,701	4,498
73	5,724	5,435	5.170	4,927	4,704	4,499	4,309
74	5,458	5,190	4,944	4.719	4,511	4,319	4,142
75	5,239	4,989	4,760	4.549	4,355	4,175	4,008
76	5,023	4,792	4,579	4,382	4,200	4,031	3,874
77	4,824	4,609	4,410	4.227	4,056	3,898	3.751
78	4,621	4,422	4.238	4,067	3,908	3.760	3,623
79	4,393	4,210	4.040	3,883	3,736	3,599	3.471
80	4,182	4.015	3,858	3.713	3,577	3,450	3,331
81	3,953	3,799	3,656	3,523	3,398	3,282	3.172
82	3,746	3 606	3.474	3,352	3,237	3,130	3,029
83	3,534	3,406	3,286	3,174	3,069	2.970	2,877
84	3,328	3,211	3 102	2,999	2,903	2,813	2,728
85	3,115	3,009	2,909	2,815	2,727	2,644	2,567
86	2,928	2,830	2,739	3,652	2,571	2,495	2,423
87	2,775	2,685	2,599	2,519	2,443	2,372	2,304
88	2.683	2,597	2.515	2,439	2,366	2,299	2,234
89	2,577	2,495	2,417	2,344	2,276	2,211	2,150
90	2,416	2,339	2,266	2.198	2,133	2,072	2,015
91	2,398	2,321	2,248	2,180	2,115	2,054	1,997
92	2,491	2.412	2,337	2,266	2,198	2,135	2,075
93	2,599	2.518	2,440	2,367	2,297	2,232	2,170
94	2,649	2.569	2,492	2,419	2,350	2 284	2,221
95	2.674	2.596	2,522	2,451	2,383	2,319	2,258
96	2,627	2.555	2,486	2,420	2,358	2,298	2,239
97	2,492	2.428	2,368	2,309	2.253	2,199	2,150
98	2,332	2.278	2,227	2,177	2.129	2,083	2.039
99	2.087	2,045	2,004	1,964	1,926	1,889	1.856
100	1,652	1,624	1,596	1,569	1,543	1,517	1,493
101	1,210	1,192	1,175	1,159	1.142	1,127	1,112
102	0,761	0,753	0,744	0,735	0,727	0,719	0,713
103	0,320	0,317	0,314	0.312	0,309	0,305	0,304

A Remarkable Volume.

COSMOGONY;

OR, THE

MYSTERIES OF CREATION.

Being an Analysis of the Natural Facts stated in the Hebraic account of the Creation, supported by the development of existing acts of God towards matter.

By THOMAS A. DAVIES.

Octavo. Elegantly bound in cloth. With many Illustrations.
Price $2.00.

TABLE OF CONTENTS.

Nature the Pathway of God.
Hebrew and English.
Language.
The Universal Creation.
English Translation.
The First Day.
Light—First Combination.
Second Day.
Third Day.
Combinations.
Granite Rock.
Theory Considered.
Clay Slate.
Mica and Talc Slates.
Stratification.
Mineral Fossils.
Fossil Sand-Beaches and Shells.
Limestones.
Sandstones.
Coal.
Inclinations of Rock Formations.
Boulder Rocks.
Metals and Precious Stones.
Quartz Rock.
Sands, Clays, and Soil.
Rock Salt and Mineral Resins.
Sulphur.
Seas, Lakes, Rivers, and Waters.
Atmospheric Air.
Vegetable Kingdom.
Fourth Day.
Heavenly Bodies.
Equilibrium.
Fifth Day.
Classification of Man and Beasts.
Sixth Day.
Ha-a-dam and A-dam.
Color of Men.
Whites and Blacks.
Scriptural Evidences.
The Flood.
Scriptural Evidences in Plain Words.
Conclusions from the Six Days' Work.
Seventh Day.

[*From the New York Observer.*]

"A remarkable book has recently made its appearance in this city, to which we desire to call the attention of the public, especially that portion of the thinking public who are accustomed to read and judge for themselves. . . . . . We have said enough of this work to show that it is a work of great labor, much curious and profound study, and worthy of a Christian scholar. . . . . . He has accomplished a great work; and if his argument will stand the searching criticism to which biblical literature and modern science will subject it, the author will have the proud satisfaction of knowing that he has made one of the most important contributions of the present day to the wall of defense which is constantly becoming more and more impregnable about the written word of God."

Sold by all Booksellers throughout the United States and Canadas.

The Publishers will send copies of this book by mail, *postage paid*, to any part of the United States, on receipt of the price in stamps,—$2.00.

G. W. CARLETON & CO.,
Publishers and Booksellers,
New York.

An Unanswerable Refutation

OF

GEOLOGIC THEORIES AS ADVERSE TO CHRISTIAN FAITH.

ANSWER TO

HUGH MILLER AND GEOLOGISTS.

BY

THOMAS A. DAVIES.

―○―

CONTENTS.

THE FALSE AND TRUE RECORDS.
GEOLOGIC TESTIMONY.
KINGDOMS IN LINES OF EXISTENCES.
WHAT THE MOSAIC ACCOUNT OF CREATION IS.
CONFLICT OF GEOLOGIC FAITH WITH SCIENCE AND THE SCRIPTURES.
THE EXPUNGING THE MOSAIC ACCOUNT OF CREATION, AND THE SUBSTITUTION OF THE GEOLOGIC BY HUGH MILLER.
FORMS IN THE FOSSIL KINGDOM.
HUGH MILLER, DISCERNIBLE AND REVEALED.
CONCLUDING ARGUMENT.
CONCLUDING ARGUMENT.—SCIENCE OF THE GEOLOGIC FAITH.
CONCLUDING ARGUMENT.—SEVERAL CONFLICTS OF THE GEOLOGIC AND BIBLICAL CHRISTIAN FAITH.

―○―

Sold by all Booksellers throughout the United States and Canadas.

The Publishers will send copies of this book by mail, *postage paid*, to any part of the United States, on receipt of the price in stamps,—$1.50.

G. W. CARLETON & CO.,

Publishers and Booksellers,

New York.

NEW BOOKS
And New Editions Recently Published by
G. W. CARLETON & CO.,
NEW YORK.

GEORGE W. CARLETON.   HENRY S. ALLEN.

N.B.—THE PUBLISHERS, upon receipt of the price in advance, will send any of the following Books by mail, POSTAGE FREE, to any part of the United States. This convenient and very safe mode may be adopted when the neighboring Booksellers are not supplied with the desired work. State name and address in full.

Victor Hugo.
LES MISÉRABLES.—The celebrated novel. One large 8vo volume, paper covers, $2.00 ; . . . cloth bound, $2.50
LES MISÉRABLES.—In the Spanish language. Fine 8vo. edition, two vols., paper covers, $4.00 ; . . cloth bound, $5.00
JARGAL.—A new novel. Illustrated. . 12mo. cloth, $1.75
THE LIFE OF VICTOR HUGO.—By himself. . 8vo. cloth, $1.75

Miss Muloch.
JOHN HALIFAX.—A novel. With illustration. 12mo. cloth, $1.75
A LIFE FOR A LIFE.— . do. ·do. $1.75

Charlotte Bronte (Currer Bell).
JANE EYRE.—A novel. With illustration. 12mo. cloth, $1.75
THE PROFESSOR.— do. . do. . do. $1.75
SHIRLEY.— . do. . do. . do. $1.75
VILLETTE.— .. do. . do. . do. $1.75

Hand-Books of Society.
THE HABITS OF GOOD SOCIETY; with thoughts, hints, and anecdotes, concerning nice points of taste, good manners, and the art of making oneself agreeable. The most entertaining work of the kind. . . . 12mo. cloth, $1.75
THE ART OF CONVERSATION.—With directions for self-culture. A sensible and instructive work, that ought to be in the hands of every one who wishes to be either an agreeable talker or listener. . . . . 12mo. cloth, $1.50
THE ART OF AMUSING.—Graceful arts, games, tricks, and charades, intended to amuse everybody. With suggestions for private theatricals, tableaux, parlor and family amusements. Nearly 150 illustrative pictures. . 12mo. cloth, $2.00

Robinson Crusoe.
A handsome illustrated edition, complete. 12mo. cloth, $1.50

Mrs. Mary J. Holmes' Works.

'LENA RIVERS.—	A novel.	12mo. cloth,	$1.50
DARKNESS AND DAYLIGHT.—	do.	do.	$1.50
TEMPEST AND SUNSHINE.—	do.	do.	$1.50
MARIAN GREY.—	do.	do.	$1.50
MEADOW BROOK.—	do.	do.	$1.50
ENGLISH ORPHANS.—	do.	do.	$1.50
DORA DEANE.—	do.	do.	$1.50
COUSIN MAUDE.—	do.	do.	$1.50
HOMESTEAD ON THE HILLSIDE.—	do.	do.	$1.50
HUGH WORTHINGTON.—	do.	do.	$1.50
THE CAMERON PRIDE.—*Just Published.*		do.	$1.50

Artemus Ward.

HIS BOOK.—The first collection of humorous writings by A. Ward. Full of comic illustrations.   12mo. cloth, $1.50
HIS TRAVELS.—A comic volume of Indian and Mormon adventures. With laughable illustrations.   12mo. cloth, $1.50
IN LONDON.—A new book containing Ward's comic *Punch* letters, and other papers. Illustrated.   12mo. cloth, $1.50

Miss Augusta J. Evans.

BEULAH.—A novel of great power.		12mo. cloth,	$1.75
MACARIA.—	do. do.	do.	$1.75
ST. ELMO.—	do. do. *Just published.*	do.	$2.00

By the Author of "Rutledge."

RUTLEDGE.—A deeply interesting novel.		12mo. cloth,	$1.75
THE SUTHERLANDS.—	do.	do.	$1.75
FRANK WARRINGTON.—	do.	do.	$1.75
ST. PHILIP'S.—	do.	do.	$1.75
LOUIE'S LAST TERM AT ST. MARY'S.—		do.	$1.75
ROUNDHEARTS AND OTHER STORIES.—For children.		do.	$1.75
A ROSARY FOR LENT.—Devotional readings.		do.	$1.75

J. Cordy Jeaffreson.

A BOOK ABOUT LAWYERS.—Reprinted from the late English Edition. Intensely interesting.   12mo. cloth, $2.00

Allan Grant.

LOVE IN LETTERS. — A fascinating book of love-letters from celebrated and notorious persons.   12mo. cloth, $2.00

Algernon Charles Swinburne.

LAUS VENERIS—and other Poems and Ballads. 12mo. cloth, $1.75

Geo. W. Carleton.

OUR ARTIST IN CUBA.—A humorous volume of travel; with fifty comic illustrations by the author.   12mo. cloth, $1.50
OUR ARTIST IN PERU.—   do.   do. $1.50

A. S. Roe's Works.

A LONG LOOK AHEAD.—	A novel.	12mo. cloth,	$1.50
TO LOVE AND TO BE LOVED.—	do.	do.	$1.50
TIME AND TIDE.—	do.	do.	$1.50
I'VE BEEN THINKING.—	do.	do.	$1.50
THE STAR AND THE CLOUD.—	do.	do.	$1.50
TRUE TO THE LAST.—	do.	do.	$1.50
HOW COULD HE HELP IT?—	do.	do.	$1.50
LIKE AND UNLIKE.—	do.	do.	$1.50
LOOKING AROUND.—	do.	do.	$1.50
WOMAN OUR ANGEL.—*Just published.*		do.	$1.50

Richard B. Kimball.

WAS HE SUCCESSFUL?—	A novel.	12mo. cloth,	$1.75
UNDERCURRENTS.—	do.	do.	$1.75
SAINT LEGER.—	do.	do.	$1.75
ROMANCE OF STUDENT LIFE.—	do.	do.	$1.75
IN THE TROPICS.—	do.	do.	$1.75
THE PRINCE OF KASHNA.—	do.	do.	$1.75
EMILIE.—A sequel to "St. Leger." *In press.*		do.	$1.75

Orpheus C. Kerr.

THE ORPHEUS C. KERR PAPERS.—Comic letters and humorous military criticisms. Three series. 12mo. cloth, $1.50
AVERY GLIBUN.—A powerful new novel.— 8vo. cloth, $2.00

Thos. A. Davies.

HOW TO MAKE MONEY, and how to keep it.—A practical and valuable book that every one should have. 12mo. cl., $1.50

Comic Books—Illustrated.

JOSH BILLINGS.—His Book, of Proverbs, etc.	12mo. cl.,	$1.50
WIDOW SPRIGGINS.—By author "Widow Bedott."	do.	$1.75
CORRY O'LANUS.—His views and opinions.	do.	$1.50
VERDANT GREEN.—A racy English college story.	do.	$1.50
CONDENSED NOVELS, ETC.—By F. Bret Harte.	do.	$1.50
THE SQUIBOB PAPERS.—By John Phœnix.	do.	$1.50
MILES O'REILLY.—His Book of Adventures.	do.	$1.50
do. Baked Meats, etc.	do.	$1.75

"Brick" Pomeroy.

SENSE.—An illustrated vol. of fireside musings. 12mo. cl., $1.50
NONSENSE.— do. do. comic sketches. do. $1.50

Joseph Rodman Drake.

THE CULPRIT FAY.—A faery poem. . . 12mo. cloth, $1.25
THE CULPRIT FAY.—An illustrated edition. 100 exquisite illustrations. . . 4to., beautifully printed and bound, $5.00

New American Novels.

TEMPLE HOUSE.—By Mrs. Elizabeth Stoddard. 12mo. cl., $1.75
THE BISHOP'S SON.—By Alice Cary. . . do. $1.75
BEAUSEINCOURT.—By Mrs. C. A. Warfield. . do. $1.75
HOUSEHOLD OF BOUVERIE. do. do. . do. $2.00
HELEN COURTENAY.—By author "Vernon Grove." do. $1.75
PECULIAR.—By Epes Sargent. . . . do. $1.75
VANQUISHED.—By Miss Agnes Leonard. . do. $1.75
FOUR OAKS.—By Kamba Thorpe. . . . do. $1.75
MALBROOK.—*In press.* . . . . . do. $1.75

M. Michelet's Remarkable Works.

LOVE (L'AMOUR).—Translated from the French. 12mo. cl., $1.50
WOMAN (LA FEMME).— . do. . . do. $1.50

Ernest Renan.

THE LIFE OF JESUS.—Translated from the French. 12mo.cl.,$1.75
THE APOSTLES.— . . do. . . do. $1.75

Popular Italian Novels.

DOCTOR ANTONIO.—A love story. By Ruffini. 12mo. cl., $1.75
BEATRICE CENCI.—By Guerrazzi, with portrait. do. $1.75

Rev. John Cumming, D.D., of London.

THE GREAT TRIBULATION.—Two series. 12mo. cloth, $1.50
THE GREAT PREPARATION.— do. . do. $1.50
THE GREAT CONSUMMATION. do. . do. $1.50
THE LAST WARNING CRY.— . . do. $1.50

Mrs. Ritchie (Anna Cora Mowatt).

FAIRY FINGERS.—A capital new novel. . 12mo. cloth, $1.75
THE MUTE SINGER.— do. . do. $1.75
THE CLERGYMAN'S WIFE—and other stories. do. $1.75

Mother Goose for Grown Folks.

HUMOROUS RHYMES for grown people. . 12mo. cloth, 1.25

T. S. Arthur's New Works.

LIGHT ON SHADOWED PATHS.—A novel. 12mo. cloth, $1.50
OUT IN THE WORLD.— . do. . . do. $1.50
NOTHING BUT MONEY.— . do. . . do. $1.50
WHAT CAME AFTERWARDS.— do. . . do. $1.50
OUR NEIGHBORS.— . do. . . do. $1.50

New English Novels.

WOMAN'S STRATEGY.—Beautifully illustrated. 12mo. cloth, $1.50
BEYMINSTRE.—By a popular author. . do. $1.75
"RECOMMENDED TO MERCY."— do. . . do. $1.75
WYLDER'S HAND.—By Sheridan Le Fanu. do. $1.75
HOUSE BY THE CHURCHYARD.— do. . do. $1.75

Edmund Kirke.

AMONG THE PINES.—Or Life in the South. 12mo. cloth, $1.5c
MY SOUTHERN FRIENDS.— do. . . do. $1.50
DOWN IN TENNESSEE.— do. . . do. $1.50
ADRIFT IN DIXIE.— do. . . do. $1.50
AMONG THE GUERILLAS.— do. . . do. $1.50

Charles Reade.

THE CLOISTER AND THE HEARTH.—A magnificent new novel—the best this author ever wrote. . 8vo. cloth, $2.00

The Opera.

TALES FROM THE OPERAS.—A collection of clever stories, based upon the plots of all the famous operas. 12mo. cloth, $1.50

Robert B. Roosevelt.

THE GAME-FISH OF THE NORTH.—Illustrated. 12mo. cloth, $2.00
SUPERIOR FISHING.— do. do. $2.00
THE GAME-BIRDS OF THE NORTH.— . . do. $2.00

Hinton Rowan Helper.

THE IMPENDING CRISIS OF THE SOUTH.— . 12mo. cloth, $2.00
NOJOQUE.—A Question for a Continent. . do. $2.00

Henry Morford.

PARIS IN '67.—Sketches of travel. . 12mo. cloth, $1.75

From the German.

WILL-O'-THE-WISP.—A beautiful child's book. 12mo. cl., $1.50

The City of Richmond.

RICHMOND DURING THE WAR.—By a lady. 12mo. cloth, $1.75

Dr. J. J. Craven.

THE PRISON-LIFE OF JEFFERSON DAVIS.—Incidents and conversations during his captivity at Fortress Monroe. 12mo.cl.,$2.00

Captain Raphael Semmes.

THE CRUISE OF THE ALABAMA AND SUMTER.— 12mo. cloth, $2.00

John S. Mosby.

HIS LIFE AND EXPLOITS IN THE WAR.—With portraits. do. $1.75

Walter Barrett, Clerk.

THE OLD MERCHANTS OF NEW YORK.— Personal incidents, sketches, bits of biography, and events in the life of leading merchants in New York City. Four series. 12mo. cl., $1.75

Madame Octavia Walton Le Vert.

SOUVENIRS OF TRAVEL.—New edition. Large 12mo. cloth, $2.00

H. T. Sperry.

COUNTRY LOVE vs. CITY FLIRTATION.—A capital new Society tale, with 20 superb illustrations by Hoppin. 12mo. cloth, $2.00

Miscellaneous Works.

MARY BRANDEGEE.—A novel by Cuyler Pine.	12mo.	$1.75
RENSHAWE.— do. do.	do.	$1.75
THE SHENANDOAH.—History of the Conf. steamer.	do.	$1.50
MEMORIALS OF JUNIUS BRUTUS BOOTH.—(The Elder.)	do.	$1.50
MOUNT CALVARY.—By Matthew Hale Smith.	do.	$2.00
THE HUMBUGS OF THE WORLD.—By P. T. Barnum.	do.	$1.75
LOVE-LIFE OF DR. E. K. KANE AND MARGARET FOX.	do.	$1.75
BALLADS.—By the author of "Barbara's History."	do.	$1.50
STORMCLIFF.—A novel by M. T. Walworth.	do.	$1.75
MAN, and the Conditions that Surround Him.	do.	$1.75
PROMETHEUS IN ATLANTIS.—A prophecy.	do.	$2.00
TITAN AGONISTES.—An American novel.	do.	$2.00
THE PAPACY EXPOSED.—Introduction by Bishop Coxe.	do.	$1.75
PULPIT PUNGENCIES.—Witticisms from the Pulpit.	do.	$1.75
CHOLERA.—A handbook on its treatment and cure.	do.	$1.00
WHO GOES THERE?—By "Sentinel," of the "World."	do.	$1.50
ALICE OF MONMOUTH.—By Edmund C. Stedman.	do.	$1.25
LYRICS AND IDYLLS.— do. do.	do.	$1.25
NOTES ON SHAKSPEARE.—By Jas. H. Hackett.	do.	$1.50
THE MONTANAS.—A novel by Mrs. S. J. Hancock.	do.	$1.75
PASTIMES WITH LITTLE FRIENDS.—Martha H. Butt.	do.	$1.50
A SPINSTER'S STORY.—A new American novel.	do.	$1.75
A LIFE OF JAMES STEPHENS.—Fenian Head-Centre.	do.	$1.00
AUTOBIOGRAPHY OF A NEW ENGLAND FARM-HOUSE.—	do.	$1.75
TOGETHER.—A new American novel.	do.	$1.50
POEMS.—By Gay H. Naramore.	do.	$1.50
GOMERY OF MONTGOMERY.—By C. A. Washburn.	do.	$2.00
POEMS.—By Mrs. Sarah T. Bolton.	do.	$1.50
JOHN GUILDERSTRING'S SIN.—A new novel.	do.	$1.50
CENTEOLA.—By author "Green Mountain Boys."	do.	$1.50
RED TAPE AND PIGEON-HOLE GENERALS.—	do.	$1.50
TREATISE ON DEAFNESS.—By Dr. E. B. Lighthill.	do.	$1.50
AROUND THE PYRAMIDS.—By Gen. Aaron Ward.	do.	$1.50
CHINA AND THE CHINESE.—By W. L. G. Smith.	do.	$1.50
EDGAR POE AND HIS CRITICS.—By Mrs. Whitman.	do.	$1.00
MARRIED OFF.—An Illustrated Satirical Poem.	do.	50 cts.
THE RUSSIAN BALL.— do. do. do.	do.	50 cts.
THE SNOBLACE BALL.— do. do. do.	do.	50 cts.
THE CITY'S HEART.— do. do. do.	do.	$1.00
POEMS.—By Mrs. Virginia Quarles.	do.	$1.00
AN ANSWER TO HUGH MILLER.—By T. A. Davies.	do.	$1.50
COSMOGONY.—By Thomas A. Davies.	8vo.	$2.00
FREE GOVERNMENT IN ENGLAND AND AMERICA.—	do.	$3.00
RURAL ARCHITECTURE.—By M. Field. Illustrated.	do.	$2.00

www.ingramcontent.com/pod-product-compliance
Lightning Source LLC
Chambersburg PA
CBHW030743230426
43667CB00007B/827